Monique David-Ménard

HYSTERIA FROM FREUD TO LACAN

Body and Language in Psychoanalysis

TRANSLATED BY *Catherine Porter*

FOREWORD BY *Ned Lukacher*

CORNELL UNIVERSITY PRESS

ITHACA AND LONDON

First published in French as Monique David-Ménard, *L'Hystérique entre Freud et Lacan: Corps et langage en psychanalyse*, in the series Les jeux de l'inconscient (Paris: Editions Universitaires, 1983), copyright © Editions universitaires–Begedis, Paris, 1983.

First published 1989 by Cornell University Press.

International Standard Book Number (cloth) 0-8014-2100-4
International Standard Book Number (paper) 0-8014-9617-9
Library of Congress Catalog Card Number 89-42870
Printed in the United States of America
Librarians: Library of Congress cataloging information
appears on the last page of the book.

The paper in this book is acid-free and meets the guidelines for permanence and durability of the Committee on Production Guidelines for Book Longevity of the Council on Library Resources.

Hysteria from Freud to Lacan

Contents

Foreword

The Epistemology of Disgust

Ned Lukacher

Monique David-Ménard's *Hysteria from Freud to Lacan* tells the story of a turning away from, an avoidance of, another story. This troping or turning occurs both within the etiology of hysteria and within the psychoanalytic discourse about hysteria. The hysteric feels an intense pleasure, an improper pleasure, that cannot properly speaking be allowed into experience. The ego is overwhelmed and frightened by this intense delight, and so it turns away. Freud's initial theory of repression is based upon hysterical repression, upon the hysteric's defense against overwhelming sensations of pleasure. "To put it crudely," writes Freud to Fliess, "the memory actually stinks just as in the present the object stinks; and in the same manner as we turn away [*abwenden*] our sense organ (the head and nose) in disgust [*Ekel*], the preconscious and the sense of consciousness turn away from the memory. This is *repression*."[1]

The difference between normal repression and hysterical repression, Freud goes on to say in the same letter, concerns the "quota of libido [*ein Beitrag Libido*]" that this "deferred internal disgust" has produced and that, because of its excess, cannot "force its way through to action or to translation [*Übersetzung*] into psychic terms but is obliged to proceed in a *regressive direction (as happens in dreams)*. Libido and disgust would seem to be associatively linked [*hängen einmal assoziativ aneinander*]." The tentativeness of Freud's attribution of the associative link between libido and disgust is

1. Sigmund Freud, *The Complete Letters of Sigmund Freud to Wilhelm Fliess*, trans. and ed. Jeffrey Moussaieff Masson (Cambridge: Belknap Press of Harvard University Press, 1985), letter of November 14, 1897, p. 280.

important, for it reveals Freud's hesitation and uncertainty concerning the relation between the psychical and the organic. For while libido, the pleasure principle, channels memories only toward pleasurable psychical sensations, disgust somehow stands in the way of this pleasurable transmission and transforms it into "nothing but symptoms instead of aim-directed ideas [*Zielvorstellungen*]." The link to disgust, the link between pleasurable psychical sensations and unpleasurable organic sensations, has already led Freud in November 1897 to the very threshold of the pleasure principle. Beyond it lies only obscurity: "The obscurity [*Unklarheit*] lies mainly in the nature of the change by which the internal sensation of need becomes the sensation of disgust." This change (*Veränderung*) marks the difference that constitutes the specificity of hysterical repression (*Verdrängung*). *Hysteria from Freud to Lacan* tells the story of this nonstory whose very unnarratability binds the discourse of the hysteric to the discourse of the psychoanalyst. The relation of hysteria to theory is the relation of the presentation of unspeakable desires to the representation of complex and sometimes necessarily obscure ideas.

The theory of hysteria is Freud's effort to describe an epistemology of disgust. What is disgust? How is it that we can experience disgust, and what traces does disgust leave in our discourse and on our bodies? The epistemology of disgust is always also the epistemology of movement and of motility (*Bewegung*; *Bewegungsfähigkeit*). More precisely, the epistemology of the movement of disgust is the epistemology of the tropological substitutions that describe the language of hysterical speech and of the hysterical body. The characteristic upward displacement of hysterical symptoms is itself, in Freud's own terms, a trope for turning away the head and nose from the object of disgust. The overriding question in *Hysteria from Freud to Lacan* concerns the site and composition of the body on which these tropological substitutions are elaborated. What *is* the object of psychoanalytic knowledge about hysteria, and what is our relation to that object?

David-Ménard organizes her analysis of Freud's first theory of hysterical conversion around a close reading of Freud's case history of Elisabeth von R. in *Studies on Hysteria* (1895). The conversion theory of hysteria was Freud's effort to account for the "change" from libidinal, psychical pleasure to symptoms of organic, physical disgust. David-Ménard reveals the inconsistencies between the clinical evidence Freud has amassed and the theoretical interpretation he brings to that evidence. Freud is here bound to a dualistic epistemology in which a psychical conflict is converted into a somatic conflict, in this case the patient's difficulty in walking and standing. Freud is here deep into the obscurity he alludes to in his letter to Fliess a few years later. Elisabeth has erotic, libidinal desires for her brother-in-law, desires whose overwhelming force and moral inadmissibility precipitate their repression. These sensations are disgusting to Elisabeth, and she refuses to acknowledge them. But these desires, however disgusting the ego might find them, will not be silenced, and they reemerge in the form of her hysterical symptoms. The analytic question here is how Freud can explain the relation between the unacceptable desire and the *particular* form of the symptoms. His answer is the associative theory of conversion, the same associative link he was to be so uncertain about in 1897. Elisabeth's legs become the privileged hysterogenic zone, he maintains, by sheer dint of the associative logic of chance that brought her legs into contact with those of her invalid father, who used to rest his legs across his daughter's lap. Freud's diffidence about the logical and rhetorical power of this explanation is evident: "If anyone feels astonished at this associative connection between physical pain and psychical affect, on the ground of its being of such a multiple and artificial character, I should reply that this feeling is as little justified as astonishment at the fact that it is the rich people who own the most money."[2]

This appeal to the undeniable empiricity of the data at hand is a rhetorical bluff whose epistemological stakes David-Ménard helps us fully grasp. There is in hysteria an epistemological break between the psychical and the physiological, a break that Freud's theory, which insists upon the continuity between these two orders of experience, refuses to acknowledge. The contact between the legs of father and daughter is but one of numerous instances in which Elisabeth's experiences of the most intense pleasure and the most intense revulsion are registered in the language of bodily position and movement. Elisabeth is walking with her brother-in-law when she first experiences those unacceptable desires. Using

---

2. Sigmund Freud and Josef Breuer, *Studies on Hysteria*, trans. James Strachey et al. (New York: Avon Books, 1966), p. 217.

the details garnered by Freud himself, David-Ménard unfolds a surreptitious language of *jouissance*, of the most intense and overwhelming sensation, which is systematically elaborated in terms of the posture of the desiring body. This realm of *significance*, this realm of significant signification, of the most intensely felt "significance," defines what David-Ménard calls the "body of jouissance" (*corps de jouissance*). It is in the realm neither of the psychical nor of the physiological but rather in the realm of the signifying discourse, which is the body of jouissance, that a too intense libidinal surge is tropologically transposed into the organic symptoms of disgust. For Elisabeth movement *is* the language of jouissance, and so its symbolic antithetical conversion takes the form of intense pain in the legs. Locked in an associationist model, Freud himself finds it difficult to take that step forward into the theory of symbolical conversion that he begins to glimpse by the end of *Studies on Hysteria*: "Confusing a complete methodological reversal, an epistemological break, with an unproblematic juxtaposition of two mechanisms, allowing himself thus to be misled by the temporal continuity of his own thoughts," Freud, writes David-Ménard, "produced a theory of symbolizing conversion dependent on associative conversion."

Although the body of jouissance is discernible in Freud's text, Freud himself does not elaborate upon it in his theoretical reflections, since his objective is to point to a synthetic process through which the unconscious conflict is directly registered in organic effects. He describes Elisabeth's love for her brother-in-law as being "present in her consciousness like a foreign body [*eines Fremdkörpers*], without having entered into relationship with the rest of her ideational life. With regard to these feelings she was in a peculiar situation of knowing and at the same time not knowing—a situation, that is, in which a psychical group was cut off."[3] Freud clearly wants to see this "foreign body" as a psychical entity and therefore is not concerned to pursue the possibility that it is constructed through another logic. David-Ménard proceeds by differentiating more precisely than Freud the specificity of this "foreign body" that occupies the enigmatic space of the conversion process. "What we have here," writes David-Ménard, "is not a psychical mechanism, but the signifying elaboration of a jouissance whose blockage or

3. Ibid., p. 206.

suspension will take shape through the symptom." The field of jouissance is radically heterogeneous and cannot be reduced to a psychical or physiological order of experience. This insight can enter Freud's text only under the sign of negation: "It is perhaps wrong to say that hysteria creates these sensations by symbolization. It may be that it does not take linguistic usage as its model at all, but that hysteria and linguistic usage alike draw their material from a common source."[4] Is it perhaps Freud's too ardent desire to discover this "common source" (*gemeinsamer Quelle*) within the primary processes at work within the unconscious that at once enables him to mark the presence of linguistic symbolization and compels him to turn away from the pressing task of determining the specific laws of symbolic conversion?

David-Ménard goes on to delineate the consequences of Freud's avoidance of the linguistic dimension of jouissance in the work of the psychoanalysts who elaborated Freud's theory of hysteria in an overtly psychosomatic direction. In so doing they were at once oblivious to the epistemological break between associative and symbolic conversion and highly sensitive to Freud's desire to discover and indeed to substantialize unconscious processes, which is to say, to make of psychoanalysis a science of the real. Their search for a homogeneous synthesis of the psychical and the somatic is an effort to posit the existence of an unconscious "substance." Here the link between the desire of the hysteric and the desire of the psychoanalyst comes into view. It was Jacques Lacan who most forcefully elaborated the theoretical consequences of the historical conjunction between these two discourses. Indeed, Lacan describes psychoanalysis as the "hysterisation of discourse, . . . the structural introduction via artificial conditions of the discourse of the hysteric."[5] "*Why,*" asks Lacan, can the hysteric "sustain her desire only as an unsatisfied desire?"[6]

Freud cures Elisabeth of her symptoms by allowing her to present to him the impossibility of satisfying her desire; this presentation becomes itself a kind of satisfaction that one calls the cure.

4. Ibid., p. 223.

5. Jacques Lacan, *Le séminaire*, book 18, "L'envers de la psychanalyse" (*1969–70*) (unpublished typescript), p. 4. Cited in Jacques Lacan, *Feminine Sexuality*, ed. Juliet Mitchell and Jacqueline Rose (New York: W. W. Norton, 1982), p. 161.

6. Jacques Lacan, *The Four Fundamental Concepts of Psycho-Analysis*, ed. Jacques-Alain Miller, trans. Alan Sheridan (New York: W. W. Norton, 1981), p. 12

Freud reports that in 1894, after the cure, he saw Elisabeth whirl by him at a dance they both attended and reports learning later that she had married. For Freud himself the presentation of the impossibility of satisfying his desire to understand the mystery of Elisabeth's divided subjectivity becomes itself a kind of satisfaction that one calls theory. Through the hysteric Freud was led to the relation of desire to language: "But this is not to say," adds Lacan, "that the relation was fully elucidated—far from it—by the massive notion of the transference." The transference between patient and analyst—and between hysteria and theory—in all its satisfying unsatisfaction, "places us," Lacan continues, "on the track of some kind of original sin in analysis. There has to be one. The truth is perhaps simply one thing, namely, the desire of Freud himself, the fact that something, in Freud, was never analysed."[7] The theory of conversion, before it describes anything else, describes the conversion of the discourse of hysteria into the discourse of psychoanalysis. "To discover," as Lacan observes, "by what privilege Freud's desire was able to find entrance into the field of experience he designates as the unconscious" would be to discover what in Freud's desire to understand the divided subjectivity of the hysteric led him to the "foreign body," to the "other" within his own subjectivity.

At the end of the letter to Fliess of November 14, 1897, in which he discussed the repressive turning away from the object of disgust, Freud proclaims the impossibility of self-analysis: "My self-analysis remains interrupted. I have realized why I can analyze myself only with the help of knowledge obtained objectively (like an outsider) [*wie ein Fremder*]. True self-analysis is impossible; otherwise there would be no (neurotic) illness. Since I am still contending with some kind of enigma [*Rätsel*] in my patients, this is bound to hold me up [*muss mich . . . aufhalten*] in my self-analysis as well."[8] Freud's abandonment of his self-analysis, and his subsequent refusal to be analyzed by any of his disciples, marks the hysterization of his own discourse as it marks the birth of psychoanalysis in the fall of 1897. Why is Freud halted on the threshold of discovering the nature of this enigmatic stranger within? The history of psychoanalysis is an

7. Ibid., p. 12.
8. *Complete Letters of Sigmund Freud to Wilhelm Fliess*, p. 281; translation slightly modified.

effect of the suspension of Freud's self-analysis. For Lacan the question of the origin of Freud's desire is the question of the Name-of-the-Father, not the question of Freud's father or that of Freud as father, not a psychological question but the structural question, the epistemological question, of the nature of questioning itself.

The desire within the question is not simply the desire of a subject. It is from within the otherness of the hysteric's divided subjectivity that there emerges the question that calls forth Freud's desire to understand. Lacan recognized that the analyst's desire to determine the hysteric's desire comes from within the otherness, the "foreign body," that divides the hysteric's subjectivity. This is precisely what enables transference to take place. Analysts should be analyzed so that they can recognize the shape of their own transference when it arises in the course of therapy and thus be able to neutralize its effect upon the course of the patient's analysis. "I have realized why I can analyze myself only with the help of knowledge obtained objectively (like an outsider)." And that knowledge is the knowledge of an enigma. One could adduce here Freud's own disgust with sexuality and his cessation, sometime during the 1890s, of all sexual activity. What "holds him up," what binds him to the stranger within his patients and within his theory, is a certain disgust with, a turning away from, the body. But this disgust is not simply disgusting, it is also intensely pleasurable; it is the enigma of how the hysteric's disgust becomes the jouissance of the psychoanalytic theorist. To undergo analysis would be to risk desublimating the hysterical desire within the psychoanalytic question.

"The field of jouissance," writes David-Ménard, "is formed through an organization of signifiers but realized in a body." *Hysteria from Freud to Lacan* is not simply about a series of approaches to hysteria from Freud to Lacan but about the hysterization of analytic discourse. Analytic discourse is itself inscribed within the field of jouissance; the desire for an impossible satisfaction, for the most intense enjoyment, is present within the logical, semantic, and syntactic elements that are represented in that discourse. The presentation of jouissance within the representations of analytic theory constitutes "the structural introduction . . . of the discourse of the hysteric" within the discourse of analysis.

Freud had much to turn his nose away from, including much pertaining to Wilhelm Fliess, whose dadaist theory of noses and whose botched operation on the nose of Emmy Eckstein are only the most grotesque reminders of the delusions to which the associative theory of conversion can lead. It is the hysteric herself who enables Freud to turn from the bizarre organicism of Fliess to the discovery of the body of jouissance. As David-Ménard astutely notes, as early as the case of Miss Lucy in *Studies on Hysteria*, Freud begins to turn away from his fascination with the sensorimotor manifestations of hysterical symptoms, and this was largely because the patient's symptoms, unlike the dramatically visible symptoms of the other patients, involved the loss of the sense of smell in conjunction with purely subjective olfactory sensations. Here, writes David-Ménard, Freud resolves the case "through an examination of the body as grasped through language." The symbolization of the desiring body, "the body informed by the signifying elaboration of desire," rather than the physiological results of "somatic compliance," becomes the object of analytic scrutiny. In David-Ménard's idiom, "the hysteric has no body, for something in the history of her body could not be formulated, except in symptoms." The hysteric smells something awful that prevents the sexualization of her body from proceeding in a normative fashion. The hysterogenic body is a kind of prosthesis for the lack of an erotogenic body. To be sure, the erotogenic body is a historically determined entity that is based upon the physiological body, but always with numerous permutations, excisions, or additions. The hysterogenic body is produced when the sexualization of the erotogenic body has been somehow disrupted. Hence "the hysteric has no body"; for some reason, the sexualization of her body smells so bad, is so disgusting, that she would rather not have a body at all. The hysteric is disgusted at the idea of pleasure, and though she refuses to think about it any further, her body—her other body, her strange hysterogenic body—has the power of thought insofar as it constructs itself through a signifying medium, constructs itself as a body of jouissance that prosthetically proclaims its will to pleasure and its lack of a physical body upon which to experience that pleasure. The "philosophic stakes in a theory of hysteria," writes David-Ménard, "amount to showing how the body thinks, and showing that what forces us to think our identity is an experience of jouissance."

In the field of psychoanalytic theory Dora is surely the patron saint of disgust. Dora is disgusted by Herr K.; her symptoms, though undramatic and commonplace (Freud even calls it a case of "*'petite hystérie'* "), are themselves rather disgusting; and finally, Freud seems as disgusted by Dora as she seems to be disgusted by him. There is no shortage of disgust when it comes to this case history and to the response it has received in recent years from feminist literary and cultural critics.[9] David-Ménard's analysis engages the sexual politics of psychoanalysis through a close differentiation of Dora's experience of the pleasures of negation, and of Dora's ability to convert pleasure into disgust. It is Dora's regressive oral disgust that negates and heightens her conflicted experience of genital sexuality. David-Ménard turns from the disgust between physician and analysand to that between the patient and her jouissance.

This case history was written at a crucial juncture in the development of Freud's theory. The analysis took place in late 1899 and was terminated suddenly by Dora on December 31. Freud wrote the case history in January 1900 but did not publish it until 1905. The Dora case history draws upon two important currents in Freud's theory: his theory of dreams and their interpretation and his theory of infantile sexuality. *The Interpretation of Dreams* was published in 1900; *Three Essays on the Theory of Sexuality*, in which he first announced his ideas about infantile sexuality, was published in 1905. Here for the first time in the theory of hysteria, thumb-sucking, masturbation, and infantile autoeroticism are significant in determining the etiology of subsequent traumatic scenes. David-Ménard reads Dora's disgust at sexuality, what Lacan calls the hysteric's "desexualization," as one side of a process whose other side is the displacement of erotogeneity that mobilizes the body of jouissance. In other words, Dora's representations of disgust actually present, in the mode of *Darstellung*, the infantile scene of jouissance, those scenes of thumb-sucking in which she enjoyed a privileged though ambivalent relation to her father, who took it upon himself to wean her of the habit. "It is by way of her mouth that she tries to present (*darstellen*) her father's sexual relationship to Frau K., but she does not actually succeed in this: it can't be swallowed, it veers off into the symptoms of voicelessness. Dora experiences

9. Cf. *In Dora's Case: Freud-Hysteria-Feminism*, ed. Charles Bernheimer and Claire Kahane (New York: Columbia University Press, 1985).

everything by way of her mouth." The infantile oral scene is a scene of "unsurpassable jouissance that catches or snags everything new, or different, that might come up in the order of jouissance." Dora's problem is that everything is oral and everything ends in disgust. Her overinvestment in oral erotogeneity had the effect of repressing genital erotogeneity. Dora buries sexual difference, writes David-Ménard, "under a jouissance that, seeking to bring everything back to itself, ends in an impasse." In conjunction with the intervening history, her mother's psychosis, her father's syphilis and later impotence, his affair with Frau K. and, finally, Herr K.'s attempted seduction, Dora's association of sex with filth and disease is not difficult to understand, and neither is the hysterogenic emergence of her infantile oral erotogeneity. Her infantile experience and her subsequent understanding of the consequences of genital erotogeneity seemed to have conspired, in Dora's case, against the formation of normative erotogeneity. In every symptom in which she represents her disgust at sexuality, her body of jouissance is trying once again to enjoy, to join in, the sexuality the others are experiencing. But the effort always fails, or rather succeeds only in pointing to its own lack, to its own failure at symbolization.

"Disgust in hysteria," writes David-Ménard apropos of Dora, "exhibits, at the heart of the conversion symptom, a passionate denial of sexual difference that seeks to attribute to the other a kind of responsibility for having 'spoiled' sexuality." This characterization of hysterical disgust as "a passionate denial" (*un refus passionné*) stands at the heart of *Hysteria from Freud to Lacan* as well, for it describes the desiring energy, the force, the nonsubjective, nonpsychological will that compels the subject onto the field of jouissance and maintains her there. The "passionate denial" issues from the body of jouissance; disgust is this "passionate denial"; disgust is this at once pathetic and hideous iteration that elaborates the symptom through the field of *signifiance*.[10] The catarrh, the discharge, the aphonia, the asthmatic breathing that result from her desperate effort, in overhearing her parents' coitus and her father's shortness

10. "It is said that passion makes one think in a circle. Certainly with hideous iteration the bitten lips of Dorian Gray shaped and reshaped those subtle words that dealt with soul and sense, till he had found in them the full expression, as it were, of his mood, and justified, by intellectual approval, passions that without such justification would still have dominated his temper" (Oscar Wilde, *The Picture of Dorian Gray*, ed. Donald Lawler [New York: W. W. Norton, 1988], p. 143).

of breath, to mark her link to their jouissance, all these symptoms that actualize Dora's disgust also constitute what David-Ménard calls "this desperate presentification" of Dora's oral jouissance. *Présentification* rather than *présentation*, precisely in order to render the simultaneity and the performativity of Freud's use of Darstellung. Disgust is both a reproach to the others for having spoiled her sexuality and a fiercely futile assertion of the utter self-sufficiency of her pathetically fragmented body of jouissance. This presentification of jouissance defines the hysterical attack, the tail wagging the dog, the prosthetic hysterogenic body rending the physical body of which it has literally lost sight.

David-Ménard's discussion of Darstellung and figurability focuses upon the organization of the hysterogenic body in terms of the occlusion of the physical body by the "thingly" character of those signifiers that become fused to certain bodily movements: "It is as if, all at once, the words covered a thing, a portion of the body, whose otherness with respect to the words that designate it is no longer apparent." When Dora poses the quintessential hysterical question, "Am I a man or a woman, and what does that mean?" her answer is structured by what David-Ménard calls "the resources of a signifying latency, of a turn of phrase or rather a syntactic organization that inscribes her sex as marked by an absence." The language of her dream, which finds Dora asking, "Where is the station [*Bahnhof*]?" points consistently to her unsymbolized genital erotogeneity through its allusions to the unattainable *Bahnhof*, the *Friedhof* (cemetery), and the anatomical *Vorhof* (vestibule). The hysterical symptom enacts the hysterogenic body's movement toward totalization, its hallucinatory, fantastic effort to make the prosthetic part into a (w)hole, a totality that is also the signifier of a lack. The analysis succeeds insofar as it enables Dora to pass through the signifying structure of the Darstellung in which she is seized and which has divided her subjectivity.

Perhaps the most original contribution of *Hysteria from Freud to Lacan* is its elaboration of the theoretical implications of the signifying medium of jouissance in the direction of a metapsychology of movement. David-Ménard's theoretical paradigm is drawn from Freud's brief but complex essay "Negation" (1925), where he describes how, through movement, negation, and judgment, the pleasure principle reshapes itself into a reality principle. Were this

xvii

not so, the child would lose itself within its own jouissance. The question, then, is the relation between motor excitations that are pleasurable and those that are at the limit—that dimension of movement that marks the contours of the body of jouissance. Freud is here concerned with the role of judgment in the primordial symbolization of the inside/outside distinction; he is concerned with the primordial part, the *Ur-Teil*, the primordial expulsion from the ego (*Ausstossung aus dem Ich*) of that *Ur-Teil* that constitutes judgment (*Urteil*). As the "pleasure-ego" (*Lust-Ich*) is transformed into the "reality-ego" (*Real-Ich*), the process of reality testing, of determining what is good/inside and what is bad/outside, and then what is internal/subjective and what is external/objective, is a process of thinking that takes place within the dimension of movement. But of course something can always go wrong here because—and this constitutes Freud's most radical philosophical gesture—the "contrast between what is subjective and what is objective does not exist from the beginning [*besteht nicht von Anfang an*]."[11] The reality-ego emerges from the pleasure-ego not by *discovering* in the realm of perception an object that corresponds to an internal image (*Vorstellung*) but rather by *rediscovering* such an object and *convincing* itself (*sich zu überzeugen*) that the object is still there independent of the ego's activity. The pleasure-ego will be encouraged to make forays into the world to rediscover those objects that afforded it, as Freud writes, "real satisfaction" but that have now been lost as a result of either maturation or prohibition. Thus the process of refinding these objects in the external world can result in "distortions" (*Entstellungen*).

At this point in the argument we come to the paragraph in "Negation" that is paradigmatic for David-Ménard's metapsychology of movement. Freud describes judgment "as an experimental action, a kind of groping forward [*ein motorisches Tasten*]," and he argues that we learn this "technique" of intellectual groping from our earlier experience of sensory groping. Insofar as sensory perception is an active cathectic process, so too is intellectual judgment; the difference consists above all in the amount of cathectic energy expended. Therefore Freud concludes that judgment involves the "primary processes" (*der primären Triebregungen*) and that affirma-

11. Sigmund Freud, "Negation," trans. Joan Riviere, in *General Psychological Theory* (New York: Collier, 1963), p. 215; translation slightly modified.

tion and negation implement the two fundamental drives of the pleasure principle: the instincts for union and for destruction. I should note the perhaps vertiginous homophony that emerges in this penultimate paragraph of "Negation" when "negation" (*Verneinung*) and "union" (*Vereinigung*) enter into such a finely differentiated proximity. The proximity between these two German words suggests that perhaps these two drives are the same, that a certain instinct for union is present in negation, and that a certain instinct for negation is present in union.

David-Ménard sees jouissance at work in the production of the "distortions" that occur when the satisfaction that had been taken in the lost object makes it difficult to rediscover such an object. Access to the symbolic order, in Lacan's idiom, becomes, in David-Ménard's idiom, the passage through motor judgment to the recognition of a lack, to the affirmation that certain lost-good-internal objects cannot be found again. Normative motor judgment would entail a certain "self-limitation of movements that create a space in which to circumscribe jouissance, to construct a body." The dimension of movement, of groping, is the order of Darstellung, the order of the presencing of the pleasure-ego's body of jouissance. The process of self-limitation involves the order of Vorstellung, of internal images that *re*present the images of perception and that signal the emergence of the reality-ego. Hysterics indulge too much in the pleasure-ego's gropings and do not leave themselves sufficient space to construct an erotogenic physical body. Obsessional neurotics, on the other hand, abandon this initial body of jouissance too precipitously and proceed too soon to the realm of Vorstellung. Both obsessionals and hysterics are unable to construct an erotogenic physical body, but for different reasons: hysterics because they experience the dimension of movement as an inward activity and are overwhelmed by desires they cannot check against reality, obsessionals because they transpose the dimension of movement outside the body and are haunted by the prohibitions rather than the desires that were originally prohibited. Whereas hysteric jouissance is always a question of the epistemology of disgust, obsessional jouissance involves the epistemology of the prohibition.

One of the most important contributions of *Hysteria from Freud to Lacan* is its clarification of the question of jouissance with reference to both language and the dimension of movement. Since Freud treats thought itself as an effect of the primary processes, which is to say an effect of jouissance, there is a certain temptation to collapse psychoanalytic theory into a critical monism. This is another version of the hysterization of analytic discourse itself. Lacan often exploits to great parodic effect the rhetorical resources of "*la substance jouissante,*"[12] a substance that knows its most immediate and forceful discharge through the foundation of a science of the real. As that aspect of pleasure that seeks to bring pleasure itself to an end, as that drive toward fusion that seeks to negate itself, jouissance is the unsatisfied residue of every desire, from which in turn the next sequence is generated. David-Ménard resists the temptation to reduce jouissance to a kind of substance, even if it is a signifying substance à la Lacan, and instead indicates, as Lacan does not, that jouissance is what divides bodily movement from and joins it to language, what orients one to the other even while keeping them rigorously distinct.

One of the lessons of *Hysteria from Freud to Lacan* is that the psychoanalytic theoretical and clinical intervention into hysteria suffers, in its own turn, from the very disgust with the body that it is attempting to cure. Furthermore, this disgust within a hysterized discourse develops a range of symptoms, from a theoretical avoidance of the dimension of bodily movement to a highly problematical aversion to feminine desire. The jouissance of psychoanalytic theories of hysteria is nowhere more clearly marked than in Freud's notion of penis envy and in Lacan's notion of the exclusivity of "phallic jouissance": "Jouissance is marked by this hole that leaves it no other path than phallic jouissance."[13] What the theory does while the theory says what it is doing, what is presented in the representation, what is discharged beneath the illusion of homeostasis, is the production, the mimesis, the emergence of *an aesthetic satisfaction, an aesthetic effect,* and this effect is produced through something disgusting, through something one would never suspect of being able to produce jouissance. Jouissance is an aesthetic text, an aesthetic-hysteric text.

"The mechanism of poetical creation [*Dichtung*] is the same as that of hysterical fantasies" (Freud to Fliess, May 31, 1897).[14] We

12. Jacques Lacan, *Le séminaire,* book 20, *Encore (1972–73),* ed. Jacques-Alain Miller (Paris: Seuil, 1975), p. 26.

13. *Encore,* p. 14.

14. *Complete Letters of Sigmund Freud to Wilhelm Fliess,* p. 251; translation slightly modified.

enjoy turning our noses away and having something disgusting to turn them away from. No less than the hysterical-poetical fantasy, the psychoanalytic fantasy that is theory enjoys the epistemology of disgust; it brings the hysterical body to the center stage of our intellectual and cultural lives and shows us that, despite all pretenses to the contrary, it has always been thus. And if we are outraged, if we are disgusted, so much the better, for disgust is like the audience's call for an *"Encore"* or, as Lacan writes it, *"En-corps,"* which we can translate rather freely here as "Bring on more bodies." Immanuel Kant wrote in *The Critique of Judgment* (1790), "There is only one kind of ugliness which cannot be represented in accordance with nature without destroying all aesthetical satisfaction, and consequently artistic beauty, namely, that which excites *disgust*."[15] Kant, however, had not read Freud's "Negation," where he would have learned the economy of the *nicht*. The hysterized discourse that is psychoanalysis teaches us that "all aesthetical satisfaction . . . excites *disgust*," and that that is precisely what makes it exciting. Perhaps the hysterization of discourse is synonymous with the becoming-disgusting of aesthetics.

15. Immanuel Kant, *Critique of Judgment*, trans. J. H. Bernard (New York: Hafner, 1966), p. 155; translation slightly modified.

Hysteria from Freud to Lacan

Hysterical Conversion and
Biological Metaphors for Pleasure

Psychoanalysis has to do with the body because it deals with sexuality; there is widespread agreement on this point. And yet beyond this vague banality, opinions differ. Some reduce the erotogenic body to the biological body, as the inventors of psychosomatics did in the 1920s. Some, following Jacques Lacan, deny that the instincts have an autonomous role in the constitution of a speaking subject in the place of the Other. In any event, they attach the erotogenic body to something other than itself in order to grant it a little reality.

In the beginning, however, psychoanalysis took a different tack. In a complex but consistent way, it linked the discovery of the unconscious to the discovery of the erotogenic body. Several aspects of this connection are worth noting. First of all, it points to the large-scale presence of hysterical symptoms in clinical practice. Whether they are viewed in a positive light (as Freud viewed the major crises he witnessed in Paris) or in a negative light (as he viewed motor paralyses), these symptoms have the body as their theater—although the status of this body remains to be clarified. The second aspect of the connection between the erotogenic body and the unconscious consists in the general assertion that a human individual is an apparatus capable of experiencing pleasure, unpleasure, and anxiety, and also an apparatus capable of thinking and speaking. The function of this apparatus is to discharge itself, and pleasure is defined as the sensation of energy discharge. But the structure of the apparatus allows it to postpone that experience; thinking is identified with the organization of the delay. Pleasure and thinking are represented here in terms of energy. The third aspect of the connection is one that Freud emphasizes repeatedly: he holds that primary satisfaction arises from discharge along motor pathways—discharge "in the direction of motility"[1]—rather than simply from a discharge of energy in general.[2] We may well wonder whether this satisfaction is mythical or real.

Freud's insistence on what he calls "discharge in the direction of motility," or the diversion of affect into bodily innervation, however, does not derive from an organicist framework. This point is the object of his report on his internship with Charcot at the Salpêtrière hospital: the visible features of hysterical paralysis do not correspond to any known or knowable organic cause. What can be seen is not necessarily defined by a physiological substratum or mechanism. Instead, in its configuration and in the problems that affect it, a hysteric's body conforms to everyday language. Hysteria is not acquainted with the anatomy of the nervous system. "It takes the organs in the ordinary, popular sense of the names they bear: the leg is the leg as far as its insertion into the hip; the arm is the upper limb as it is visible under the clothing" (*SE* 1:169). For a part of the body to be affected as popular speech would have it, and not as

1. See "Project for a Scientific Psychology," in *The Standard Edition of the Complete Psychological Works of Sigmund Freud*, ed. James Strachey, 24 vols. (London: Hogarth Press, 1953–74), 1:311, 317, 333 (in subsequent citations this edition will be designated by the abbreviation *SE* followed by volume and page numbers). Freud reaffirmed this principle in 1926 in "Inhibitions, Symptoms and Anxiety" (*SE* 20:94–95). Freud actually uses two terms, "motility" and "motion," in ways that are difficult to distinguish. "Motion" occurs more frequently in discussions of the psychical apparatus. "Motility" also appears in "Project," however, even with respect to the discharges with weak energy that characterize the system of consciousness (p. 311). In "Inhibitions, Symptoms and Anxiety" the expression "discharge through motility" (p. 95) refers to a specific action implying a relationship with an object that is external to the body itself and that makes the achievement of pleasure possible. "Discharge through motion" sometimes means energetistic discharge in general, whether thinking or pleasure is involved. But most often the first of these expressions designates the enactment of bodily movements in the experience of sexual jouissance or in symptoms, which presupposes a momentary cessation of representations.

2. Although pleasure, and thus motor discharges of weak intensity, may be secondarily associated with the work of thought, which distributes energies along diversified paths, in another sense the transformation of these energies into movement is opposed to such distribution, and pleasure is opposed to thought. By "energetistic discharge in general" we mean discharge that involves the pleasure of thinking. By "motor discharge" we mean discharge that also triggers bodily movements in the ordinary sense.

anatomy requires, the body must in some sense belong to the order of language. Instead of an injury to the arm, according to Freud, we have an injury to the idea of an arm. The subject may forget the idea of an arm, however, even while he maintains the use of his arm. Hysterical conversion thus differs from other types of symptoms, since in hysterical conversion affect is withheld from conscious influence and is diverted into bodily innervation (cf. *SE* 2:164). When Freud listens to motor symptoms instead of looking at them, he is thus by no means refusing to take into account the fact that they involve the body. To describe the specificity of these symptoms, he first used the confusing term "conversion" for the process by which an initially psychical affect would pass into bodily innervation. Later he found a better way of identifying the body in question by saying that hysterical symptoms and crises constitute a pantomime of sexual pleasure.

In these attempts to define the body that is at stake in hysteria, the reference to language makes it clear that the physiological body is not what is involved, even though the symptoms in question are not to be identified exclusively with discourse either. Instead, what is played out in the body takes the place of a discourse that cannot be uttered. Now, this is a decisive turning point; and when Freud speaks of thinking in terms of energy, when he speaks of pleasure in terms of energetistic or motor discharge, his formulations can no longer be accused of organicism.

Even as the clinical theory of hysteria was being developed, the close connection between the erotogenic body and the unconscious was being inscribed in Freud's formulations in a different way, one that no longer concerns hysteria alone but involves the psychical apparatus in general.

The expression "psychical apparatus" is ambiguous here, since this apparatus is a material framework capable of experiencing pleasure, pain, and anxiety. Let us therefore abandon the terms "corporal" or "psychical," so as to recall the statement with respect to which Freud never wavered: the sensation of pleasure corresponds to a motor discharge of energy within that framework. In articulating this general conception of pleasure, was Freud emprisoned by the image of the erection and relaxation of the penis or by the spectacle provided by hysterical crises? Not at all; for even though these images remain present in his general formulation, the notion of an apparatus that discharges itself immediately, or mediately, also leads to a reflection on the death instinct in its relation to sexual pleasure or *jouissance*.[3] The ultimate case of an apparatus that would, by discharging itself immediately, nullify all internal tensions and then return to the inanimate state represents that excess of sexual jouissance that always threatens stable configurations in the existence of a human subject. Death is not biological death here, but rather disorganization, of which sexual life in its delights—that is, its excesses—is always the correlative.

With such a reading of Freud's energeticism, which describes the specific aspect of human reality that can be delineated by the terms pleasure, unpleasure, and anxiety, we are led to abandon the idea that these experiences would affect a substratum that could be called body or mind; such notions prove wholly inadequate here. Moreover, it appears that the term mental or "psychical" is a confused one that has been created to designate something that is not organic and that refers to what is usually called thought.

For in his "Project for a Scientific Psychology" Freud brings off a tour de force in representing by a single model the pleasure–unpleasure–anxiety apparatus on the one hand—that is, sexual jouissance—and on the other hand thinking in its unconscious and conscious mechanisms. Freud's aim here is not to provide a theory of knowledge, as philosophers do. He is simply seeking to conceptualize the relation between sexual jouissance and the elaboration of thought. Bypassing the psychological distinction between psychical and somatic, and the philosophical distinction between mind and body, he represents the difference between experiencing sexual

3. We shall thus use the term *jouissance* to refer to sexual pleasure in this character of excess that links it to the death instinct. [In the translator's note accompanying his English translation of Lacan's *The Four Fundamental Concepts of Psycho-Analysis* (New York: W. W. Norton, 1978), Jacques-Alain Miller includes the following discussion of jouissance: "There is no adequate translation in English of this word. 'Enjoyment' conveys the sense, contained in *jouissance*, of enjoyment of rights, of property, etc. Unfortunately, in modern English, the word has lost the sexual connotations it still retains in French. (*Jouir* is slang for 'to come.') 'Pleasure,' on the other hand, is pre-empted by '*plaisir*'—and Lacan uses the two terms quite differently. 'Pleasure' obeys the law of homeostasis that Freud evokes in *Beyond the Pleasure Principle*, whereby, through discharge, the psyche seeks the lowest possible level of tension. '*Jouissance*' transgresses this law and, in that respect, it is *beyond* the pleasure principle" (p. 281). For the same reasons, I shall retain the French term *jouissance* in this translation. —TRANSLATOR'S NOTE]

jouissance and thinking as a difference in the level and distribution of energy within the apparatus, or as a relation between the structure and the function of that same apparatus: the structure of the so-called neuronic system serves to block quantities of energy from the paths of discharge; these quantities can then be distributed along associative paths instead of being discharged in conformity with the function of the neuronic system. To think is to defer sexual gratification, by developing chains of representations that maintain only a tenuous link with the memory of the objects that initially gave rise to pleasure. Or rather—for this opposition is still too simplistic—there are three fundamental moments or phases.

In the first place, sexual jouissance corresponds to the fact that the apparatus, fully cathected with a charge of desire, triggers the signal for discharge when it is in the presence of a desired object. All thought work is temporarily abandoned. The discharge here is doubly determined: the apparatus is emptied of all the accumulated energy of its desire, *and* the process entails a triggering of motility within the body. The second type of operation Freud describes is the operation of judgment: here the bridges between thought and the desire for sexual jouissance are not burned; but perceptual cathexes that are partly similar—that is to say partly dissimilar—are compared with memories of desired objects. When the two cathexes coincide, the apparatus may stop thinking and start experiencing jouissance, as in the previous case.[4] The third operation consists in disconnecting the representation from the hope of sexual jouissance. The process that takes place within the apparatus may neglect motor discharge and seek only the representation of the identity of one object with another one that is perceived for the first time. These operations of thought still have an energetistic component of weak intensity; but the reference to a weak circulation of energy is independent of the passage to motor discharge in which sexual jouissance consists. Thought can be developed in relative autonomy with respect to sexual desire proper: it remains related to that desire only in a representative way by the choice of the objects among which it establishes relations.

If the third moment of the Freudian schema is singled out for

---

4. "Project," *SE* 1:346, 347, and 350. Here discharge sometimes designates sexual gratification, sometimes only jouissance taken in the representation that Freud calls belief.

emphasis, the experience of satisfaction turns into a mythical "first time," which would involve the order of need, sexual desire proper being elaborated as a quest for rediscovery but also as mourning for the lost object. Jacques Lacan's reading takes this tack:[5] the Freudian machine represents desire in its relation to language; the displacements of weak energy materialize the circulation of signifiers. The only point of access to sexual jouissance comes about through the possibility, programmed into the machine, of hallucination.

"Judgment, thought, and so on," Lacan says, "are discharges that are energetistic inasmuch as they are inhibited. This is the construction that will always remain Freud's own when he says that thinking is an act maintained at the level of minimal cathexis. It is a simulated act, in a way.[6] It must be admitted that there is a reflection of the world, given that experience obliges us to posit a neutral perception—I say neutral from the point of view of the cathexes, that is a perception having minimal cathexes" (*Le moi*, p. 137). Here Lacan acknowledges the Freudian concept of thought as inhibited discharge, by and large, but his own aim is something else again: the formation of *a reflection of the world* in the apparatus. Lacan wants to localize what he himself calls the Imaginary and finds in the Freudian schema only as a lack (p. 125). Indeed, Freud does not raise the issue of object orientation here, or the issue of the relation to the other as to an image of oneself, and he does not define consciousness as a reflection of the world. To be sure, in the schema of the apparatus there exists a special system (ω) that registers not quantities of energy but frequencies and that corresponds to what Freud calls the signal of consciousness. This is a decisive cog in the machine, decisive because of the uncertainties that affect its operation: for this signal may be triggered either when quantities of energy arriving from the external periphery of the apparatus, that is, from reality, transmit information to ω or when a charge of internal desire—quantities coming from the internal periphery—triggers the same signal of consciousness or the same reality index. In the

5. *The Seminar of Jacques Lacan, Book 2: The Ego in Freud's Theory and in the Technique of Psychoanalysis, 1954–1955*, ed. Jacques-Alain Miller, trans. Sylvana Tomaselli (New York: W. W. Norton, 1988), chaps. 7–10.

6. Simulation, for Freud, is precisely not a purely representational activity. When the "imitation value" of a perception is involved, it is because we are dealing with motor discharge, which Freud calls primary judgment. See "Project," *SE* 1:333.

second case we have a hallucination, not a perception. And no subject masters the difference between the two; this difference can be assured only if the intermediary system (ψ) multiplies the associative—that is, memory-based and representative—connections; on this condition alone, these ramifications play the role of an effective filter when significant quantities approach these neuronic regions (ψ). Only on this condition can the signal of consciousness avoid switching on inappropriately.

In this view of consciousness, its traditional prerogative of putting the subject into relation with a perceived reality is no longer guaranteed. But Freud's interest does not hinge upon the constitution of an image of the world. A signal is not necessarily a light of consciousness that would introduce us to the problematics of consciousness as the elaboration of a reflection of reality. For Lacan it goes without saying—although the self-evidence of the proposition does not constitute the object of any justification—that the signal of consciousness is the visual reflection of the self and of objects. And it is on this point that Lacan veers away from the Freudian schema with his own conception of the "mirror stage," of the body as an image of the body, and of narcissism.

But Lacan's text in effect becomes polarized by the question of the visibility of the self and of objects and by a conception of knowing envisaged in its relation to the register of the Imaginary. Now this is not at all the case for Freud. When Freud speaks of the triggering, at a given point in the system, of the signal of consciousness, nothing suggests that that signal gives off any reflection; he is concerned only with an *index of the presence* of something; that is what interests Freud, since it is the crucial factor that has to be regulated in order to avoid catastrophes such as hallucinations or hysterical crises. The effect of the index of presence is to trigger a motor discharge. Freud is interested in the signal produced in ω, because it makes the apparatus pass from representational operation to motor operation and because this may come about in the absence of any object allowing actual sexual gratification. The importance of ω hinges entirely upon this risk. Moreover, when Freud deals with the relations between thought and reality—that is, with representational and reproductive activities that are seeking identity even though they have given up the right to discharge (*SE* 1:329, 332)— he is no longer interested in ω. Unlike Lacan, Freud is not con-

7

structing a theory of knowledge as a relation to an imaginary world or rather, as an imaginary relation to a world. He is merely describing the way the activities of thought and, at times, of perception are rooted in the experience of sexual jouissance. That is why he defines consciousness as providing indexes of qualities; and he never specifies that these indexes are predominantly visual or that they open the way to the elaboration of a reflection of the world. Indexes of qualities may just as well be auditory, tactile, gustatory, or olfactory; there is no reason to suppose otherwise. They consist simply in the subject's sudden feeling of the undeniable presence of something that he desires to enjoy sexually and that triggers a motor discharge, that is, produces jouissance in his body. Now the structure of the apparatus represented by Freud makes it possible to show that this feeling is in itself by no means a guarantee of the actual presence of that "something." The more the subject develops his representational, associative, and cognitive activities, the more he will be prey to the risk of experiencing a jouissance that is not connected to any "something." If the Freudian categories are to be opposed to the Lacanian ones, we should rather say that in the "Project" Freud is attempting to conceptualize the relation between the Real and the Symbolic. The Imaginary is not a predominant consideration here, for the body is not conceived as an image of the body; it is not a representation or a fantasy, but it corresponds to the moment of realization of sexual jouissance, which Freud always calls "discharge in the direction of motility" and which presupposes a moment when thought is suspended. For Freud, then, the body is not reduced to a representation of the body. Instead, the motor discharge in which sexual jouissance consists presupposes the temporary abolition of representations.[7] Between sexual jouissance and thought, in fact, we find relations of proximity and reciprocal exclusion.[8] Thus in the Freudian model the experience of satisfaction cannot be said to be purely mythical: Freud is not merely contrasting a mythical satisfaction of a need with a nostalgia for that satisfaction that would constitute the core of sexual desire proper.

7. The term representation has two different meanings in turn here. It first designates the image of the body and the fantasy as imaginary, then the activity of thinking as judgment and reproduction.
8. On the persistence of this theme in Freud see, for example, "Notes upon a Case of Obsessional Neurosis" (the Rat Man case), *SE* 10:244.

He contrasts sexual desire, inasmuch as it is realized in experiences of jouissance, with desire that is inhibited in its realization but capable of satisfying itself with representational activities. In the latter case, the only shred of evidence that thinking is rooted in sexual desire lies in what might be called thought's tireless energy or exigency, which confers upon it the character of absolute necessity in a subject's existence: this may take the form of obsessional symptoms or delusions, but it may also appear as the elaboration of an artistic, philosophical, or scientific work. Perhaps the specific logic, grammar, and style of such works also make it possible to grasp the way they arise on the basis of a sexual desire that has renounced the possibility of realization but that does not cease to assert itself in these productions of thought. To demonstrate this would be the task of another book.

But so far as our present topic is concerned, since the body in psychoanalysis is not reduced to a representation of the body, it has seemed indispensable to create a term that would designate it. When we are concerned with what may or may not be realized in sexual jouissance, we shall speak of the "motor imaginary" and not of the Imaginary in the strictly Lacanian sense. Epistemologically, we are thus taking care not to relegate to the sidelines Freud's idea that sexual satisfaction is produced by a discharge that puts motility into play in the body, once we have understood that this idea, for Freud, is not at all organicist or biologistic. Clinically, the notion of a "motor imaginary" will also make it possible to account for what is going on in what is called conversion hysteria, in which the passion for the visible is never found all by itself but is always linked to a crazy—or else inopportunely triggered—hope of realizing, through and on the body, a sexual jouissance to which the subject is committed. This is what Freud calls the conversion of affects or bodily innervation.

Freud always considered the concept of hysterical conversion both indispensable and mysterious. The notion was present in the earliest formulations that allowed him, distancing himself from Pierre Janet, to abandon any psychopathology based on the idea of degeneracy, and it persisted through all the experiments and all the reworkings by means of which Freud attempted to shed light on the unconscious. This continuity is not without a few solid paradoxes, which are explicitly formulated in the *Studies on Hysteria*, with

9

reference to the treatment of Elisabeth von R, for example: "The mechanism," Freud wrote, "was that of conversion: i.e. in place of the mental [*seelische*] pains which she avoided, physical [*körperlich*] pains made their appearance. . . . I cannot, I must confess, give any hint of how a conversion of this kind is brought about."⁹ Freud never wavered in this posture of acknowledging the presence of mystery. At certain moments in his reflection, he advised against letting oneself be blinded by these paradoxical symptoms: "Anyone who studies hysteria," he notes, "soon finds his interest turned away from its symptoms to the phantasies from which they proceed."¹⁰

In 1908 and 1909 Freud broke away from the complications of conversion. He did so not by explicitly criticizing the notion, but by speaking differently about its object: hysterical attacks, he now maintains, are nothing but "phantasies translated into the motor sphere, projected on to motility and portrayed in pantomime."¹¹ The notion of pantomime, if it were developed, would perhaps make it possible to escape from the psychical and somatic categories to which, on the contrary, the notion of conversion rivets us. But Freud in fact never goes so far as to attempt such elucidation. And when he returns to pay close attention to the specificity of symptom formation in hysteria and in obsessional neurosis, he abandons conversion to its "peculiar obscurity"¹² and hopes to find himself on more familiar ground with obsessional neurosis. Nevertheless, this relinquishment does not amount to negligence, since at the same time the affective states in general are understood as hysterical attacks (*SE* 20:93).

How are we to understand Freud's faithfulness to formulations that maintain a mystery since they posit at the same time a heterogeneity and a homogeneity between what is called psychical and then, depending on circumstances, the corporal, organic, or somatic?

Retrospectively, if we survey the later Freudian developments that spoke a different language, we may be inclined to be impatient:

---

9. Sigmund Freud and Josef Breuer, *Studies on Hysteria*, SE 2:166.

10. "Hysterical Phantasies and Their Relation to Bisexuality," *SE* 9:162.

11. "Some General Remarks on Hysterical Attacks," *SE* 9:229.

12. "Why the formation of symptoms in conversion hysteria should be such a peculiarly obscure thing I cannot tell" (*SE* 20:112).

if there is a mystery involving hysterical conversion or the passage from psychical energy into somatic innervation, it is because the idea of the psychical is a confused notion to begin with. We can understand how Freud fastened upon this concept when he was comparing organic paralyses and hysterical paralyses: since a given paralysis of the arm corresponded to no neurological cause but sometimes could be relieved by narratives, Freud declared that what was involved was an injury to the idea of the arm; and the idea of the arm was deemed psychical—since it was not organic. But the term "psychical" begins by abolishing the relation between representations and discourses on the one hand and the erotogenic body on the other; and when that relation surfaces again in certain symptoms, we hear about a mysterious passage into the organic realm. The circle closes when Freud is led to say that that conversion concerns not only hysteria but all states of affect. Since the medical body is kept at bay only through the term "psychical," however, there is no question of giving it up; its obscurity is simply recognized and accepted.

Yet this retrospective overview is too concise. It does not account either for the complexity of what Freud confronts under the label of "hysterical conversion" or for the importance this question has had in the history of psychoanalysis and in the establishment of what is called psychosomatics.

For Freud himself, even before he put forward the notion of erotogenic body or of instinct, the obscurity of hysterical conversion arose from the fact that that conversion was at once a causal and a symbolic phenomenon. The mechanism of conversion signifies the passage, the transport, the transposition of something—energy or affect—from the psychical domain into another that is heterogeneous to it, the body. How are we to reconcile these three terms: passage, transport, transposition? The passage has to be conceived both as the effect of causality and as a symbolic shaping, a transcription. The patients Freud listened to saw their symptoms form when they began to reach for a line of reasoning such as the following: "This can't go on any longer, so I'm to be paralyzed." But that reasoning was, precisely, unformulated: the "symbolizing conversion" is, to be sure, not easy to conceptualize. But it is all the less so when the categories available for its conceptualization are those of the psychical and the organic.

This distinction is not problematic in itself, and in any event there is a precedent here: the study of a human subject as a compound made up of two substances was inaugurated by Descartes in his treatise *The Passions of the Soul*. The clear distinction between body and soul (mind), far from signifying that there can be no relation between them, on the contrary allows us to know their possible relations. It is only because there is nothing spiritual in the order of the body and nothing corporal in the order of the soul that what is produced in each substance has effects on the other. In the body, everything is movement; the body does not think in any way. But for any perceptive act of consciousness, an external object has to set our corporal machine in motion; this machine will provoke the perception by way of the animal spirits and the pineal gland. And that causal action of the body on the soul is confirmed, in the absence of any external object, in the productions of the imagination. Conversely, there is nothing corporal in the soul; and its actions are acts of will that have, among other powers, the power of governing the body.

It is correct to say[13] that the Cartesian soul is not the psyche of the late nineteenth century. However, the Cartesian dualism is the basis not only of neurology, which distinguishes the voluntary and involuntary nervous systems, but also of psychosomatic theory. The notion of emotion, a central one for psychosomatics, designates after all a causal action of the psyche on the body. The psychosomaticians, moreover, were well aware of this:[14] their discipline is based first of all on a dualism of substances that makes relations of reciprocal causality conceivable.

But when we are talking about hysterical conversion, these dualist principles—even though they are present in our terminology—become unusable because the hysterical body thinks.[15] When Elisabeth was paralyzed, it was because she felt helpless, because she told herself she could no longer walk as before. Here and here alone

13. Georges Canguilhem, "Qu'est-ce que la psychologie?" in *Etudes d'histoire et de philosophie des sciences* (Paris: Vrin, 1968).

14. Thus Jean Delay considers the Cartesian theory of the pineal gland to be an intuition verified by contemporary research on the hypophysothalamic region: see his *Introduction à la médecine psychosomatique* (Paris: Masson, 1961), pp. 12–13.

15. That psychoanalytically the hysterical symptom, hinged to the realization of a jouissance, does not accede to the representation of the desire does not mean that epistemologically it must be said to think.

do we have the nub of the riddle of the "leap into the organic." How can we understand that a thought, which is initially psychical, becomes a physiological mechanism without ceasing to be a thought?

Furthermore, the dualist principles become unusable for a second reason: when we are dealing with hysterical conversion, a monism of affect is couched within the duality of the corporal and the psychical. Certain of Freud's texts seem to encourage this drift: if we substantialize libido or affect, we will seek to determine in what cases they remain or do not remain within the psychic domain. Breaking free of the specific features of symbolizing hysterical conversion, certain analysts will later propose to extend the concept of conversion to the entire field of what is to be called, following Franz Alexander or Felix Deutsch, psychosomatics. Deutsch[16] will search for the secret of conversion in a metabiological order that antedates the differentiation of the psychic and the psychological. There is a future, then, for the obscurities of conversion.

These paradoxes constitute a point of departure that affects the entire history of psychoanalysis. From Freud to Lacan, there will always be two sides to this question, epistemological and technical, that play off against each other in a curious way. The obscurity of the phenomenon seems to involve an issue in the history of science: How can a thought be diverted into bodily innervation while at the same time it remains a thought—given that the hysterical symptom takes the place of an utterance? There is no solution to this problem within the framework of a dualist epistemology. But from a different viewpoint, that of analytic technique, Freud suggests that this question not be overemphasized. That he loses interest in the symptom in its specificity, in 1908, signifies that as he listens to his patients he does not take into account the difference between one hysterical symptom and another. This omission inaugurates a division. One group, analysts drawn to psychosomatics—such as Felix Deutsch and Franz Alexander—could be considered the only ones who remained interested in the role of the body in hysteria; they drew hysteria into the orbit of emotional disturbances.[17] The others—Freud, Melanie Klein, Lacan—are interested in the structure

16. Felix Deutsch, "Zur Bildung des Konversionssymptoms," *Internationale Zeitschrift für Psychoanalyse*, 1924, no. 3, pp. 380–92.

17. Ibid., and Franz Alexander, *La médecine psychosomatique* (Paris: Payot, 1962).

of hysterical fantasies without making further concessions to the fascination exerted by the body that the hysteric patient exhibits and that the analyst no longer takes into account, since he is listening (rather than looking). In the Lacanian tradition, listening to signifying plays on words involves language and "innervations" in the same way. Thus Octave Mannoni writes: "A psychoanalyst dreamed the following dream: he was setting the table and certain articles of silverware kept turning out of the proper alignment. That is the entire dream. There were no associations. The analyst hazards the polysemic: 'That turned out badly. . . .' In 'that turned out badly,' the reader cannot fail to recognize the same form as in 'You are not on an equal footing' in *Studies on Hysteria*, and there the interpretation did not apply to a dream. *The effects of polysemy are expressed just as well, as we can see, in the imagery of dreams as in symptomatic bodily attitudes.*"[18]

In the numerous works in which Jacques Lacan develops and refines his analytic listening to hysterics, the emphasis falls exclusively on the complexity of identificatory relations.[19] If we follow the successive readings of the Dora case in the history of psychoanalysis,[20] do we not end up saying that the essence of hysteria is played out in the traumatic relation to the maternal, a relation affecting every demand that, addressed to a man, derives from that relation its absolute character and that, for that reason too, takes the form of a violent refusal? In treatment this is the most difficult aspect to analyze, but it is the crucial one. The question of conversion would thus be secondary. But for Lacan himself things are more complicated: the epistemological problem turns out not to be eliminated but to be disconnected from the clinical question. With respect to Dora, Lacan insists on the identification with a man, which directs the interrogation of the hysteric toward femininity; and that has nothing to do with the form of the symptom. Elsewhere, however, when he attempts to conceptualize the relation between desire as a signifying organization and instinct, conversion

18. Octave Mannoni, *Clefs pour l'imaginaire, ou L'autre scène* (Paris: Seuil, 1969), pp. 45–46; emphasis added.

19. Jacques Lacan, "Intervention sur le transfert" (1951), in *Ecrits* (Paris: Seuil, 1966), p. 215; and his unpublished seminar "L'envers de la psychanalyse" (1970–71), January 14 and 20, February 11 and 18, 1971. See below, pp. 74–75 and 92.

20. "Sur l'hystérie," special issue of *Revue Française de Psychanalyse* 37 (May 1973). See also *L'hystérie*, special issue of *Confrontations Psychiatriques* 1 (1968).

and the difficulties it raises come back to the surface. Lacan mentions the problem, in fresh terms, with respect to false pregnancies, for example: "What did she show by this? One may speculate, but one must refrain from resorting too precipitously to the language of the body. Let us say simply that the domain of sexuality shows a natural functioning of signs. At this level, they are not signifiers, for the nervous pregnancy is a symptom and, according to the definition of the sign, something intended for someone. The signifier, being something quite different, represents a subject for another signifier."[21] We may be tempted to speculate. Hysteria, which resists the signifier by relegating the body to the rank of signs, invites this, but. . . . Lacan stays away from speculation! His new formulation of the mystery of hysteria is at the same time generalized, however. There is a double movement in Lacan, partially analogous to what was taking place in Freud: the latter recommended detachment from the paradoxical symptom, but in a certain way he generalized its import first through his conception of pleasure as a sensation of discharge, then by introducing (in 1915) the notion of instinct, which inherits some of the obscurities of conversion—"limiting concept between the psychical and the somatic." Lacan is interested in the determination of desire by the symbolic order, whether hysteria or some other structure is involved. Nevertheless, hysteria indicates something about sexuality in general: sexuality, as if it were itself hysterical, "shows a natural functioning of signs." We need not insist on this; to do so would be to positivize unduly the body that comes into play in the instinct! The entire Lacanian solution to the question of the relations between desire and instinct consists, on the contrary, in positing that these two registers are articulated because each one in its own order includes an essential moment of negation. The object of the instinct fills in for an empty space, and the subject is a vacillation between two signifiers. As the objectal void and subjective gap converge, sexuality—biological as well as instinctual—and language would be articulated. We can see why Lacan did not pay sustained attention to the epistemology of conversion, which always positivizes the body to a greater or lesser degree in order to determine its status. But this recourse to the negative cannot stand as a solution to the

21. Lacan, *Four Fundamental Concepts of Psycho-Analysis*, p. 157. (Cited hereafter as *FFC*.)

problem: when two or three series—biological sexuality, the determination of the subject by a system of signifiers, and instincts—are heterogeneous, their heterogeneity is not abolished because each of these series presents a negative aspect. And the Lacanian recourse to topology extends to the unconscious in general the difficulty raised locally by hysterical conversion, by positing the necessity of conceptualizing the former in spatial terms—though such a conceptualization is the correlative of "a certain impotence in your thinking" (*FFC*, p. 209). We are not so far removed after all from Freud's reflections on the obscurities of hysterical conversion, although the language has changed considerably.

But the Freud/Lacan confrontation reveals that the epistemological question and the technicotheoretical question, though they may be distinct, and even precisely because they are, are not without connections: to polarize attention on the fascinating obscurities of hysterical conversion is, in the guise of epistemology, to obstruct the paths of the symptom in analytic practice and theory. But to neglect entirely the role of the body that comes into play in hysteria in order to be able to listen to it and analyze it does not do away with the body's fascination, which reappears in the theory, generalized. How might we unravel a few threads of that skein?

Chapter 1

The First Theory of Conversion

Pain in Physiology and Psychoanalysis

What is hysterical pain? The paradoxical encounter between clinical observation and hysteria can be formulated as this question, which Freud takes as a starting point in his account of the case of Elisabeth von R. The question implies a new assessment of what a doctor is asking when he interrogates a patient; or rather, the patient's answers themselves oblige the doctor to reconsider what his questions ordinarily imply. What does it mean to localize pain, to describe it? The pain in Elisabeth's legs is "of an indefinite character" (*SE* 2:135) according to the prevailing organic nosography. There are tests designed to show pain as the sign of a causal connection between a sensory experience and an objective process, but these tests seem to have failed. Elisabeth is in fact suffering from a painful fatigue. Freud can say that her pain emanates from the front of her right thigh, adding that it also extends to other areas in both legs; and yet these details do not suggest a line of inquiry that might lead the investigation back to a previously identified problem. But the atypical character of Elisabeth's pain does much more than signify a lack or question mark, an incomplete knowledge of physiological problems and their manifestations; it also implies a new status for the body that is involved in what the patient tells the doctor about her complaints. Hysteria and hypochondria are both opposed in this sense to ordinary organic pain, that is, to those aspects of pain usually noted by clinicians for the purpose of developing a physiological interpretation. Freud presents his interlocking modifications of the medical examination and the patient's relation to her problem with particular clarity. In an organic illness or in the organic approach to illness, the patient's awareness of it is invoked as a still confused but already informative description of the nature of the problem. The effort to localize the pain indicates the patient's attitude: he turns his own experience into material for an inquiry into causes. The language of his pain is reformulated as information about his sensations. In hysteria and hypochondria, on the contrary, the body seems to be a pretext for language. Here the body is not so much the object of the hypochondriac's discourse as the territory or field in which that discourse operates. As if something were slipping out of control in the obligatory reformulation whereby pain becomes medical information, the hypochondriacal subject provides information in excess. His discourse offers a plethora of description and objectivization, for its very repetitiveness demonstrates both the necessity and the impossibility of finding out what is causing the pain. The way the hypochondriac remains on the terrain of the body-object even while undermining it is one way of subverting the pertinence of the body that medical practice has constructed.

However, the hypochondriac's pretext-body differs from the hysteric's.[1] Though the hysteric's language remains on the terrain of the suffering body that is to be described, it does not serve to stamp that body with an inexpressible profundity or to assert, along with the body's reality, its incomparable character. Hysterical pain, which does not lack physiological characteristics—they are atypical, to be sure, but they are nevertheless real—comes up again in another register. Freud points this out: Elisabeth's problem is important to her, but something else has gotten her attention. The paradoxical nature of her problem is described first of all by way of a lexical paradox: Freud uses the intellectualist term "attention" to designate something quite different from the relation of a confused knowledge to a physiological process under investigation that is presumed to be the cause of a pain initially expressed in an anarchic, irrational manner, as in a dream language. Here the term "attention" refers to pain that still has a physiological basis but that also

1. This Freudian distinction leads us to limit our research to hysteric conversion. The reevaluation of the somatic that is based upon hypochondria is another undertaking entirely.

serves as signifying material—that is, as the constitutive element of a language lacking in cognitive aims.

The ambiguity of the body here might be compared with the dual aspect of the linguistic sign: pain could offer an example of the material basis of every signifier. And phonology, which identifies the elementary vocal oppositions of a language, deals with physiological objects—sounds—whose characteristics can be inventoried with the help of delicate physical instrumentation. Moreover, the physical reality of these objects is bracketed, as it were (and not actually suppressed), so that the objects (sounds) can be defined as signifiers, as systems of differential abstract elements whose organization makes it possible to build a description of the structure of a language.

Hysterical pain, like any reality grasped within a signifying structure, has to be known in its two sides or aspects. Yet the notion of attention does not account very well for this duality. If we were looking for other, comparable phenomena, we might turn for example to Husserl, who analyzed the status of mathematical idealities in his "Origin of Geometry."[2] In geometry too an abstract entity exists in a coherent language only because elsewhere it is an element within a system of material written signs. The paradox in geometry is that the ideality of mathematical notions has as its condition for existence the materiality of the written signs, a materiality that alone ensures or even produces by its permanence the universality of these notions.

Hysterical pain is not a mathematical ideality. But it is the material element of a language in which, without ever losing its physiological reality, hysterical pain supports another type of reality whose ambiguous status—in the proper sense of the term—Freud indicates by speaking of hysterogenic zones.

"In the case of Fräulein von R., however, if one pressed or pinched the hyperalgesic skin and muscles of her legs, her face assumed a peculiar expression, which was one of pleasure rather than pain" (*SE* 2:137). By mentioning the patient's expression here, Freud is referring, albeit obscurely, to the ambiguity of the hysterical body.

2. In Jacques Derrida, *Edmund Husserl's "Origin of Geometry": An Introduction*, trans. John P. Leavey, Jr., ed. David B. Allison (Stony Brook, N.Y.: Nicolas Hays, 1978), pp. 162–64.

The idea of bodily expressivity, a commonplace notion that is extremely difficult to develop, leads us to refine our comparison with the double aspect of linguistic signs. In a language, when physiological phonic elements are grasped within a signifying system, they unquestionably keep their physiological reality: the problem of preserving magnetic tapes or of setting up the appropriate physical conditions for electronic sound recording suffices to illustrate this. But the materiality of the hysteric's body raises a different question. What is expressive—that is, what constitutes the language of the hysterical subject—is not merely a pain; it consists of bodily movements that, though they may be organized around the pain, nevertheless continue to exist in a physiological body that is defined by its own mechanisms. Not only does pain seem to be the signifier of satisfaction, in this instance, but the reality of the body—always in some measure physiological—is also, apparently, what brings about the relation of signification between the two aspects of pain. Not only is a double aspect of the sign analyzed in the object by two heterogeneous although inseparable procedures, but these two aspects combined in one are also confused in the body itself: "She cried out—and I could not help thinking that it was as though she was having a voluptuous tickling sensation—her face flushed, she threw back her head and shut her eyes and her body bent backwards" (*SE* 2:137).

The function of this description is not easy to specify. It focuses less on the body subject to physiological study (although that body continues to be present) than on the body we all perceive, the body that is seen and offered to view. That the body is in motion need not lead us to begin by seeking the components or the physiological consequences of its movements, even though these exist, but rather might lead us to consider its movements as the perceptible appearance of a signifying system or a language that plays upon the visible.

The situation is even more complicated than in the case of ordinary language signs. Although the physical reality of language signs is always present, it is heightened, as it were, in the sense of the Hegelian *Aufhebung*, within the reality of the signifying system. No one would ever think of continuing to view the sounds of a language as physical data pure and simple. *In hysteria, on the contrary, the body's signifying reality is masked, as it were, and may go unrecog-*

nized, because it is produced by way of movements. The continuing tendency, in the history of psychiatric thought, to analyze hysteria through its physiological manifestations by differentiating them from the other complaints they resemble shows how difficult it is to comprehend the ambiguity of the body in hysterical symptoms.[3] Freud's language itself offers evidence of this. His description of the movements of Elisabeth's body concludes with the following notation: "None of this was very exaggerated but it was distinctly noticeable" (*SE* 2:137). What a peculiar remark, under its anodyne appearance! What does *exaggerated* mean? Might we not say that, from the standpoint of a medical description that relates visible signs to a physiological foundation, the manifestions may appear inadequate, whereas at the same time it is undeniable—*distinctly noticeable*—that the movements in question are bodily manifestations arising from another type of reality?

Perhaps the difficulty may be expressed another way. Whereas the linguistic sign is resolutely ambiguous,[4] the hysterical body has more than two faces, for the movements perceived provide a way of approaching this body initially endowed with a sort of self-evidence that disintegrates or not depending on whether the movements are related to a physiological foundation or to the signifying but nonverbal order, to what is "offered to view."

Perhaps we need to allow for three views of the body: the perceived body, the physiological body, and the body that we shall later call the motor imaginary. Or we may do better to note that the perceived body does not hold up on its own, *since, in the end, bodily movements are perceived variably according to what one is expecting to find in the first place: the physiological body or the imaginary one.*

We cannot settle these questions for the time being. Still, it is important to note how the different levels of the body's reality are interrelated. The difficulty of conceptualizing the body's status in hysteria arises because in reality its physiological aspect is not separated from its symbolic value—as might happen in a play on words that is not simultaneously acted out by the body. From the stand-

<hr />

3. H. Baruk and L. Von Bogaert attempt to delineate hysteria by taking the visible as their criterion; see *Congrès des médecins aliénistes et neurologistes de langue française* (Paris: Masson, 1935).

4. In the sense defined here, which does not include the notion of double articulation in linguistics.

point of unconscious structure, it is surely not irrelevant that the subject's language is deployed in the realm of the visible and thus is open to confusion with movements that belong to the physiological arena. This is not to suggest that the subject simulates organic problems for the doctor's benefit, for that perspective simply attributes to the hysteric unconscious a medical nature consonant with the doctor's point of view. We are suggesting rather that, within the realm of unconscious symbolizations itself, what is "offered to view" entails an attempt to cancel out symbolization by way of action.

Critique of All Ontologies of the Body

If we are to arrive at an adequate conceptualization of what is "offered to view" in hysteria, we have to follow Freud, who had his own way of analyzing pain, and free ourselves from what Gaston Bachelard called the substantialist obstacle,[5] a realist approach to the body that grants ontological priority to physiological constructs.

In the case in point, the substantialist obstacle treats physically constructed movements as the essence of all perceived reality; it reproduces the Cartesian approach that Bachelard attacks so forcefully. Descartes thought that any scientific approach worthy of the name had to establish its own physicomathematical foundations and build its complex constructions up from the rationally evident character of simple elements; that requirement ensured the ontological value of science. Descartes appears to be undertaking a radical critique of the privileges of sensory experience; he seems to be establishing a discontinuity between such experience and the construction of the real. But no sooner is the method for acquiring knowledge unique, no sooner is it supposed to give us the essence of things, than the apparent discontinuity dissolves.

If the physicomathematical essence of every perceptible phenomenon can be determined, the discredit into which sense perception has fallen is overcome: there is at least *one* relation of identity between what is perceived and what is constructed. The perceptible is always the appearance of the physicomathematical, so that its consistency never wavers in the end. By demonstrating the neces-

5. *La formation de l'esprit scientifique*, 5th ed. (Paris: Vrin, 1967), chap. 6, p. 97.

sity of a non-Cartesian epistemology, in *Le nouvel esprit scientifique* (1963) Bachelard denounces the collusion of an ontological conception of science with trust in the data of primary experience. If appearances can be grounded through reference to a language and to a unique method of acquiring knowledge, suspicion with respect to appearances can be nipped in the bud: the observer would not trust in the sensory appearance of things, of course, but in order to account for things would always take the same direction, since there exists a true thought for each datum of perception.

By requiring us to renounce this tranquil univocity of being, Bachelard's reflection on the plurality of scientific methods and languages opens up the gap between what is perceived and what is constructed. Even in this case, however—even if the schema of the atom proposed by Nils Bohr and inspired by celestial mechanics has had to be criticized as an image, since it applied improperly to the sphere of the atom a conception of the relation between a body's mass and its speed that was valid only in another realm[6]—the fact remains that, from celestial mechanics to quantum mechanics we remain within the field of physics. The sensory apprehension of a phenomenon is disqualified, it splinters under the multiplicity of methods of construction of the superobject, but objects and superobjects belong to a single domain, that of physics. And the possibility of such a bracketing of the perceptual order is supported by the fact that within the atomic order, for example, phenomena can no longer arise independent of the specific experimental procedures that cause the superobject to appear.

In psychoanalysis, and particularly when the body is in question, the obstacles are more numerous and more dangerous. First of all, we have to give up the idea that perception would be an appropriate terrain on which to identify effects of the unconscious order. We then have to give up the idea that there is a simple, univocal relation between the order of our own perceptions and the nature of the phenomenon under consideration.

But even after we have made this break, the fact remains that we will continue to perceive motor manifestations in symptoms. The physicist's situation is different: once he has criticized every representation of the atom—whether naive or well informed, they will still all be inadequate—he will no longer be tempted to rely upon

6. *The Philosophy of No: A Philosophy of the New Scientific Mind*, trans. G. C. Waterston (New York: Orion Press, 1968), pp. 118–19.

perceptual appearances, for the autonomy of his object does not emerge in that way. The psychoanalyst, on the contrary, even if he knows that the order of desire must not be confused with his perceptions of his patient, will nevertheless continue to perceive that order. Even though he knows that the erotogenic body cannot be conceptualized in the same way as the organic body, he will still be dealing with symptoms that stem from the organic body as well.

This means that the symptom he is seeking to understand and whose components he is attempting to isolate continues to present itself to him with the same confusion. The psychoanalyst mistrusts what he first perceives as thoroughly as the physicist does, if not more so, but when he reconstructs the symptom the perceptual confusion is not eliminated. He does not construct a superobject that assigns a place to the perceptual residues. The analyst mistrusts the perceptual data as much as the physicist does, but in the analyst's case these data are not reorganized by an instrumental technique that dissolves their appearance.

In the very definition of a symptom, in the approach to what is called a symptom, the persistence of the perceptual order, even when this order is misleading, will not be eliminated. Through this persistence, the dialectics of immediate experience and reconstructed experience is thus radicalized in that it is distanced in two different ways from what Bachelard had to say about the sciences of nature. This dialectic obliges us to understand how a single phenomenon arises from two different orders of truth that will always remain confused in our immediate apprehension of the phenomenon. And it demonstrates that we have to give immediate experience a role to play in the approach to the object itself, even though we know that experience is deceptive. In physics, epistemological obstacles may arise again and again in new forms, but at every stage they can be eliminated. In psychoanalysis the epistemological obstacle of primary experience cannot, on principle, be dissolved: it is inseparable from the clinical approach.

Conversion in Theory (Innervation) and Practice (Pleasure-Body)

An epistemological study of the idea of hysterical conversion requires a retrospective reading of Freud's texts. To indicate the trends of thought that crisscross and sometimes contradict each other in the notion of conversion as Freud uses it, we shall be guided by what psychoanalysis has gradually delineated as the place of the unconscious. In what follows we shall use Freud against Freud, inquiring why in his later discussions of hysteria he maintains the idea of conversion, which in many respects acts as an obstacle to the discovery of the autonomous order of the unconscious.

As he studies the case of Elisabeth von R., Freud sets out to understand symptom formation in astasia-abasia by distinguishing the cause (*Verursachung*) of the illness from its specific determination (*Determinierung*), that is, the modalities of its installation. It can be shown that the second of these terms not only introduces a certain degree of specificity with respect to the first but also undercuts the dualist tonality of the first term.

Freud's working procedure can be described as follows: he sets out to try to comprehend the relation (*Zusammenhang*) between the history of the illness as a set of psychic particulars and the illness itself.[7] An underlying assumption here is that we are confronting two heterogeneous series (*SE* 2:144): there is at first no relation between the history of the girl's unhappiness and her painful loco-motor symptoms. When Freud comes to understand the relationship, the terms he brings together are no longer the same ones: what is at stake turns out to be something other than an effect of causality or an association between something in the soul (*das Seelische*) and something in the body (*das Körperliche*). The dualism posited between these two orders ends up being specified in turn along two different lines, causal and associative.

Freud wonders first of all whether the relation between the *See-lisch* and the *Körperlich* might not be explained by the coincidence in time—the hypothesis of a temporal accident of association here increases the heterogeneity of the two series—of a painful experi-ence and physical pains. Perhaps Elisabeth, reliving these coinci-dental events in memory, had transformed her bodily pains into a symbol of her soul's pain.[8] This first hypothesis as to the symbolic nature of a relation between body and soul (Freud suggests it may be a matter of substitution) continues to depend upon a metaphys-ical opposition between two orders of reality; this opposition re-

---

7. See, for example, *Studies on Hysteria, SE* 2:139.
8. Ibid. The term indicating pain is always *Schmerz*, for body and soul alike.

quires that something pass, in causal fashion, from one order to another.

To resolve the enigma of the relation between soul and body, which have no relation, to understand how Elisabeth's difficulty in coping with life might have transformed itself into a pain in her legs, Freud tries to find out what events and psychic impressions are connected with the initial appearance of her pains. And on this point too, what he finds eventually leads him to modify the question itself.

But the first answer he gives ascribes the major role to the passage of something—a pain in the soul—to the body. At the end of the first period of treatment, Elisabeth spoke of an intolerable conflict between her passionate inclination toward a young man and her nursing duties toward her father. Freud sees this as a psychical conflict, and he finds its intolerable character sufficient reason for its transformation into physical pain, into a problem with walking.

Freud thus inaugurates a mode of explanation whose value he reaffirms throughout the entire text devoted to Elisabeth. At the end of the analysis, at a more "precise" level in the archaeological stratification of the patient's unconscious, the etiology of the illness is summarized as follows: Elisabeth's scarcely formulated, barely conscious love for her brother-in-law contains something intolerable; the conflict between that inclination and the unseemliness of the death wishes she had entertained with respect to her sister suffices to explain why the pain in her soul was transformed into physical pains or, rather, why it became fixated on rheumatic pains, which had a prior, independent physiological existence.

Conversion is this transformation of a soul conflict, characterized as pain, into physical pain, either a preexisting pain that is reinforced in the process or an entirely new one. Thus conversion plays on several registers: it presupposes a natural heterogeneity between soul and body and an associative link between them that is made possible when occurrences in each zone coincide temporally; but at the same time it calls for a causal mechanism that Freud spells out in two forms, clinical and metapsychological. In his narrative of Elisabeth's treatment, pain is what brings two incompatible orders into sudden communication, to the point that one spills over into the other. Prior to the distinction between *Seelisch* and *Körperlich*, the term "pain" makes possible a secret equivalence between the two

26

orders. It is only when Freud thinks he has discovered a so-called psychical conflict that is painful to the point of being intolerable that the substitution of the physical for the psychical can be conceived. A single word, "pain" (*Schmerz*), has the function of rendering the two independent orders homogeneous so that the passage from one to the other may occur. This passage is no longer merely an associative link but becomes a sort of transsubstantiation.

This somewhat magical function of the word "pain" in Freud's text is corroborated by the other formulation we mentioned, which constitutes its exposed, self-evident dimension: the conversion could not be conceived without the theory of affect. Elisabeth "repressed her erotic idea from consciousness and transformed the amount of its affect (*Affektgrösse*) into physical sensations of pain" (*SE* 2:164). The notion of affect certainly presupposes the same homogeneity of *Seele* and *Körper* as does Freud's use of the notion of pain: if the psychical is evoked in terms of affective charge, then the energy of affect can be conceived as transformed into somatic innervation and ultimately into an inhibition of the locomotor functions in astasia–abasia.

Conversion theory is thus not averse to inconsistency: dualism is at the service of a loose theory of symbolism just as it is twice being called into question by a monist conception of affect that corresponds, in Freud's theoretical summaries, to the attention focused on what he designates globally as pain.

In his well-known texts on "metapsychology," Freud illustrates a conception of science that is not dependent upon the issues that metaphysics sees itself obliged to settle immediately. The philosophical confusion surrounding the notion of conversion provides a clear-cut example of this. Our task is then to attempt to see whether and to what extent this confusion may be fruitful or if, instead, the theory of hysteria progresses despite the confusion.

The Other Body in Transference

To tell the truth, when we follow Freud's undertaking attentively, we can hardly avoid some astonishment if we limit ourselves to the official and eclectic discourse on conversion, for in fact what is essential is played out elsewhere, alongside or by way of the confusion and the contradictions we have pointed out. In principle,

the search for the inaugural moment of conversion remains dependent on the presumed dualism, on the heterogeneity of two series,
psychic history and motor problems. But the actual search brings to
light a different order of reality, one that escapes the psychical-
physiological alternative and that we shall designate as the order of
the pleasure-body. After the discovery of the first motif of conversion, the transformation of mental pain into physical pain as an
effect of the intolerable nature of the conflict, Freud reveals his
scruples. This general formula is not enough for him; his attention
is drawn to the details of the process (*SE* 2:150) about which
Elisabeth herself, unsatisfied with the improvements in her condition, informs him. One day, at the beginning of a session, she
asserts that she knows why her pains are localized precisely in her
right thigh: that is the spot where her father used to rest his leg
every morning while she was changing his bandages. This would
be a mere detail if Elisabeth's legs themselves had not at the same
time begun to "speak" during the sessions, thus revealing, in a
certain relation with the linguistic elaboration of fantasy, the true
ground of conversion. The body that suddenly appears in treatment
(or the one Freud suddenly identifies) is defined in the first instance
not physiologically, but as one of the terms of an alternative in
which the other is the narrative of a painful memory. In this emergence of the pleasure-body, played out, narrated, and lived in
transference, pain is always present, but it changes meaning.

The patient was free of pain when we began to work, Freud says.
But when he aroused a memory by a question or by pressure on her
head, an impression of pain first arose, and much of the time so
strongly that the patient trembled and sought the painful spot with
her hand. This pain, once awakened, persisted as long as the patient
was overcome by her memory; it reached its apogee when she was
on the verge of expressing the essential, decisive point and disap-
peared with the last words of her communication. Freud does not
stop paying attention to the symptom here, for he learned to use
Elisabeth's pain "like a compass." But his attention changes direction: we no longer have mental pain or moral torment on the one
hand and physiological impressions on the other; we no longer have
an association between a psychic history and a physiological symptom either, but rather have the homogeneous and not yet com-
pleted history of a body of pain and pleasure. Pain here is the

activation of a body that can no longer express itself; hence the inhibition of functions is reevaluated, is recognized as a consequence of the revival, in the symptom, of a scene that has never been completely elaborated in language. *Between the symptom and the scene related, there is thus no longer any difference in nature*, though there is an essential distinction involving the organization of desire. The *Seelisch/Körperlich* dualism posited two separate substantial orders; the distinction between them tended to be annihilated by conversion theory. Nothing remains of that schema here: when the order of the suffering body (in the symptom) and the elaborating body (in language) is brought to light, no substantialist interpretation is required. This order of reality does not aim to unify the psychical and the physiological by presupposing something beneath or beyond them; it does not need to take them into account at all. To grasp their coordinates does not mean salvaging all the rest; on the contrary, it means distinguishing an order of reality through its particularity. The homogeneity invoked to characterize what is played out in the love scenes that are recounted or in the symptom as it reforms itself presupposes no totalization of body and soul. In this sense, in Freud's text, despite the excessive clarity of his discussion of conversion, we confront an epistemological break.

In yet another way the attention to details removes us from the categories of the psychical and the physiological. Just before Elisabeth's legs began to speak during the sessions, something she said had introduced an element of doubt into Freud's quest for a primary and fundamental scene of conversion. Once again the discovery of the multiplicity of traumatizing scenes imperils the opposition between the psychic and the physiological by revealing the field of fantasy, which cannot be labeled psychical without the risk of misunderstandings.

Had the conversion really taken place at the moment when Elisabeth, returning from a ball where she had been with her lover, found her father's condition worse than when she left? On the contrary, during this period several scenes seem to have occurred that draw the symptom into something like a dotted line. In particular, Elisabeth, who complained during treatment that her feet felt cold, also reported that she had frequently leapt out of bed barefoot at night in response to her father's call. This detail illustrates the reversal we pointed out earlier. The scene corresponds exactly to the symptom to the extent that the symptom continues it. There is no longer an association here between mental pain and physical pain, since physical pain belongs in a paradoxical way to the realm of what Freud elsewhere calls the *Seelische*. This realm is no longer psychical, then, and the symptom is not the product of a conversion but a continuation of the scene. And if we are obliged to conceive of an associative relation between the scene and its residue, this associative theory requires that we give up positing, between the terms it connects, an inherent heterogeneity that would characterize the psychical and the physiological. Progress in the description of the new realm will thus require a theory of symbolism. Because the detail of Elisabeth's bare feet becomes the crucial element, it reverses the official discourse on conversion, calls into question the blend of dualism and incipient monism that it presupposes, and brings to light the inadequacy, if not the complete rout, of the notion of association between events and symptom. We are not dealing here with the connection between an event and an emotion that would be signaled by—that is, would choose for itself—an arbitrary reference point in a heterogeneous and concomitant physiological phenomenon, which left room for the idea that chance had a role to play in the association. In the scenes as well as in the symptom, the continued and, in Jacques Lacan's sense,[9] unrealized life of a desiring body enters into play. On this point we can grasp the still undispelled obscurity of Freud's thought: the notion of association, at the very moment when it brings to light a new area, makes it impossible to grasp its coordinates, for the notion remains caught up in the opposition of the psychical and the physiological, overshadows the desiring body, and prevents the formation of a theory of symbolism.

The Search for the Psychical, or the Importance of the Structure of Scenarios

The proper status of fantasy, in this observation, can be grasped only in opposition to the categories identified above, which form a system. When Freud places his confidence in the dualist conception of conversion, he is seeking a beginning, a "first time" for conver-

9. Lacan: "A register that has nothing unreal, or dereistic, about it, but is rather unrealized" (*FFC*, p. 23).

sion that would mark the passage from the psychical realm into the organic. Any pain that had appeared before the intolerable conflict would thus be left aside, considered purely organic. But the whole story of Elisabeth's treatment is punctuated by her reliving, in her transference and through her narrative, what we shall designate as bedroom scenes and summonses.

According to one of her earliest memories of this sort, during the time she was nursing her father Elisabeth was forced to take to her bed one day, suffering from rheumatic pains. While in this state of immobility she had been surprised by the visit of a man, a relative she had been unable to receive; the impression was all the stronger because the same scene, played by the same protagonists, was repeated two years later. In reporting this story, Freud expresses his disappointment at being unable to find any "psychical motive" for Elisabeth's confinement to bed; the scene took place before the occasion of the intolerable conflict that exhibits the first moment of conversion, so that the episode in which Elisabeth's immobility originated is connected to a purely physiological problem. Freud's search for an intolerable psychic conflict causes him to miss the importance of the scene's structure, which in itself constitutes the psychical element he is looking for. Here we can see how treating a physiological problem as autonomous effectively reinforces the search for an association between a psychical conflict and a physical ailment. Their linkage, which is the crux of "conversion theory," blocks access to the order of the pleasure-body: the manifest physiological data monopolize the analysis, and the phantasmic character of the narrated scene is dismissed. We can only note that it was at this moment of the treatment, and as if in protest against that dismissal, that Elisabeth's legs began to speak insistently through their pain.

From the barefoot scene to the scenes in which a male visitor surprises Elisabeth in her immobility, an inversion is accomplished, as in a dream. In one case she had been answering her father's nocturnal summons, leaping barefoot onto the cold floor. In the inverse case, a man had surprised her when she was immobilized and incapable of responding to his call. Surprise, a man's summons, immobility or abrupt motor response—this sequence will be replayed at the end of her analysis, at a particularly fruitful moment.

In the middle of a session, hearing a man's footsteps in an adjoining room and perceiving a voice asking questions (*Fragen*) in a pleasant tone, Elisabeth got up, asking Freud to interrupt the session, for it was her brother-in-law asking for her (*nach ihr frage*). This statement was followed by the reappearance of pain in her legs. Pain is produced in the influx of the fantasy, or rather the *acting in*. And the notion of conversion is too simplistic to help us understand this mobilization of Elisabeth's body at a given moment of her discourse: Passage of the energy of affect from the psychical to the physiological? But this sidesteps the problem of the nature of the pain. Why does the pain arise immediately after the *acting in*? What hurts Elisabeth at the very moment when the conversion is starting up again? The idea that pain is the inhibited motor innervation (she gets up) begs the question, through a physiological metaphor, of what unconscious process is being played out at that moment. What, in the economy of Elisabeth's desire, does that sudden mobilization of her body represent, during the reliving of an intolerable scene experienced at the borderline of hallucination?

Freud's official discourse on conversion makes it doubly difficult to recognize these questions. The first time, in Elisabeth's memory of her rheumatism, the effective reality of the physiological problem excuses him from ascribing value to the scene of a man's visit in which the problem turns out to be brought up again, reawakened. Conversely, in the scene involving the bed—or rather the sofa— and the hallucinated surprise visit, the notion of conversion, linked with that of affect, prejudges the nature of Elisabeth's pain and precludes any inquiry into its relation to the act. Conversion keeps the implications of this moment from being noticed—this moment in which Elisabeth, having come as close as she can to the essence of her pain, can only relive it in words for a moment, in hallucinatory fashion. She can only act it out through her body, can only reproduce it in the imaginary register, to such an extent is she still caught in its grip.

This inversion of an active motor response to a summons by a man (her father or her brother-in-law) into the symptomatic and painful immobility in which she no longer responds to masculine calls is a strange exchange indeed. Is not the true scene of the analysis and of what Freud calls the psychic conflict situated at this juncture of body and language that Elisabeth's story sets before us, if only we were able to understand it? What is her body if not the agent that desires to hear the words of a man and that immobilizes itself because she forbids herself to have this desire?

Once the structure of the scenes is thus understood, the very notion of the conflict is turned upside down. Freud gives two successive versions of it: after the narrative of the ball scene, what Elisabeth cannot bear is thought to lie in the opposition between her desire for a young man and her nursing duties. But this psychologizing formulation explains nothing, for she has created this conflict herself: No one prevented her from going off to dance, certainly not her father, who on the contrary encouraged her to do so. What, then, is forbidden to her? The responsibilities she feels toward her sick father are only a pretext here. We do not find an intolerable mental pain that had to be converted into physical pain.

In the episode of love for her brother-in-law that saw the crystallization of the symptom and the return of the repressed, the terms of the conflict are spelled out. What is intolerable here is that, in order to love her brother-in-law, she had to wish for her sister's death. But once again a psychological summary conceals the true question: Why does the desire for a man arise here only in connection with a desire for the death of a woman for whom she was sometimes mistaken? In her treatment, indeed, the narrative of Elisabeth's relations with her brother-in-law leads into memories of events in which third parties had mixed up the two sisters, as if they were not distinct persons. In Elisabeth's associations, why is there this resemblance, this threatening proximity that perhaps forbids a relationship to a man or connects that relationship with death? It cannot be denied that, when Freud makes his triumphant summary of the facts of the psychical conflict—"Everything was now clear" (*SE* 2:157), he is simplifying in the name of some conception of the psychological and social incompatibility of certain feelings. The notion of the psyche provides for the simplification by resolving rather too readily the question of the nature of the intolerable situation that made Elisabeth ill.

We might follow up by pointing out, for example, that during her father's illness, when she was more or less remonstrating with him for it, Elisabeth did not fall ill herself. Her illness began when she actually offered to take his place after his death, when she proposed to replace him at her mother's side, in order to restore the luster of the house. In short, in the material this case presents, we might see the problem of the bisexuality of hysterical fantasies take shape as the true heart of the conflict. To do so would be to use Freud against himself. But such is not our intention. We shall focus on noting how, in every respect, *the first version of the conversion theory misreads the material it summarizes.* The duality of registers we would be presupposing were we to rely on this version of the theory, if only so as to abolish it magically at the moment—presumably the unique moment—of conversion, confuses the erotogenic body with the physiological body and reduces the order of fantasy to the merely psychological.

Symbolic Conversion and Associative Conversion

In *Studies on Hysteria*, Freud's radical modification of his approach to ailments, of his strategies for acquiring knowledge, is carried out with a certain hesitation and with some ambiguity that is at once concealed and summarized in the distinction between two mechanisms of conversion that he finally acknowledges: in Elisabeth's case, he defines an associatively created functional paralysis and a symbolic functional paralysis. How and why is this distinction made? Freud lingers over its justification on several occasions, [10] and it obliges him to confront numerous examples of conversion and in particular to juxtapose Elisabeth's story with Frau Cäcilie's. He devotes a lengthy discussion to determining whether the possibility of a purely symbolic conversion, without any prior organic problem, has to be admitted. Is it conceivable that Elisabeth found her legs paralyzed because she thought she was in a bind she could not get out of, that "she could not take a single step forward" (*SE* 2:152)? Freud leaves the question unanswered until his closing discussion, and the position he adopts is complex; so far as Elisabeth is concerned, the conversion by symbolization did not occur in the absolute. It reinforced and complicated the psychic pains that had already become significant through associative conversion, that is, through the temporal coincidence between a traumatizing event and a pain: "The circumstances indicate that this somatic pain was not *created* by the neurosis but merely used, increased and main-

10. The most representative passages are the following: *SE* 2:142, 144, 149–50, 152–53, 174 ff.

tained by it" (p. 174). Freud recognizes the possibility of conversion through pure symbolization, however, and he takes as his example the pain in her forehead Frau Cäcilie had suffered during adolescence (p. 180), which was attributed to her grandmother's piercing gaze.

In spite of the clarity of Freud's explanations, what is at stake in this discussion remains confused. Far from being complementary, the two modes of conversion are in fact contradictory if we are concerned with the status of the body they presuppose. Symbolization cannot reinforce conversion through association. This alternation belongs not to the object Freud is studying, but to the way he comes to know it: he begins by analyzing the ailment as consisting of associatively created pains; then, changing his problematic, he discovers the possible ground of another body and of another pain. But he is unable to "hold on to" this new point of view, and he adopts a confused compromise between his earlier way of thinking about hysteria as associative conversion and the new way, whose nature he has merely glimpsed and the possibility of which he maintains even as he acknowledges that it remains mysterious.

Freud's Questioning of Elisabeth von R.

To understand this unstable point in the Freudian perspective on hysteria, we have to compare the modifications of his problematic in the course of the treatment narrative (*SE* 2:150–53) with the conclusions that he draws in his attempt to synthesize (pp. 174–75).

On one decisive page, in fact, he explains how he found himself obliged to make a drastic change in his approach to hysterical patients. He had set out in search of a precise correspondence between pain and some event that could be identified as its cause. Now what was described as monosymptomatic hysteria turned out to be a multifaceted pain determined by multiple events. Without altering his view of the chance association between pains and events, Freud undertook to establish a detailed geography of Elisabeth's body, initially using this approach to interpret the vicissitudes of the symptom in the course of her analysis. The pains in her right thigh refer to her nursing care of her father; their extension to her whole leg is associated with memories of her first love—with her father, once again—whereas the left part of her body seems to retain only more recent memories: pains arise there when she recalls her sister's death and her two brothers-in-law. The multiplicity of pains and scenes Freud has discovered changes nothing in his conception of the spatiality of the body: the pains, atypical ones as we know from the start, are envisaged in themselves, as autonomous phenomena, except that their frame of reference is not organic, as medecine would have it, but psychic. Freud progresses in his analysis of Elisabeth's pains by correcting the superficial method that considers the hysterical symptom in its global aspect, and he discovers a multitude of juxtaposed symptoms. We pass from macromolecules to micromolecules; we change scale, not object; pain remains pain, attached to some zone of the body; that is, conceived with reference to its spatial element (*SE* 2:149–50).

Now this quest comes to nothing, for a reason that is presented at first as "purely technical": the attempt at delimitation (*Abgreizung*) of the painful zones corresponding to each psychic circumstance does not succeed, for *the patient's attention turns away from these relationships*. This difficulty, which is indeed one of technique, reveals the theoretical impasse of Freud's initial method and makes it necessary to redefine the very object of the quest. More precisely, as the *attention* that Elisabeth pays (or does not pay) to the spatiality of her pains becomes noticeable, Freud begins to ask her different questions, begins to understand something new. From this point on he is interested in the way the symptomatic complex of abasia *in its entirety* could have been constructed on the basis of painful zones.

It is not a matter of returning to the point of departure; this new global view of the symptom is not the same as the one according to which the classical theory of hysteria referred to monosymptomatic ailments. With the search for the spatial characteristics of Elisabeth's pain, a certain abstraction, a certain autonomization of pain, is abandoned in favor of an inquiry as to Elisabeth's bodily *positions* when she is in pain and when she finds herself, according to her own accounts, in intolerable situations.

"What was the origin of [your] pains in walking? In standing? And in lying down?"[11] More than the detailed geography of her

11. *SE* 2:150. In the new question Freud is asking, the spatiality of the body becomes explicitly metaphorical. In the phrase "Woher rühren die Schmerzen im Gehen, im Stehen, im Liegen?" the words *woher rühren* might be translated successively as "Where do they come from? What do they grow out of?" (*Gesammelte Werke*, 18 vols. [Frankfurt and London: Fischer, 1952–68], 1:214; cited hereafter as *GW*.)

pains, the reference to bodily positions strikes Elisabeth as relevant, for she reorganizes the story of the intolerable things she had experienced in terms of the positions she had occupied in those scenes: thus she found herself standing near a door when her father was brought back to the house suffering from a heart attack, a situation in which her terror immobilized her as if she were rooted to the spot. Other scenes that brought horror together with the standing position then imposed themselves, in particular the one in which she stood as if spellbound (*gebannt*) at her dead sister's bedside.

This interest in bodily positions, coming after the examination of pains, is more than a mere nuance; it indicates a complete break. Positions and pain are not homogeneous phenomena here: to take pain as the starting point for clinical investigation means necessarily to consider it as an element of the disorder one is attempting to construe. In an organic inquiry pain is a subjective fact, an indication of an objective physiological fact: it is autonomized because it is considered the psychic reflection of a network of causally linked facts. And it is itself an element of that chain, that is, one of the facts whose subjective character changes nothing: pain, the reflection in consciousness of a fact, is in this perspective a fact of the same order. [12] In his search for associations between pains and events at first thought to be unique and later recognized as multiple, Freud is searching for relationships among facts. We have seen that he ends in an impasse.

A position is indeed not a fact; or more precisely, if we are seeking to understand the genesis of hysteria, we must not consider it primarily as a fact. To be sure, a position can be described spatially in relation to coordinates chosen by an observer, but thus considered a position does not count as a symptom in itself. Since it has such importance in the history of the problem, something must have conferred this importance on it. Pain represented a fact that presented the nature of a symptom in an immediate way: its spatial and physiological component was coupled with conscious reflection in a coincidence such that the self-evidence of what had to be taken as a symptom was unavoidable. To the contrary, it is not at all self-evident that a position counts as a symptom. If Elisabeth accepts Freud's question about her bodily positions, whereas she

12. See above, p. 12. This does not contradict the idea that the information provided by the sensation of pain is only confused knowledge that has to be rectified.

refuses to respond to questions about her pains, it is because something has given certain positions special significance for her—has made them symptomatic. The new object of Freud's research is now clearer: something "corporal" is indeed at stake in the importance attributed to positions, but the bodily component does not have in itself, as pain does, the status of a symptom already defined by the correlation between a location and an informing sensation. The positions that are traumatizing and symptomatic for Elisabeth could not be so naturally, that is, in terms of the theoretical framework that classifies everything Freud is looking for into the material of psychical or organic phenomena and into the material of pain, the junction between the psychical and the organic.

This new order of reality, which is not a fact in terms of the theory of association between physical pains and psychical events, and which poses a challenge to that theory, is shown by Freud to consist in a certain relation on the subject's part to her own bodily positions, to a configuration that has reality in spatial terms but derives its influence from what makes that reality significant for the subject. That a subject adopted a certain position in a given scene does not explain why that position has become symptomatic and is even accompanied by pains unless we see what is expressed by the *attention* she has conferred on it. The origin of hysteria lies in this attentive relationship of a subject to her own body. It is clear that the impasse Freud encountered in his first line of inquiry consisted indeed in a technical difficulty, but in the sense analytic technique introduces here, at the very core of the thing it is naming, precisely the patient's attention.

To move from pain to position is thus to make a fundamental change in the object under investigation, in the order of reality to be considered symptomatic: a spatial order no longer defined by the refraction it undergoes in a pain-ridden consciousness, and a view of pain that, while recognizing it in its reality, no longer autonomizes it so as to construe it. Nor is pain abstracted, to that end, from the situations in which it is produced. To consider painful positions here is to insert bodily spatiality within a different strategy for acquiring knowledge. Instead of retaining from the pain that is speaking only whatever may serve as an indication of some organic problem—that is, the flash of consciousness that says (or merely thinks) "I hurt"—we need to listen to the language of the pain, since pain reveals precisely that other space we are looking for: the history of the attention that a subject has paid to her body, and to certain of its positions, in preference to other possible cathexes. Taking an interest in the positions of Elisabeth's body means focusing our inquiry on the type of attention to her body that was responsible for what we are calling hysterical conversion.

A New Definition: Body-Magic

The signifying elaboration of a jouissance precipitates in a body-magic.

This new focus may seem to take us far from the question we started with, which targeted the distinction between associative conversions and symbolizing conversions. But a reading of the very brief text in which the shift in problematic comes about reveals that this is not so at all. Having shown what reorganization of her history is delineated, for Elisabeth, when the privileged cathexis of her body is invoked, Freud adds:

> This whole chain of memories might be expected to show that there was a legitimate connection between her pains and standing up; and it might indeed be accepted as evidence of an association. But we must bear in mind that another factor must be proved to be present in all these events, one which directed her attention precisely to her standing (or, as the case may be, to her walking, sitting, etc.) and consequently led to the conversion. The explanation of her attention taking this direction can scarcely be looked for elsewhere than in the circumstance that walking, standing and lying are functions and states of those parts of her body which in her case comprised the painful zones, namely, her legs. It was therefore easy in the present case to understand the connection between the astasia-abasia and the first occurrence of conversion. (*SE* 2:150–51)

Let us not be too ready to take Freud's newly established clarity at face value or to accept his claim that the relationship is "easy . . . to understand," for this text is on the contrary a difficult one. It would be impossible to speak of associative relations between pains and position *if there were not some other moment that brought these relations into play—put them into effect.* This passage confirms our observation that here Freud is abandoning the idea of associative conversion as a connection between facts that are conceivable within the framework of the principles defined above. Something has to cathect facts that are unimportant in themselves so they can become circumstances of the illness. This "something" is first presented as responsible for a certain orientation of the subject's attention toward her bodily positions. And in the following sentence the net is drawn tighter: the "something" that cathects certain unimportant facts, turning them into circumstances of an illness, is that attention itself, in the focus it adopts.

Finally, it is on the level of this cathexis of the body—without which the conversions identified as associations would not count as such—that Freud situates the origin of the conversion process. Now, what are we to understand by the attention that makes certain of Elisabeth's bodily positions both meaningful and intolerable to her, if not precisely that order of reality that makes the body a symbolic object,[13] one that can never be defined solely by natural spatial coordinates?

When Freud privileges Elisabeth's painful positions in the questions he puts to her, he is defining a different scene, a new breeding ground for the illness called hysteria. To say that Elisabeth suffered from hysteria is to say that everything that happened to her and preoccupied her took on existence for her through its manifestations at the level of bodily positions or states. Thus we can clarify what Freud refers to as the focusing of attention on bodily positions. The text we have cited states clearly that the conversion process is resolved on these grounds: it presents conversion as a result of the focusing of attention. We may wonder whether the two are not rather the same thing; the idea that psychical conflicts are converted into physical pain, to use Freud's earlier terminology, is expressed in his new language as follows. To construct her identity, a subject retains—from everything that makes up her life—scenarios in which her body is at stake: not her entire body, but certain of its movements, states, or positions. These manifestations have characterized her body in the empirical course of events, to be sure; but after the cathexis in question, they survive in what henceforth takes on the value of a symptom. To explain conversion

13. We are referring here to the meaning the term has for Freud in "Some Points for a Comparative Study of Organic and Hysterical Motor Paralyses," *SE* 1:160–72.

is to reconstitute the history of that cathexis and to stop seeking a cause for effects that are identifiable as symptoms.

In Elisabeth's stories of scenes that took place at the same time as the fixation of her symptoms, Freud highlights one moment in particular. At a time when the entire family was reunited for a holiday, after her father's death, Elisabeth had an opportunity to go walking (*gehen*, *Spaziergang*) alone with her brother-in-law, and she derived a pleasure from this that she could not express to herself without anxiety. The choice of her body as the signifying material for a psychical conflict—to use the earlier language—did not come about arbitrarily or by chance, since this stroll tête-à-tête represented an experience of jouissance for Elisabeth: a real and forbidden jouissance, pleasure and pain, this experience was repeated in her treatment, for Elisabeth continued to live through it and to refer back to it as an issue that was not yet resolved. She got up right in the middle of a session, for example, thinking she had heard her brother-in-law's voice, and indulged in bittersweet memories—as Freud says—in an orgy of pain. The symptomatic pain here indeed takes on a tinge of jouissance that the subject can neither give way to nor give up. It is a fragment of an erotic scene experienced in the manner of a hallucination, as Freud says in 1908 and again in 1931.[14] Pain in this context no longer has the autonomy it had in the construction associating the physical dimension with the psychic.

In the same manner, the seated position became intolerable for Elisabeth after she returned, alone and nostalgic, to the paths she had taken with her brother-in-law and sat down on a stone bench, for once allowing her painful jouissance to express itself. As we recall, by the time she returned from that walk, her illness had taken over; her family characterized it as pain due to overexertion (*SE* 2:151).

This new itinerary makes it possible to characterize the texture of the attention that a hysterical subject brings to bear upon the positions of her body. The last part of the text cited above provides an outline: through trivial events of her daily life, the positions of Elisabeth's body, the configuration of the spaces she occupies, and her empirical situation with respect to other objects or persons always refer to another scene, to a space of jouissance. This is an

14. "Hysterical Phantasies and Their Relation to Bisexuality," *SE* 9:163–64; "Inhibitions, Symptoms and Anxiety," *SE* 20:111–12.

imaginary space in that it parallels the empirical coordinates of the ordinary situations of life, imaginary too in that for Elisabeth *it "precipitates" and in that sense converts* the approach of any reality into the configuration of a jouissance-body that she never recognizes but continues to pursue in a quasi-hallucinatory fashion. This makes her body a sort of magic place in which everything is played out for her, without her. Yet it is also a real space, in a double sense: the forbidden jouissance that is always about to erupt, that alienates Elisabeth from the perpetual hallucination of her body in what she experiences, is also delineated in her body as she perceives that body and as an observer can identify it while limiting it to the phenomenon labeled "pains." But the reality of the painful sensations does not exhaust the reality in question, for the order of sexual jouissance circumscribes a specific reality: the one in which a subject's identification is played out through a certain relation of her jouissance to language.

On that issue too the new hand dealt in the approach to hysteria has something more to tell us. Is not what Freud identifies here as attention to bodily movements and positions precisely what has left traces of its elaboration in the wordplays through which Elisabeth expresses her helplessness? In this history of a forbidden jouissance that in fact *converts* all experience into body-magic, not everything has the same value. In the situations from which Elisabeth draws the signifying material of her desire, only certain elements are selected: certain positions and therefore, in her symptoms, certain pains. The magic of jouissance that traverses Elisabeth's existence is not exercised in all directions, does not mobilize all her physiological functions. Something gives it a configuration, that is, limits; and that "something" is language: *Alleinstehen* ("standing alone"); *nicht von der Stelle kommen* (unable to "take a single step forward," rooted to the spot as if "spellbound"); *keinen Anhalt haben* ("not having anything to lean on"): all these expressions that assign the symptom its form bear witness to the fact that the orientation of Elisabeth's attention toward her bodily positions, the very terrain of conversion, consists in a discourse that determines the scenario of which her body is at once the theater and the instrument.

The use of the term "attention" to translate *Aufmerksamkeit* risks concealing this point of articulation between the imaginary of that magical jouissance and its limiting hold over the expressive apparatus. *Merken* means to notice; the attention Elisabeth pays to her bodily positions or functions designates that what is retained from any experience is marked or written through the involvement of the body. At the very least, the etymology of the term *Aufmerksamkeit* allows us to outline that problematic here and to glimpse a new meaning for the word "conversion."

The Hysteric Body: Omnipresent or Unfindable?

We are thus led to an initial conclusion concerning the gap that arises between consideration of pain and consideration of the attention the patient pays to her bodily positions. The subject in question in the symptom is defined as something other than a relationship or a combination of psychophysiological phenomena; it is defined as the mainspring on the basis of which the order of these phenomena can appear. Not that we are confronting a substantive reality that would antedate the distinction between body and psyche. The establishment of a new field of knowledge usually reveals nothing more fundamental about reality than was known before. The theory of hysteria in no way requires an ontology of the body.[15] Still, in the narrow reality of the unconscious, those psychophysiological phenomena can no longer be conceived directly without some indication of how they have become real to the subject. This can only mean that what is at stake in the symptom arises exclusively from previously identified phenomena through the intermediary of signifying effects. Where Freud's study focuses on the attention a subject pays to certain of her bodily coordinates, it must be understood that the subject has no immediate, natural, direct relation to her body (any construction that combines two positive realities, the physiological and the psychical, erroneously supposes the opposite). We are now on the path that will lead to the text on negation. We must start from the fact (a strange fact in the light of those that the theory of associative conversion was in the process of constructing), or rather from the principle, that the subject's relation to reality—for example, to physiological reality—is highly problem-

15. In the sense in which Maurice Merleau-Ponty used the term in *Phenomenology of Perception*, trans. Colin Smith (New York: Humanities Press, 1962) or in *The Visible and the Invisible*, ed. Claude Lefort, trans. Alfonso Lingis (Evanston, Ill.: Northwestern University Press, 1968).

atic; and we must suppose that the subject can perceive her own body only by way of a certain type of symbolization of her desire. Her perception of her body is never primary, nor is it ever independent of the history of a jouissance that is signified in that perception. That is why it is inappropriate to treat pain as autonomous, to abstract it from the language it uses so as to reduce it to sensation within a determinable physiological process—not because it would be impossible or absolutely incorrect to do so, but because, if one begins that way, with that strategy for acquiring knowledge, one rules out by definition any possibility of access to the grounds on which hysterical conversion is triggered. A reversal of direction is required for this to become apparent: this break in Freud's thought is what we are attempting to situate.

The hysterical symptom changes meaning completely if we refuse to continue to abstract pain, sensory impressions, motility, from the history of a pleasure-body [*un corps de jouissance*] that is organized by expressive linkages. We had been conceiving of the symptom as a positive reality, for no other realities had been available to us for speaking about the subject. If the new object of study consists in the subject's cathexis of certain positions, the subject's problems may be viewed—must be viewed, perhaps—as a bracketing of some of her bodily coordinates. As we know, Freud comes to insist more and more clearly on the importance of negative hallucinations,[16] anesthesias, in hysterical symptoms. He could not have moved in this direction without reevaluating what are known as sensory impressions, motility, pain. What first appears as a psychically motivated *production* of pains and physiological problems, as a production of some positive element in the body, must now be understood, owing to a radical change in Freud's thought, as a deficiency in the subject's symbolization of her body. So long as we are limited to the theory of associative conversion, we are blinded by the body's physiological reality, or rather by the visible nature of the reality we are defining in this way; we are blinded by the spatiality we have identified, and we no longer succeed in thinking that the hysteric's problem lies in her lack of a body. The failure in the symbolization of her desire, the prohibition of jouissance that polarizes the history of her body, simultaneously eradicates the

16. Freud was following up on some of Breuer's comments about the case of Anna O.

reality, even the perceptual reality, of that body. This eradication is the underside of the obtrusive hysterical symptoms. Once again the epistemological import of this break in Freud's argument is clear. In the absolute, he does not deny the reality of the physiological problems that arise in hysteria, but he shows that the exposure of that order of reality—which is indeed identifiable—makes it impossible to know on just what grounds hysteria is formed. This is not the way to get at the problem. Any search for associations between the psychical and the physiological realms must lead to an impasse, for it implies a misunderstanding as to what is being sought.

Symbolic Conversion and Attention

In Freud's study of Elisabeth's case, new directions are suggested, yet one crucial issue remains ambiguous. Freud states clearly that the new focal point, that of *Aufmerksamkeit*, the directing of attention to bodily positions, requires a critique of the associative conception of conversion. The relation between attention and the wordplays that constitute it is not clearly set forth, however, although this relation alone allows the subject in treatment to regain access to her blocked history. Freud asserts that conversion is played out on the terrain of *Aufmerksamkeit*, attention. He also declares at one point that the painful element invoked to account for conversion into physical pain consists in *Elisabeth's symbolic elaboration of her own impotence.*[17] But in his own text he separates conversion through symbolization from the identification of this new terrain. As if the etymological affinity of what is called "attention" [*attention*] with a process of writing, indeed of symbolization, had not been noted and studied. It is as if the German term "deserved" its translation as "attention."

There is a real contradiction in Freud's argument here. If we follow its progression in detail, the act of listening to the speaking body—and this alone—sets Freud on the path toward redefining hysterical conversion. He is preparing for his return to the vicinity of hysteria, his renewed questioning of Elisabeth—the import of which we have noted—when he discovers that her painful legs play

17. Cf. *Studies on Hysteria, SE* 2:152. What was *painful* in all this was her feeling of helplessness, the impression of being unable to "take a single step forward."

a role in the discourse of her treatment, begin to "join in the conversation" (*mitsprechen*) (*SE* 2:148).

Because he relies on this speaking pain as a trustworthy compass, he finds himself compelled to give up his initial search for an association between specific bodily locations and psychical circumstances, for that quest led to the suppression of the discourse of those pains, or rather of those speaking pains. Elisabeth's attention was being turned away from these relationships, which is to say that the pain was being reduced to silence, was being denatured, drawn away onto inappropriate grounds. When Elisabeth begins her narrative all over again, starting from a new question by Freud about the positions she finds intolerable, she discloses the history of the onset of her symptoms. The rules of this scenario of jouissance are organized around recollected wordplays. *Thus we find a relation of identity between the attention paid to bodily positions and the order of the jouissance that is realized in a body and organized by the signifier, by wordplays.*

In Freud's mind, however, this identity remains masked, obscured by the use of the term *attention*. In the intellectualist tradition, particularly in the Cartesian theory of knowledge, attention as a matter of principle rejects the value of any thought that does not have knowledge as its goal. In the extreme case, true thought—that is, thought that is attentive to its object—is thought without language, intuitive thought, for such thought coincides with the object of its knowledge.[18] At the very least, the language of such thought must play a purely instrumental and intermediary role, must lack texture of its own, must be completely at the service of the thought that orders it, and must be transparent to that thought's aim. The words one uses are not neutral. The term "attention" in the Freudian text makes it impossible to conceive of precisely what the term seeks to designate, namely:

—a thought that has a pleasure-body as its theater (for the philosophic stakes in a theory of hysteria amount to showing how the body thinks, and showing that what forces us to think our identity is an experience of jouissance;

—a language, a speaking pain, that does not have as its function the production of knowledge of *signifiance*;

18. Cf. "Rules for the Direction of the Mind," in *The Philosophical Works of Descartes*, trans. Elizabeth S. Haldane and G. R. T. Ross, 2 vols. (Cambridge: Cambridge University Press, 1931), 1:7–8.

—in other words, finally, a thought or, better yet, a knowledge that exists nowhere else but in this signifying discourse.

The term *Aufmerksamkeit*,[19] understood in the sense of attention, risks presenting conversion as a process of thought without language whose realization in a body thus becomes mysterious. When he points out the importance of Elisabeth's bodily positions in the scenes that preceded the onset of her illness (the walk with her brother-in-law, its repetition in nostalgic solitude), Freud himself presents the patient's thoughts as thoughts without language; he does not relate them to the signifying nodes that give the symptoms their configuration. "[Her thoughts] were once again concerned with her loneliness and the fate of her family; and this time she openly confessed to a burning wish that she might be as happy as her sister" (*SE* 2:151).

That the burning impact of this desire never left her afterward, that its impact consisted in her inability to walk, stand upright, or remain seated, is explained here by the temporal coincidence of the unbearable scenes and those bodily positions. The body, in its symbolic tenor, is no longer presented as the place where this conversion originates; conversion through symbolization is invoked only as a limited complementary mechanism dependent upon association.

How the Mystery of Conversion Is Constructed

In psychoanalytic literature, the prevailing view maintains that hysteria is a symbolizing conversion; and this conversion is always evoked as spectacular and mysterious. Freud always recognized the possibility of such a conversion, while acknowledging that he did not know how one might bring it about in oneself. In an article published in 1966, Jean-Paul Valabrega adopts the same perplexed tone: he proposes to retain the term conversion even though he says that it is obscure and that what is converted or somatized is not well understood.[20]

Our own reading of Elisabeth's case may allow us to deconstruct this mystery by showing that it arises out of a methodological

19. *Merken*, one should recall, means "to notice."
20. Jean-Paul Valabrega, "Entretien avec J.-P. Valabrega: Les conceptions actuelles en médecine psychosomatique," *Revue de Médecine Psychosomatique et de Psychologie Médicale* 8, no. 1 (January–March 1966).

inconsistency. The hysteric symptom is construed as a mysterious and spectacular mechanism when one abandons the attempt to specify the coordinates of the terrain on which it originates. "This can't go on any longer, so I'm going to be paralyzed"—this summary, scarcely a caricature, of the symptom's genesis is advanced with all the more complacency in that Freud is at the same time giving up the attempt to explore the field of jouissance that is formed through an organization of signifiers but realized in a body. Just before she fell ill, Elisabeth had admitted her desire to herself, undisguised, *unverhüllt*. This lack of disguise indeed refers to the symbolic elaboration of the scenarios of jouissance she was dealing with during that period. The symptom of astasia-abasia is established when something is arrested in the development of Elisabeth's awareness of her own jouissance: what is realized in her body is that canceled-out knowledge. That knowledge, the signifying elaboration of a desire, does not consist in any awareness of her own identity that the subject might acquire by reflecting on a psychic conflict. What we have here is not a psychic mechanism, but the signifying elaboration of a jouissance whose blockage or suspension will take shape through the symptom. No symbolic conversion is possible except on this terrain where the body of jouissance is elaborated through the signification of a desire to which it fixates itself.

On this terrain, the wordplays enacted in the body lose their spectacular and mysterious character. Conversely, the symbolizing conversion is highlighted when it is isolated from this place of origin. Freud's entire closing discussion of Elisabeth's case bears the stamp of that isolation (*SE* 2:174–81). He wonders whether a hysterical symptom might not—all the same—be produced by pure symbolic conversion, which would amount to dispensing with associative conversion. Referring to the story of another patient, Frau Cäcilie, he grants that hypothesis: the headaches that were always present during her treatment were directly related to the look with which her grandmother used to "pierce" her forehead. But the hypothesis of the signifier's direct hold on the body remains here as a possibility salvaged in extremis although with its mystery intact, for as a clinical exception it confirms the rule according to which every mechanism of symbolic conversion is dependent upon a conversion through association.

To summarize and conclude, the ambiguity of the term *Aufmerk-samkeit* opens the way to a contradiction in the theory of conversion. Freud declares that the new terrain discovered, that of the patient's cathexis of certain coordinates of her body as repetition and signs of scenarios of jouissance that have remained as it were in suspension, is properly speaking the place of origin of hysterical conversion. Only that "other moment" activates the associations between the patient's pain and the events that had seemed, in a misguided analysis, to be its cause.

If, as we have shown, the attention paid to bodily positions and the signifying organization of jouissance are the same thing, then conversion has as its mainspring that seizing of the body in the signifier. In other words, conversion is always and fundamentally what Freud identifies, sometimes uniquely, as conversion by symbolization. Conversion by symbolization cannot be conceived as just one mechanism among others in hysteria—the third, the most obscure—for it is the fundamental mechanism. Beyond this, Freud implies a critique of the notion of association, a notion that is provisional and not very rigorous. Thus it cannot be said that this mechanism arises later than the notion of association in the genesis of hysteria: what is invoked here as posterior in fact involves the attempt at knowing, not the object to be known. Freud spoke first of conversion by association, then, as he discovered another terrain (the imaginary subjection to a jouissance that owes its real configuration to signifying nodes), he made it necessary to criticize the theory of associative conversion. But he did not act accordingly; instead, confusing his own attempt at knowing with the object to be known, confusing a complete methodological reversal, an epistemological break, with an unproblematic juxtaposition of two mechanisms, allowing himself thus to be misled by the temporal continuity of his own thoughts, he produced a theory of symbolizing conversion dependent on associative conversion. The earlier mode of thought asserted itself: the terrain of that other body linked to the imaginary and to the signifying discourse of jouissance becomes murky once again, which is to say that conversion by symbolization appears mysterious in comparison with the "self-evidence" of an association between psychic and organic elements.

The self-evidence of associative conversion, as well as the exceptional nature of conversion by symbolization alone, imposes itself, according to Freud, on the basis of clinical evidence. Is this really so? At what point in his investigation does Freud think he has furnished the proof of a conversion mechanism that has been initiated by an association between conflict and pain?

Do the clinical facts invoked really exhibit the associative mechanism and the absence of a symbolizing conversion? Is it not rather the restrictive conception of such a conversion—the *sporadic* identification of jouissance making its manifestations spectacular—that makes it impossible to recognize the extent of the order of the body seized by signification?

The analysis of Frau Cäcilie's neuralgias leaves little doubt on this point. The recognition of a mechanism of associative conversion that would open the way to conversion derives its necessity from the isolation, from the preliminary abstraction that fails to recognize the true purport of the symbolizing conversion. Frau Cäcilie suffers, among other symptoms, from atypical facial neuralgias. Against the advice of her doctors, who had sought the cause in a dental infection and were prepared to proceed with the unnecessary extraction of seven teeth, Freud recognized the hysterical nature of the problem, which yielded to hypnosis. By a movement of thought that is more antinomic than dialectical, Freud then opposed the symbolic nature of the symptom to organicism: "When I began to call up the traumatic scene, the patient saw herself back in a period of great mental irritability [*Empfindlichkeit*] towards her husband. She described a conversation which she had had with him and a remark of his which she had felt as a bitter insult. Suddenly she put her hand to her cheek, gave a loud cry of pain and said: 'It was like a slap in the face.' With this her pain and her attack were both at an end."[21]

There is no doubt about it, symbolization is occurring here; she felt (*Sie hatte gefühlt*) as if she had really received a slap in the face. Now "everyone will immediately ask how it was that the sensation of a 'slap in the face' came to take on the outward forms of a trigeminal neuralgia, why it was restricted to the second and third

21. *Studies on Hysteria*, SE 2:178. Freud's play on the word *Empfindlichkeit*, essential to the symbolism of the symptom, is lost in the English "irritability." For a more accurate rendering of the scenario of erotic struggle between protagonists, *Empfindlichkeit* might be translated as "sensitivity."

branches, and why it was made worse by opening the mouth and chewing—though, incidentally, not by talking" (*SE* 2:178).

This text appears characteristic of the divergent directions of thought that crisscross in Freud's first elaboration of a theory of hysteria, directions of which traces remain in numerous contemporary psychoanalytical studies. On the one hand, Freud is breaking new ground: the feeling of a slap in the face is not accompanied by the feeling of a blow actually received, independent of the circumstances. It does not work for all blows, so to speak: her husband's words have such a magical effect on Frau Cäcilie's body only because she has already been feeling "great mental irritability" toward him. In other words, appearances notwithstanding, the blow in question is not isolated and sudden; before the striking effect of the husband's words, something in Cäcilie's body offers itself to similar blows, or provokes them. It may be said that this simply puts the problem at one remove. But no: the problem is displaced onto another terrain—that of the "mental irritability" that provokes, calls for, the blows. We are on the terrain of a jouissance that is articulated in a demand and that sometimes short-circuits the signifying elaboration, converts it into a sensory hallucination—one that is rigorously determined, however, by the signifying organization of the desire that is fixated on it.

Here we may borrow Freud's own terms: the origin of Frau Cäcilie's hysteria is the focusing of her attention toward her sensations. To grasp the mechanism of conversion amounts to reconstituting the history of that orientation, allowing it to pick up its threads where the symptomatic nodes confuse warp and woof.

But in fact this focusing of attention, suggested by the kinship of the terms designating the tenor of the patient's relationship to her husband and the form of the symptom, is not really exploited by Freud. More rapidly even than in Elisabeth's case, the terrain of hysteria is covered over and the symbolizing conversion is pinpointed as a miracle. Freud isolates it and, abandoning this attempt to conceptualize it, opposes it to the physiological construction even as he remains a prisoner of the latter.

The "everyone" who is astonished that an impression can produce the physiological phenomenon that it signifies through a metaphor is a man for whom the relation of body to language cannot come into existence, for want of being conceived by way of specific concepts—a man for whom physiological science functions not only as a science but as an imaginary discourse establishing a model for all possible bodily reality.

Since the terrain of jouissance is scarcely indicated, since even in its unavoidable effects it is reinterpreted by a psychophysiological discourse, there is no reason to be astonished that it is no longer identified among the clinical facts but that, on the "near" side of the terrain and serving as its foundation, as it were, one finds an associative conversion through *Gleichzeitigkeit*, simultaneity (*SE* 2:178). Frau Cäcilie's first attack of neuralgia here does not seem to warrant a detailed account: a painful look had brought to the surface a reproach that led her to repress another series of thoughts. In spite of—or because of—the vagueness of these indications, Freud recognizes a case of conflict and of self-protection. "Association through simultaneity" signifies that a neuralgia of organic origin, and thus completely heterogeneous to the conflict, becomes from this point on the sign of a reminder of the repressed conflict.

In this construction of conversion through the chance encounter of two independent and heterogeneous series, the notion of association functions clearly as an epistemological obstacle in that it prevents the pursuit of an investigation of the nature of the pain experienced and of the illness in question. Freud concludes, indeed, that the appearance of the neuralgia at that moment would not be understood without a recognition of the existence, during the same period, of facial or dental pains. When he adds that this was not implausible, furthermore, since Frau Cäcilie was then in the early months of pregnancy, he comes full circle: no further question on the relation of this pregnancy to the aforementioned psychic conflict is possible.

Freud's next example further confirms that he is caught in a closed circle. Another superficially symbolic symptom is linked, once again, to its presumed associative foundation: a pain in the legs, an inability to walk that appeared just as the doctor was taking the patient's arm to have her leave the room was reproduced and resolved in the analysis when the patient formulated her fear of not knowing "what stance to take" at the family meal she had to attend. But Freud adds that this symbolization was superimposed on an organic ailment: the proof is that the patient had remained so long in her room only because her feet hurt.

This canceling out of any further question about pain, this dualist interpretation of the simultaneity of conflict and pain, is all the more astonishing here given that this simultaneity was understood in an entirely different way before the full-fledged return of "associative conversion." When Elisabeth's legs became involved during the analytic sessions, and especially the day she got up, thinking her brother-in-law had called her, before she was struck with violent pains, it was clear that the symptom was a part of the scene being relived, that there was no chance element whatever in their supposed association; it was clear that the simultaneity of the phenomena in fact pointed to the homogeneity of a field that articulates body and language. Freud even noted that, in the latter part of the treatment, which brought to light the meaning of these violent pains triggered by the hallucinated summons from her brother-in-law, Elisabeth yielded to bittersweet (*schmerzlichsüss*) memories, to painful delights.[22]

Little is left of this insight by the time of the final synthesis, which is regrettably just that, a synthesis. In the official version of the conversion theory, there are three successive phases: the physiological base made up of the common pains of existence; the "opening" properly speaking of the conversion process through the cathexis of a pain or physiological function that is contemporary with an intolerable conflict and that becomes a signal for its recollection; and finally the refinement, the spiritual aroma, of the symbolizing conversion that reworks the material prepared by the association. Associative conversion through simultaneity is what connects, what accomplishes the synthesis between, word games and bodily events that are otherwise without common measure—or the synthesis between conflict and pain.

In fact, the task that had been assigned to the notion of conversion by association remains unfulfilled to the end, for we are confronted with a term that applies to no object, refers to no real process that it would allow us to understand. What is more, this expression serves

22. *SE* 2:156. Yet another example (pp. 171–72) confirms that the mnesic symbol is not a pain that is radically heterogeneous to the conflict, but a piece of a scenario of jouissance: the episode of the "pricking sensation" in Rosalie's finger.

only to confuse things, to render unrecognizable an unknown order of reality glimpsed in spite of itself. It is the name given to a dream of synthesis involving successive and irreconcilable apprehensions of a single phenomenon: hysteria. It thus corresponds in the Freudian argument to a moment of confusion owing to idealism—if, as Marx said in his critique of Hegel, idealism consists in projecting onto the object the thought process through which one apprehends it, in transforming into the genesis of reality the successive phases of the knowledge of reality one has gained.

It is indeed a genesis of conversion that Freud claims to provide through his dream of an articulation between a physiological problem, association through simultaneity, and symbolization. But this projection onto the object is not a simple displacement: what Freud presents as a synthesis involving the object he is concerned with is in fact a necessary break in the problematic. Epistemologically, this point is laden with consequences: when one begins with a medical description of the pain and its symptoms, in order to approach the terrain of hysteria it is necessary to make a clean break, after which there is no turning back. When the place of origin of the conversion has been defined as the direction of the subject's attention toward the positions of her body, it is inconsistent to return to a phased construction of the conversion—first the purely physiological problem (rheumatism, in Elisabeth's case), then the association, then the symbolization, for the third viewpoint presupposes a critique of the other two and represents a different approach to the problem, a different strategy for acquiring knowledge. This means that between the psychophysiological construction (or the psychosomatic one, to use more contemporary terminology) and the psychoanalytic undertaking, a choice must be made. To be sure, one may be content to describe the organic manifestations that are bound to surface in cases of hysterical conversion: Elisabeth's example suffices to show this. Her unconscious cathexis of her bodily positions puts into play something of her organic body *as well*. Freud's emphasis on the importance of these positions makes it possible to see how. Her bodily positions are decisive for Elisabeth in that they represent fragments of scenes of jouissance that she retains as presenting elements (*Darstellbarkeit*) of her desire. To say that hysteria is at stake here is to assert the consideration of that order of reality as the only legitimate one. But this does not mean that the positions in question cannot be identified at the perceptual level at the same time. A position, when it is conceived as an element of presentation in an unconscious scenario, may have an identifiable aspect in an empirical or organic observation: if hysterical cramps perpetuate a scenario of jouissance, they can also be perceived by an observer (whereas the scenario of jouissance cannot), and they can be accompanied in the long run by organic problems. There is no mystery here when one conceives of the articulation between the unconscious order and the organic order as the opposition between two methods that have the same object: the two methods do not have the same pertinence with respect to the problem of hysterical conversion, since only the analytic approach is constituted so as to conceptualize the problem. The physiological approach, on the contrary, is absolutely unequipped to say how symptoms arise from hysteria. But this does not prevent this approach from using its methods to cathect the body of a hysteric.

The confusion begins when the disjunctive articulation of two methods is transformed into a causal relation that would presuppose the homogeneity projected onto the object of these two in fact divergent methods: *as soon as we say that the unconscious produces effects in the organic realm, we are headed for that confusion*, even if the two orders are distinguished. For we are presupposing a sort of substance that would be the synthesis of the unconscious and the organic and in which transfers, causal mechanisms, could be produced. The Freudian idea of a phasing of "conversional" mechanisms on the basis of a physiological body playing the role of zero-degree fantasy does not present such a caricatural aspect. But it is on the basis of this sort of synthesis that certain first-generation psychoanalysts justify mixing hysteria and psychosomatic problems together. Thus in 1924 Felix Deutsch proposed to look for the secret of conversion in a metabiological order that would precede the differentiation of the psychic and the biological.[23] As opposed to this research for a "protobody," for an *Urleiblichkeit*, we would do well to follow Freud when he shows the insistence of the unconscious order (which is in no way a more worthy ontological reality than the others) in what is called at first, and in a necessarily confused way, the body.

23. "Zur Bildung des Konversionssymptoms," *Internationale Zeitschrift für Psychoanalyse*, 1924, no. 3, pp. 380–92, especially pp. 387–89.

Appropriate and Inappropriate Uses of the Psychic/Organic
Opposition: The Problem of the Psychosomatic

In its complexity, the Freudian theory of conversion thus seems
to indicate two paths, two approaches to hysteria. Only one of
these, the newer but also the more difficult to maintain, can account
for hysteria as such. The other direction, purportedly based on the
notion of associative conversion, reduces the body of jouissance to a
combination of psychic and somatic elements. Freud's itinerary
thus implies that we do not confront the realm of psychosomatic
problems on the one hand and that of hysterical conversion on the
other but face a single problem: the status of the unconscious body.

Now, the idea that hysteria was one thing and psychosomatic
ailments quite another emerged over time in the history of the
psychoanalytic movement. But oddly enough, this distinction was
put in place through a redefinition of hysteria from the viewpoint of
psychosomatics, that is, through a return to prepsychoanalytic categories.

These shifts led to a reevaluation and a distortion, between 1912
and 1930, of what Freud had begun to establish. What brought
them about? This question can orient our reading of the *Internationale Zeitschrift für Psychoanalyse*. The topic of hysterical conversion is under continual discussion during these years; and though
the term psychosomatic dates from Franz Alexander's work in
1945, numerous scholars were at work well before then on the issue
of the "leap into the organic." We need to make one observation at
the outset: whereas for Freud the theory of associative conversion
and the isolation of the pleasure-body in spectacular manifestations
never cause the newly observed terrain to disappear, other texts on
the contrary (indeed, precisely those that promote the idea of psychosomatic ailments) muddle the coordinates of that terrain. Let us
look at two examples, beginning with a text by Felix Deutsch. In
his 1924 article on the formation of conversion symptoms, Deutsch
criticizes the idea of the "leap into the organic," seeking to show
that what appears to perception as a symptom has been in prepara-
tion long since, both in the organism and in the subject's psyche.
Deutsch is answering a question Freud raised in *Studies on Hysteria*.
Starting from a description of the organic—and in this instance
motor—symptom, he looks to the patient's anamnesis to discover
what might account for the symptom's specificity. The description

of the symptom is carried out in two registers in turn: in medical terms, the circulatory problems mentioned are presented as atypical in that only the foot is affected; the patient's circulation remains otherwise normal. The symptom's history is also atypical: a doctor had considered amputation but then decided to hold off, since circulation had been temporarily reestablished along collateral paths. After that episode the patient had gone to see Felix Deutsch, telling himself that it was perhaps a nervous condition. Deutsch subscribes to the physiological description of the circulatory problem while writing it off as atypical. He does not ask himself what the atypicality may signify, or whether the symptom might not lead to an overly rapid passage from the problem perceived to the problem constructed physiologically. The objective sign that is deemed to indicate the problem's physiological basis is the absence of pulse accompanied by the coldness of the foot. Without questioning the modalities of this attribution, Deutsch then falls into step with his patient, so to speak, or at least moves to the psychic realm, to the psychogenesis of the symptom of conversion, which he first recognized as organic. He wants to explain, in his own terms, how the psychic *rejoins* the organic, and he is primarily interested in the first series. Summarizing the data gathered in the anamnesis, he first establishes correlations between psychic determinations and what he calls the symptom's form, without further explaining that expression.

The patient showed difficulty walking, for in so doing he was *illustrating*[24] his impotence: "This isn't working, this can't go on [*es geht nicht*]." The correlation established between the patient's psychic impotence and his organic problem becomes clearer in the assertion that the foot serves as symbol for the penis in the following scenario: the patient finds himself compelled to remain standing on the pavement to tie his shoes because he has the feeling that his foot has gone limp and is quivering in his shoe. From this point on the problem of conversion becomes inextricable: by summarizing as he does the so-called psychic elements and the so-called organic elements—which include the circulatory problems as well as what happens to the patient's foot when he stands still—Deutsch renders himself unable to ascribe any status to that other body that is

---

24. Emphasis added. The German term translated by "illustrate" is *dokumentieren*.

nevertheless profiled in the second description of the symptom. Only the insistence on its *form* suggests its place in the theory: but "form" is opposed to "content" and, as these concepts are elaborated, the other body of the symptomatic scenario remains subordinate; in particular, the question of its relation to the organic aspect of the problem is definitively eliminated, since everything involved in the scenario falls into the psychic category. Deutsch's method, in this summary of a case that begins with a presentation of the treatment results, goes hand in hand with his theoretical bias concerning the psychic nature of the symptom's genesis. A first step has been taken: in the very rich material revealed by the patient's narratives, his foot comes up over and over again. The author notes this quite precisely, yet the foot remains lodged between the psychic and the organic. Fifteen years earlier, a sentence about *claudicatio* intermittens ("a mysterious ailment, full of traps") had left a lasting mark on the patient, who was reading a medical book. This mystery referred him also to his mother's slight limp, and to an event of his childhood in which he had supposedly tripped his mother, making her fall on her own leg. But these remarks in themselves do not clarify the status of the body, for they are categorized among the "psychogenic preparations for conversion."

Deutsch next examines the second series, the history of the patient's prior circulatory condition, his latent tendency toward circulatory cramps, which could perhaps be considered the residue of an infectious illness that had long since been cured, when the first signs of conversion appeared. But in pursuing the links between two heterogeneous series, one does not eliminate their heterogeneity; at the crucial moment, as the author himself admits, conversion remains as mysterious as before. The enterprise turns out to have been ambiguous from the outset. Deutsch is attempting to understand how the psychic rejoins the organic: does he mean to determine only the moment of their encounter? Or does he mean to determine what event allows a latent organic ailment to take on meaning for the unconscious? This indeed seems possible;[25] from this viewpoint Deutsch is doing what he set out to do, but he is aiming at something else at the same time. He is analyzing the psychic and physical factors in order to find, as he puts it, their point

25. In fact, this first phase itself turns out to be ill constructed; see below, pp. 74–75.

of psychophysical contact—which is to say that in the end he consecrates the mystery of conversion even as he claims to resolve it.

In a negative way, this article shows us that conversion as mystery reappears whenever the organic body and the erotogenic body are confused and whenever one retains, conceptually, just one of the two terms—as Deutsch does—while seeking a point of psychophysical encounter. The term retained eradicates the history of a subject's desire, insofar as this history is inscribed on his or her body. If we are capable of identifying the order of phenomena to which all the clinical material of Felix Deutsch's patient referred, if we are capable of understanding its relation to onanism, we may then be able to redefine hysteria as a fixation that is proof against onanism, favored by an organic problem just as other neuroses are favored by some event that is itself external to the history of the desire but that becomes a good terrain and a good pretext for the constitution of a neurosis. This approach would never abolish the difference between the organic and the erotogenic, but it could explain the possibility of their strange alliance, tying in with Freud's suggestions in his discussion of somatic *compliance*. When all is said and done, the specificity of his remarks notwithstanding, Deutsch continues to fall short of what the Freudian expression invites us to consider.

A second exemple is even more telling. S. Feldmann,[26] in an article published a little earlier than Deutsch's, analyzes a case of blushing. The method he uses to account for it appears at first glance less elaborate, more narrative than Deutsch's: he tells how things came about, without framing the narrative within the theoretical problem of conversion. After a lecture, a student had come to see him, very interested in his teaching but unable to ask any questions in public, because he would have turned beet red. The narrative, like the treatment, embarks this time not on an analysis of the physiological atypicality of a given symptom, whose psychogenesis would thus have to be sought, but on the actualization, in transference, of the symptom of blushing and of the patient's defense against it. The pertinent correlations have changed: they are concentrated on the relation between the symptom replayed and the

26. S. Feldmann, "Über das Erröten," *Internationale Zeitschrift für Psychoanalyse*, 1922, no. 1, pp. 14–34.

symptom related. Between the actualized blushing and the narrated blushing no heterogeneity analogous to the one that separates the psychic order from the physiological is ever introduced.

This latter point indicates the homogeneity of a new register of the body in treatment. The patient immediately refers his symptom to the onanism that had provoked its first appearance: in a dream of that period, the patient saw himself urinating at a street corner, in a long stream, beside his father.

What Deutsch called the *"form" of the symptom* here takes on the status of an exhibitionist scenario: the patient recalls that when he blushes he feels handsomer, and at the same time he cannot bear it for fear people are making fun of him. But there is nothing psychic in this exhibitionism, which the author defines rather as a component of the scenario and its avatars: to exhibit oneself or to blush points up the insistence of a long experience of pleasure that has always been situated at the point of articulation between body and language that we are identifying. The patient's uncle had said to his five-year-old nephew on his lap: "This child would be quite good-looking if his nose weren't too big; we ought to trim it a bit." The proximity of a loved one's body refers the patient back to another memory: he found himself one day leaning up against his mother, who was not fully dressed and was not feeling well. Pressing his nose and his face against his mother's breast, he smelled a particular smell that provoked in him a sort of orgasm that for a long time afterward he sought to repeat by rubbing his penis against the maids' legs. During the treatment, these stories were accompanied by a dream in which an elephant's trunk was so large that it was connected to his penis. The intersection of these elements does not provide us with a psychogenesis: after mentioning this dream, Feldman makes explicit the penis–nose equivalence in the substitution of blushing for an erection. But in these displacements we do not leave the body of jouissance. In his patient's anamnesis, Deutsch sought the origin of the latter's interest in his own foot. Right after reading the book on *claudicatio intermittens*, he had begun to monitor his pulse. In this formulation the foot remains an external object chosen for its psychic nature; what is more psychical, after all, than interest in the vocabulary of classical psychology? Similarly, in the tripping episode, what the subject was doing to his mother was defined as a event capable of giving rise to, or of nourishing, a *feeling* of guilt. Feldman's study, on the contrary, makes the patient's body, in the anamnesis as well as in the symptomatic and transferential actualization, the terrain of desire's exercise and elaboration. Everything the author notes here circumscribes the space of the erotogenic body, whereas Deutsch draped the clinical material with markers that left it shapeless.

The uncovering of a homogeneous field does not suppress all differences. It defines them independently of the metaphysical question of conversion: the pertinent correlation, as we were saying, involves the relation of what happened with what was said, a relation that in this case encompasses that of body and language. Between the drive actualized in the body and the drive elaborated by language is established in many respects a relation of exclusive disjunction: it is by suspending the act that the narrative delivers up the erotic configuration of the body that that act was still putting forth only as an enigma. This difference, essential for characterizing types of elaboration of desire or of drives, confirms that the body/language duality has nothing to do with the psychical/physiological duality; between what is realized in the body and what is elaborated in speech, one can identify the same disjunctive relation as between the forms of the symptom. The suspension of the act through narrative has its counterpart in the fact that the patient, if he abandons himself to exhibitionism, if he displays himself, is thereby relieved from blushing. From the act to language and from the symptom to its constituents, we do not depart from scenarios of pleasure. Symptom and language constitute two moments of their elaboration: to be sure, in treatment the patient speaks of his body, but it is less a matter of discourse on the symptom, as in Deutsch's formulation, than of another elaboration of what was happening in the body. To account for the terrain of treatment, it is necessary to show either that the body in the symptom already participates in language, or else that, in language, the body is never, properly speaking, the object of a discourse. The beginning of the treatment illustrates this perfectly: for the young man to speak after the lecture is to put his body on stage while avoiding blushing. It is not to speak about blushing; it is to speak in order to make blushing exist in the mode of suspension.

The question of hysteria, here, is defined essentially as no longer that of conversion but rather that of the body's insistence as terrain where the drive is actualized. To this extent we are invited to reflect on the notion of the act in psychoanalysis in relation to the act of an erotogenic body that allows us to situate the hysterical symptom and onanism reciprocally.

Feldman's article, however, does not go that far. In it we note a displacement of stress, not a suppression or a critique of the notion of conversion. He reverses the order of factors but still calls upon the old notion—locally, so to speak, and in such a way that the notion does not abolish the erotogenic body. He mentions that the blushing represents for the patient an experience converted from his "beauty complex," favored by an overactivity of the sebaceous glands alongside the nose. This physiological problem faded in the course of the analysis.

The phenomenon always arises from a dual dimension. The physiological fact is never immediately identified with the unconscious order; in our example, the organic situation indicated took on value for the unconscious after the patient himself had the thought, or heard someone say, that he had a shiny nose. Blushing as a symptom dates back to the symbolic reprise that brings into play the unconscious cathexis of a perception and of things overheard.

A question now arises: If we are determined to distinguish the erotogenic from the organic, can we nevertheless acknowledge that the symbolic, the unconscious cathexis, would "command" a displacement toward the upper part of the body of the physiological component that accompanies jouissance? In the case in point, how is the substitution of blushing for erection brought about? Is the insistence and the repression of the signifier "blood" connected with the smell of the patient's mother that could also direct a displacement of the sanguinary engorgement of the penis toward the nose? Feldmann does not answer this question, or rather he maintains its ambiguity. According to the first representation of the case, which we have just recalled, he continues to refer to the idea of a leap into the organic, even if the bank from which it is appropriate to jump is called the pleasure-body and no longer the psychic realm.

But another way of understanding the case is suggested, at a pivotal point in the text, that would dissolve the mystery of conversion. Feldmann notes that his patient favored one onanist and exhibitionist scenario in particular: he massaged the sides of his nose, which made him sneeze and thus gave him a reason to blush without shame. Does this anodyne element not constitute the middle term that explains what he designates by the displacement of the erotogeneity of the penis toward the nose? It is henceforth pointless to suppose that the importance of the signifier "blood" in the patient's desire would mysteriously command a physiological displacement of the sanguinary engorgement of the penis toward the nose: the subject's relation to his nose is played out on two levels at once. The phantasmic importance of the shininess of his nose only reinforces this brilliance physiologically, because it stimulates massages that are acts of perceptive reality having physiological consequences at the same time as they are the actualization of an onanist drive.

Must we then seek in all cases of hysteria this missing link that dissolves the mysteries of conversion?

Chapter 2

From the Theory of Conversion to the
Theory of Erotogenic Zone Displacement

Initial Shifting

The notion of conversion, as we have seen, is vague and even contradictory. In Freud's first theory of hysteria, this idea lent some credibility to the obtrusive self-evidence of symptoms; conversion theory sought to trace that self-evidence to an origin that would make manifest the change from the moral order to the physical. The problematic of conversion by association attests to Freud's search for a "first time" of conversion. Nevertheless, the worm is in the fruit. From the outset, Freud viewed the emigration of some psychic element in a process of bodily innervation as a transposition belonging to the order of language. If conversion is the diversion of psychic energy into bodily innervation, there is no need to suppose that the body speaks. Yet at the very same time, Freud was using terms that implied a *grammaticality* of symptoms,[1] even for the mechanism of association. As for conversion through symbolization, when Freud sought to describe the change of register of affect, he relied upon terms he had been using ever since *Studies on Hysteria*, terms that appeared repeatedly in later texts: conversion is a transformation (*Verwandlung*, GW 1:233), a transposition (*Umwandlung*, *Versetzung*, GW 5:4), and more clearly still a transcription (*Transkription*, GW 5:63). Nearly all these terms present the ambiguity we have observed in Freud's thought concerning the nature of the process under investigation. They offer the illusion of homoge-

1. Cf. *Studies on Hysteria*, SE 2:151. Even in the texts that speculate on associative conversion, Freud uses a term that stems both from local determination and from grammar: the painful zone had developed through *apposition*.

neity between the order of nature as constructed by physiology and the order of language, which is not a natural reality.

Let us take as our hypothesis[2] the suggestion that, to develop a cogent theory of hysteria, we must free ourselves of metaphors like these that perpetuate confusion about the *object* of a theory of hysteria. This is not merely a secondary issue, for as the investigation of the symbolism of symptoms comes into focus the object of study itself is transformed. We have noted that in Elisabeth's case Freud gradually shifted the emphasis onto a different moment or factor— *ein anderes Moment*—that single-handedly brings into play the correspondences between psychic phenomena and physiological phenomena—that makes these correspondences operative (*SE* 2:150). The same expression, focusing the investigation on *ein anderes Moment*,[3] is repeated and amplified in Freud's study of Dora's case. At the point where he is evaluating the role Herr K.'s seduction of Dora (the stolen kiss) played in symptom formation, Freud remarks: "The stimulation of her lips by the kiss was no doubt of importance in localizing the feeling at that particular place; but I think I can also recognize another factor in operation" (*SE* 7:29). In other words, a process of physiological excitation of the body triggered by a specific incident does not in itself account for the formation of a hysterogenic zone. What does Freud mean when he speaks of "another factor"?

The Epistemological Importance of Negative Systems: The Hysteric Has No Body

Many of the cases presented in *Studies on Hysteria* attracted attention because of the dramatic and compelling nature of the symptoms exhibited; not so for Dora's case. Freud himself calls it a case of "*'petite hystérie'* with the commonest of all somatic and mental symptoms: dyspnoea, *tussis nervosa*, aphonia, and possibly migraines, together with depression, hysterical unsociability, and a *taedium vitae* which was probably not entirely genuine."[4] The hysteric's body no longer fascinates him, no longer holds the answer he

2. Subject to recognition, as well, of the limits that such a proposition will not fail to encounter.

3. French translators have rendered the German term *Moment* as *facteur*, "factor," in *Studies on Hysteria*, and by *mobile*, "motive," in Dora's case. [The *Standard Edition* gives "factor" in both instances (*SE* 2:150, 7:29). —TRANSLATOR'S NOTE]

4. "Fragment of an Analysis of a Case of Hysteria," *SE* 7:23.

is looking for. From this point it is a short step to his assertion in 1908 that anyone who studies hysteria soon loses interest in its symptoms ("Hysterical Phantasies and Their Relation to Bisexuality," *SE* 9:162).

This displacement of emphasis comes about because, although hysterical symptoms do maintain a very close relation with the sensorimotor functions, it has become clear that these functions cannot be understood apart from the history of the subject's symbolization of her own body. The remarkable motor symptoms displayed by Anna O. and Elisabeth were the focus of attention only inasmuch as the equation established between the body and corporal innervation was really taken literally. Freud proceeds to show with increasing clarity that in psychoanalysis, and especially in the investigation of hysteria, one cannot rely on the idea of a bodily sensorimotor system that would be independent of the history of the symbolization of the desiring body. His essay on negation and Lacan's rereading of it have taught us that the subject of desire maintains no immediate or natural relation with the real world. It is not that that world does not exist; but the subject's relation to it is unverifiable, is not self-evident, notwithstanding psychology's claim that perception is the elementary act of psychic life. Reality exists for us only inasmuch as language structures our desire, inasmuch as grammar contributes its resources to the construction of that desire. If this is true of our relation to the objects of the world, it is hard to see how our relation to our own bodies could be any different. A human being is not a consciousness that organizes organic phenomena; we cannot conceive of our own bodies as sets of bodily innervations for the good reason that our bodies exist for us inasmuch as we symbolize them.[5] It is now clear where this reversal leads: from the omnipresence of the hysteric's body to the eyes of a fascinated observer, the study of sensorimotor functions permeated by language leads us to say that that ostentation is only the obtrusive side of the hysteric's absence with respect to her own body, for want of its symbolization. The hysteric has no body, for something in the history of her body could not be formulated, except in symptoms.

This change of direction in the theory of hysteria, which dismisses the idea of conversion, is suggested as early as 1895 in the

5. And not through knowledge of them.

cases in which Freud is not especially concerned with motor symptoms. Thus in Miss Lucy's case we cannot succumb to fascination with the hysterical body, for where her problems involve the sensory rather than the motor sphere they appear in their negative guise, their aspect of lack. Ordinarily—for example, in Breuer's description of Anna O.'s symptoms—his references to anesthesias (that is, to the subject's absence with respect to her own body) are overshadowed by the compelling nature of the motor problems caused by her contractures. Such a presentation shows the body as a positive entity and thus makes us imagine that autonomy accompanies its visibility; hence we assimilate the order of the body to the order of bodily innervation. In Miss Lucy's story, on the other hand, her symptoms are manifested only, or principally, by a lack: anosmia, or the inability to smell.

How do sensory symptoms relate to language? Our brief glance at Miss Lucy's case allows us to state the question clearly, in the form it takes later on in Dora's case. The opening of Freud's account puts in place two aspects of the symptom: anosmia, that is, the suppression of olfactory sensations, and a positive hallucinatory counterpart for this deficit—that is, the subjective olfactory sensations that Miss Lucy quickly identifies as the smell of burnt pudding. Here is the first link between sensoriality and symbolization. For an anosmia that is connected with such contrapuntal precision to a highly significant odor could hardly involve a mute body. Indeed, Freud goes on to note that Miss Lucy was suffering from a heavy head cold; however, *he does not attempt, as he did in Elisabeth's case, to construct the hysterical symptom on the basis of a zero-degree fantasy viewed as purely organic.* It is pointless, in this case, to try to find out how the symptom was constructed on the basis of organic pain or to identify conversion by symbolization as a complication of conversion by association. Organicism may remain of interest in other respects, but as Freud's study of Miss Lucy's case unfolds, this interest is never focused on a possible relation between the hysterical symptom and an organic problem from which it is presumed to arise. The problem is resolved during treatment, and it is clarified in the text through an examination of the body as grasped through language. Only *at the end* of his narrative does Freud remark, without compromising his interpretation of the case: "I must leave it an open question, however, how far her nasal disorder may have played a part in the impairment of her sense of smell" (*SE* 2:121).

67

The case thus manifests a change of method, and nowhere more clearly than in the analysis of the first scene Miss Lucy narrates. She traces the odor of burnt pudding back to a day when she received a letter from her mother that led her to waver between her daughterly duties and her responsibilities to the children she was taking care of and who were fond of her. Just as she was representing the conflict to herself, and in spite of the fact that she had completely lost her sense of smell at that time, she smelled pudding burning in the kitchen. If, in a productive moment in which something of a still ill-defined conflict is articulated, the meaning that permeates or works through sensoriality can remove a functional inhibition, must we not conclude that ordinarily the repression of this signifying sensoriality is what inhibits the function?

The sense in which we have been speaking of pleasure-body is now clear. Sensoriality—in the case at hand, the sense of smell—does involve the body, but a body informed by the signifying elaboration of desire. And to situate the proper order of the hysterical symptom is to activate that sensoriality, to give it voice in the symptom's history. This can be achieved only if sensoriality is considered in itself; Freud makes no further attempt to construct it on the basis of some primordial problem that would be purely organic.

His change of method appears to be aided by the fact that an olfactory problem does not serve as well as a motor problem to satisfy a quest for correspondence between some place in the body that is presumed to have been inhabited by a purely organic pain and events that are presumed to have made that place symbolic, to have turned it into the *Merkmal*, the sign recalling a conflict. Sensory ailments thus allow a first approach to the reality of the erotogenic body, whose conceptualization, with all the difficulties such a conceptualization entails, is indispensable to a theory of hysteria. But the autonomy of a bodily domain permeated by language can appear only with the discovery of infantile sexuality. Until Freud pushes his analyses back that far, the reality proper to the erotogenic and hysterogenic zones cannot be clearly delineated.

Outline of a New Approach: The Displacement of Sensations

In his discussion of Miss Lucy's treatment, Freud's problematic undergoes only a limited transformation. The analyst highlights three significant scenes that modulate the life of the symptom.

Freud's interpretation of the first of these scenes, accounting for the burnt pudding odor, still falls within the framework of conversion theory. All the elements are present: the supposed psychic conflict; the olfactory sensation, which turned up just when the conflict was being experienced most sharply; and thus the junction of the two, the use of the olfactory sensation as sign (*Merkmal*) of the conflict. "The conflict between her affects had elevated the moment of the letter's arrival into a trauma, and the sensation of smell that was associated with this trauma persisted as its symbol" (*SE* 2:116).

But Freud is not satisfied with these correspondences. He goes on to look for yet another moment that would bring them into play, for he is hard put to see why it should have been a smell, and that particular smell, *if it had nothing to do with the conflict*, that became the mark, the scar, of the conflict. Now, as it happens that smell, and Lucy's sense of smell in particular, is not unrelated to the conflict: to account for this, the idea of a psychic conflict has to be abandoned. After Lucy has recalled the first traumatizing scene, her symptom does not improve, or not very much. Freud then proposes an interpretation that brings into play an unconscious love Lucy has for her employer. Lucy accepts the interpretation, and in the aftermath her symptom is displaced (in the sense that displacement, *Verschiebung*, has in dream interpretations), for she then begins to smell cigar smoke. Freud does not speak of transference, as he later does in Dora's case. But in what we have been calling up to now the life of the pleasure-body continued in the symptom, or sensoriality, which exists for a subject only inasmuch as it is shaped by the symbolization of her desire, we now have to recognize the problematic of displacement.

The second scene Lucy recalls presents the sense of smell in an entirely new way. One day her employer had forbidden her to do what the luncheon guest, the head accountant, had done—to kiss the children on the mouth. Now that day, as usual, there was an odor of tobacco smoke in the dining room. Orality and the sense of smell figure on both sides here: in the symptom, but also in the trauma. It is not *by chance* that the smell became the sign of the trauma, since Lucy's employer, instead of addressing her as a woman, spoke up to forbid her to kiss the children—spoke to her, in other words, as he would to a servant. Some element of Lucy's desire for this man—the desire for a kiss, an oral desire perhaps—thus turns out to be forbidden, blocked. The so-called traumatizing events have Lucy's erotogenic body as their place of impact, which means that nothing passes from the psychic to the organic. Once this point is clear, another way of considering the formation of hysterical symptoms is indicated, namely, via displacements of erotogeneity. We have just identified such displacements in two ways. In the modifications of Lucy's olfactory symptom, we found representations displaced in a dreamlike manner that led to the lifting of the anosmia; the burnt smell gave way to the more specific smell of cigar smoke, focusing the signification of the symptom on Lucy's relation to her employer and to Freud.

But the prohibition on kissing the children is traumatizing only through its connection with an orality constitutive of Lucy's desire, and perhaps with what, in Dora's case, Freud calls a displacement of erotogeneity—a notion he will depend on much more than on conversion to define hysteria. Now how are these two displacements related? Can *Verschiebung*, as a stylistic device of dreams, as metonymy, also become a localized displacement of something onto the body? Is this how we are to conceptualize the displacements of erotogenic zones in hysteria? What is the place that imposes itself in the use of the term *Verschiebung*, dis*place*ment?

Not until his study of Dora's case does Freud show the conditions under which one can elaborate what he outlined in Lucy's case, the foregrounding of the erotogenic zones and of their history. Unlike Felix Deutsch, with his repeated and single-minded insistence on somatic compliance as the distinctive feature of hysteria,[6] Freud puts the question in different terms as early as 1905. To explain the traumatic nature of the scene in which fourteen-year-old Dora was seduced by Herr K., it is not enough to say that an affective energy connected with an intolerable conflict was discharged in sensory or motor innervation. Freud points out here, as he did in *Studies on Hysteria*, that such an explanation is unsatisfactory, since the symptom (Dora's cough or Elisabeth's rheumatism) existed before the supposedly traumatizing scene. This difficulty would have remained purely technical, would not have spurred a renewal of the problematic, had it not led Freud to extend his investigation back to early childhood. That decision—*"Bis auf die Kindheit zurückgreifen"* ("we must go back to her childhood" [*SE* 7 :27])—does not simply

6. "Zur Bildung des Konversionssymptoms," *Internationale Zeitschrift für Psychoanalyse*, 1924, no. 3, pp. 380–92.

imply some supplementary clarification of the theory of somatic compliance. The extension of the analysis back to childhood subverts the first theory of hysteria, for the discovery of an infantile sexuality persisting in the symptom brings to light an autonomous erotogenic body that can no longer be defined in relation to an underlying organic foundation of the symptom.

"I should without question consider a person hysterical in whom an occasion for sexual excitement elicited feelings that were preponderantly or exclusively unpleasurable; and I should do so whether or no the person were capable of producing somatic symptoms" (*SE* 7:28). The indifference to somatic symptoms here does not mean that all consideration of bodily involvement will be ruled out, but it means such consideration must be cast in new terms. The body can no longer be synonymous with motor innervation.

In the three new criteria set forth for the symptom—reversal of affect, displacement of erotogenic zones, avoidance mechanism— the first two bring into play a new notion of the body. Disgust can be conceptualized only as a modification—a rejection—of an experience of jouissance that can be conceptualized only within a body, as Serge Leclaire points out.[7]

In *Four Fundamental Concepts*, Jacques Lacan suggested that the reaction of disgust should be understood as a process of desexualization.[8] Does the fact that the sexual object inspires disgust mean that it is tilting toward reality and presenting itself as a hunk of meat? Is this what is at stake in the scotomization (unconscious exclusion from the field of consciousness) of certain parts of the erotogenic body proper and of the body of the other in hysteria? Such does not seem to be the case. The hysteric's approach to sexual difference takes on the aspect of a refusal. There is something about the body of the other that the hysteric cannot "take," cannot swallow, inhale, or touch, according to the circumstances; but this refusal is played out in the erotogenic order, as Freud's discussion of displacement of erotogeneity makes clear. Lacan, here as elsewhere, proceeds rather too quickly to identify the body with a lack of erotic enjoyment (*un*

7. *Psychanalyser* (Paris: Seuil, 1968), p. 6.
8. "It is in the function in which the sexual object moves towards the side of reality and presents itself as a parcel of meat that there emerges that form of desexualization that is so obvious that it is called in the case of the hysteric a reaction of disgust" (*FFC*, p. 172).

manque à jouir) that takes the shape of a piece of meat, a corpse, or a stone. The formation of hysterical symptoms presumably strengthens the arguments against such identification—witness Miss Lucy's case, or Dora's.[9]

Herr K. had hugged and kissed Dora. The word "disgust" characterizes Dora's immediate reaction, as she herself describes it during treatment. Displacements of sensation, on the other hand, characterize the modalities according to which this experience is inscribed on her body. When he compares the physical contact between Dora and Herr K. in the seduction scene with the marks that contact left on Dora's body, Freud speaks of a first displacement combined with a reversal of affect. Instead of a pleasurable genital sensation, an unpleasurable feeling cathects the mucous membrane of the alimentary canal; disgust lingers in the form of a slight repugnance for food. Here we can see how displacement has to be understood. Something, to be sure, has the body as its theater, but no libidinal substance moves from the stomach to the alimentary canal.

In the second displacement Freud identifies, the positive aspect of the symptom reappears, as the visible aspect of a process that consisted initially in a scotomization. Dora suffers from a sensory hallucination, from a sensation of pressure on the thorax—her denial, her refusal to take into account the existence of Herr K.'s sexuality and her own, leaves its trace in her feeling of suffocation. Once again, no substantive element moves from one place to another; in this sense nothing is displaced. When the notion of displacement of an erotogenic zone appears, it does not involve the idea of somatic innervation; instead, it refers us back to the first model of 1895, which distinguished perceptual neurones from memory neurones, or it refers us to the image of the mystic writing pad, which allows us to understand how an incident can be inscribed without being experienced, as in the case of disgust. "This perception [of Herr K.'s erect member] was revolting to her; it was dismissed from her memory, repressed, and replaced by the innocent sensation of pressure upon her thorax" (*SE* 7:30). Here Freud seems to *acknowledge* Dora's perception. According to the argument we have been developing, however, that Dora's perception has

9. On the inanimate as ultimate signified see, for example, Lacan's unpublished seminar, "La relation d'objet," December 5, 1956.

disgust as its tonality means that the reality of sexual difference, which confronts Dora here (and which is never a perceptible reality without first being a symbolizable reality), is not really acknowledged at all. To say that a perception was set aside, shunted onto memory, is to say that the perception occurred only in the mode of denial.

Every aspect of this experience is played out upon the body, but only through the symbolic elaboration or nonelaboration of the desire that conveys perceptions and feelings. That we are dealing here with a body other than the one implied in conversion by association and in somatic compliance is confirmed when Freud spells out the forms of displacement. Dora's oral zone, which had been "over-indulged . . . by the habit of sensual sucking" (*SE* 7:30) had been an important erotogenic zone from her earliest childhood. The association of the psychic and the somatic had seemed partly fortuitous; in erotogenic zone displacements there, chance no longer plays a role. What appeared in indistinct form in Miss Lucy's case—that the so-called traumatic scenes actually represented moments in which something of the order of jouissance sought expression when a seemingly external event brought the infantile body back to life—is explicitly posited only when the relation between the symptom and infantile sexuality is clarified. What proved to be intolerable in Herr K.'s declaration, and what accounts for Dora's feeling of disgust and for her erotogenic zone displacement, has something to do with her past as a thumb-sucker (and both Dora and her father recalled that childhood habit). Perhaps we need to go further and juxtapose this intolerable element to sexual difference, in Herr K.'s relation to the oral experience that linked Dora to her father as to a maternal figure, since it was her father who had attempted to wean her from her thumb-sucking. As we know, Lacan's reading of the Dora case points up the importance of the screen memory tied to her thumb-sucking[10]—a memory in which Dora sees herself "sitting on the floor in a corner sucking her left thumb and at the same time tugging with her right hand at the lobe of her brother's ear as he sat quietly beside her" (*SE* 7:51)—since Lacan also suggests that the importance of the father's (ambiguous) role in the history of the formation of his daughter's erotogenic body cannot be overestimated. According to Lacan, Freud failed to

10. *Ecrits* (Paris: Seuil, 1966), p. 221.

note that Dora was reliving this relation in transference. In this view the treatment failed not, as Freud suggested, because he himself had failed to display enough affection in the therapeutic relationship (*SE* 7:109), but because of the unanalyzed maternal position that he revealed in expressing this very scruple and that put him in the same place as Dora's father. This interpretation is doubtless partly correct, so long as Dora's thumb-sucking is not reduced to the homosexual component of her desire. To put it another way, her orality and her homosexuality are themselves complex: they consist as much in her relation to a complicitous father as in her fascination with Frau K. Did Dora's father, as he weaned his daughter from her thumb-sucking, play the role of a prohibitory mother or that of a complicitous companion? Since we are compelled to answer "both," we are brought back to the history of the erotogenic zones.

Somatic Compliance Called into Question by the Return to Childhood

"*Bis auf die Kindheit zurückgreifen*": this return to childhood does not simply mean that more memories are elicited from the patient, but means also that the life of the erotogenic body can appear in its autonomy, can cease to be conflated with an initial moment at which the problem would have been purely physiological. Freud relates symptom formation to this specific order.[11] Everything takes place in Dora's throat. We no longer need to presuppose a zero degree of fantasy. The problematic of *somatic compliance*, inherited from the first conversion theory, can be relativized. Freud initially defends this notion (*SE* 7:40–42) for polemical reasons, but after the significance of Dora's childhood thumb-sucking is brought to light things are turned upside down. Dora's tendency to cough and to lose her voice does not have to be explained by some organic condition that would have suddenly turned into the reminder of a psychic conflict. Freud notes, on the contrary, that patients who eventually suffer from anesthesia and hysterical afflictions are precisely those for whom a given bodily location has had a particular erotic significance. His formulations sparkle with unequivocal clarity: "An intense activity of this erotogenic zone at an early age thus

11. Jacques Lacan, unpublished seminar, "L'envers de la psychanalyse," February 18, 1970.

determines the subsequent presence of a somatic compliance on the part of the tract of mucous membrane which begins at the lips" (*SE* 7:52). In this discussion Freud is less concerned with arguing over priority (What is more fundamental, the organic predisposition to throat ailments or the erotic status of Dora's throat as signifying material and as the theater in which the chronicle of sexual difference is simultaneously staged and erased?) than with establishing the autonomy of a new domain, that of the erotogenic body. When he discovers the importance of thumb-sucking and of fantasies involving a sexual relationship transacted by mouth, it would not be correct to say that he deems the physiological construction false. It is more accurate to say that the earlier method, the one that sought to comprehend the formation of hysterical symptoms by way of an underlying organic foundation, turns out to have functioned as an epistemological obstacle. The erotogenic body is not the organic body, and it cannot be defined on the basis of the organic model. Thus the notion of somatic compliance is indirectly subject to criticism not by virtue of some intrinsic error, but by virtue of its function, because of what it prevents us from comprehending.

On one particular point, however, the resulting consideration of the erotogenic body does seem to call physiology directly into question. There exists a physiological science of sensations that does not presuppose that the feeling body is a speaking body. Now if we follow Lucy's history, and Dora's, it is not clear that the relation of human sensoriality to language can be dismissed without an act of reduction that is detrimental to scientific construction and that is at the same time inadequate with respect to the object that the science in question is claiming to explain. Thus Dora creates her own throat irritations in a quasi-hallucinatory fashion—the hallucination being enacted in her body—because in so doing she brings about the presence, in the sense of Darstellung, of a sexual scene. Her coughing and throat-clearing can be analyzed as behaviors that stimulate organic phenomena through habit. But *once we begin* to analyze the hysteric symptom in this manner, we can no longer conceptualize it as the renewed enactment of a fantasy in which, since childhood, Dora has been simultaneously formulating and setting aside the problematic of sexual difference in an appeal addressed to her father. A human subject has the inherent capacity to

75

stimulate sensations in herself that can also be analyzed as so-called objective realities, for reasons that have to do with the necessity for a symbolization of her desire.

In this sense the erotogenic body antedates, in principle, the physiological body. We must not understand this as an ontological proposition, however. To be sure, it is always appropriate to consider the body, even the hysteric's body, as a physiological object. But a scientific enterprise is not undertaken without a precise explanatory aim. The physiological construction and the psychoanalytic construction do not square off in the absolute like two axiomatics developing a neutral or undefined terrain. They have specific problems to respond to; and that is why, in the case in point, the one is better than the other. The first may be understood as an impasse with respect to what the second is able to articulate.

Here we can see what it means to say that, although there is no absolute notion of truth in these experimental sciences, which are defined by the order of phenomena they seek to account for, not everything has equivalent value. The theory of somatic compliance equates the speaking body with a physiological body and establishes its own primary task as that of understanding the relation between them. In so doing it proves to be mistaken, because it prevents comprehension of the very phenomenon it sought to understand in the first place; it no longer refers to that phenomenon except by allusion. The discovery of infantile sexuality, through analysis, reopens the question by making it possible to trace the history of the symptom, and by that very token it posits the necessity of conceptualizing a different body.

The Essential Problem:
Erotogenic Zones and Hysterogenic Zones

Freud has changed direction in his clinical definition of hysteria. His point of departure is no longer conversion, but rather is the close and specific relationship that symptom formation maintains with the history of the erotogenic zones. In *Three Essays on the Theory of Sexuality* (1905), the link between erotogenic zones and hysterogenic zones is made explicit (*SE* 7:183).

From the outset, an essential question underlies the apparent banality of a definition. Must the erotogenic body be construed as different from the physiological body? How can the erotogenic body be defined with respect to the physical body? "An [erotogenic zone] is part of the skin or mucous membrane in which stimuli of a certain sort evoke a feeling of pleasure possessing a particular quality [*bestimmte Qualität*]. There can be no doubt that the stimuli which produce the pleasure are governed by special [*besondere*] conditions, though we do not know what those are. A rhythmic character must play a part among them and the analogy of tickling is forced upon our notice. It seems less certain whether the character of the pleasurable feeling evoked by the stimulus should be described as a 'specific' [*besondere*] one—a 'specific' quality [*Besonderheit*] in which the sexual factor would precisely lie" (*SE* 7:183).

This is the earliest passage, to my knowledge, in which Freud questions the adequacy of the vocabulary of physiology to provide a clear description of the bodily order involved in sexuality. What is a sexual stimulus, as he first reconsiders the term? With reference to what the smell of burnt pudding indicates about Miss Lucy's relationship with her mother and her employer, for example, to speak of a sexual stimulus is to speak metonymically at the very least. When some element of Miss Lucy's erotic life is evoked and, however briefly, elaborated, when the prohibition that impedes her respiratory functions is, however briefly, lifted by the return of the unresolved conflict that it had been stitching up, the "stimulus" involved is the report of an event, the reception of a letter, with a signifying constellation: that is, it is not a stimulus at all. Just when the "pulsative" function[12] causes the unconscious to close back up on the smell of burnt pudding, which modulates and confirms some aspect of an orality constitutive of Lucy's desire, a metonymic process intervenes. But this is not a reason why the knowledge that accounts for this symptom work should fall into step with it. To designate this productive moment in Lucy's instinctual life in terms of sexual stimulation is to replace the signifying constellation by a single one of its moments, the one that takes on meaning with respect to a physiology of pleasure—that is, with respect to a discipline that cannot take the signifying constellation into account. This is not only a displacement, it is a displacement that annuls, that renders unthinkable what it ought to subsume. Perhaps this is

12. *FFC*, chap. 5.

where we find an explanation for the impasses of a physiology of pleasure. In the text cited, uncharacteristically, Freud confronts the following question head on: In what can the "specific" quality of the sensation of pleasure consist? In other words, in what order of reality is it to be conceived? Despite his identification of certain special conditions definable in physical terms, Freud declares that the sensation of pleasure cannot be defined in the register of psychophysiology. *The sexual element, in a given experience, cannot be exhibited as a specific relation between a stimulus and a sensation; the sensation itself is not specific, that is, cannot be made to correspond to a physical "montage" as a way of defining its particularity.* Freud is by no means giving up the effort to spell out the nature of pleasure: however, the quality of the stimulus, which is not a physiological specificity, refers rather to the relationship of the signifying constellation of a desire to a surface body.

The second noteworthy point in *Three Essays* lies in the identification of a bodily order distinct from the one suggested by energetistic metaphors for pleasure. "The character of erotogenicity can be attached to some parts of the body in a particularly marked way. There are predestined erotogenic zones, as is shown by the example of sucking. The same example, however, also shows us that any other part of the skin or mucous membrane can take over the functions of an erotogenic zone, and must therefore have some aptitude in that direction. Thus the quality of the stimulus has more to do with producing the pleasurable feeling than has the nature of the part of the body concerned. A child who is indulging in sensual sucking searches about his body and chooses some part of it to suck—a part which is afterwards preferred by him from force of habit; if he happens to hit upon one of the predestined regions (such as the nipples or the genitals) no doubt it retains the preference" (*SE* 7:183).

The only notion of the body involved here is a highly unscientific one. As early as 1893, in "Some Points for a Comparative Study of Organic and Hysterical Motor Paralyses" (*SE* 1:169), Freud declared that hysteria "takes the organs in the ordinary, popular sense of the names they bear" and that as a result it was absurd to define it as simulation. Nearly ten years later, he makes this intuition more explicit in the idea that any part of what is called the organic in a different language or terminology can serve as an erotogenic zone, that is, can be the place of realization connected with a signifying constellation, so long as it is part of the skin or mucous membrane. The decision to translate *Haut* as "skin" and not "epidermis" supports the contention that the scholarly language of physiology is inappropriate—and may even be highly misleading—when what is at stake is knowledge of the pleasure-body.

Even so, the nature of this body continues to pose a problem. What is meant by "skin" or "mucous membrane"? Is Freud referring here to the precise meaning of these terms in physiology, or do the physiological realities supply him instead with a suitable realistic image allowing him to describe the erotogenic body insofar as it may be any place whatever, internal or external, in the body that a different language characterizes as organic, provided it can function as imaginary surface involved in the signifying constellation of a desire?

Lacan takes up this question again in *Four Fundamental Concepts*, without resolving it once and for all, in response to a question by Dr. Mathis: To what, in the body that a different language calls organic, can be applied what Lacan defines as the rimlike structure identifiable in the trajectory of the drive? Dr. Mathis's question suggests an extensive interpretation of the notion of erotogenic zone, since every part of the body can be described as including skin or mucous membrane. "One question concerning the rim-like structure. When it is a question of the mouth and the anal rim, do you locate the eroticization at both extremities? Where do you place what may occur at the level of the oesophagus, at the gastric level, in sniffing, in vomiting, at the level of the trachea? Is there something profoundly different there from what you have articulated at the level of the lips?" (*FFC*, p. 172).

We can begin to glimpse the importance of this discussion. The traditional form of the question—What aspect of the body can have as its function the hysterical symbolization of desire?—has to be redefined as follows: Can every part of the organism function as material for an instinctual construction, materializing the rimlike structure of that apparatus—which, even though it is imaginary, nonetheless produces pleasure? The surface of the body, or the body as surface, comes into play twice. First as the real surface, that is, the surface that the subject can perceive. This surface, whether internal or external, has the minimum of so-called objective reality for the subject that physiology presupposes when it constructs a psycho-physiology of sensation. But this surface reality, even if it is per-ceived by the subject as a bodily reality, stems—this is its second occurrence—from an instinctual montage in which the surface, the real surface of the body in which the jouissance is inscribed, is only raw material for a construction that makes the body the place of the imaginary itself, or the imaginary as place.

To describe the status of the erotogenic body, then, we need concede only one point to the physiology of the organism. Physiol-ogy is built upon an initial acknowledgment of the subject's own perception of her body. This order of perception also comes into play, though in an entirely different way, in the psychoanalytic construction of the body, as the imaginary and real place of jouis-sance. Between the body as it intervenes in the unconscious and the body as it functions as an organism there is no relation, for these two realities appear only in two disciplines that lack any common model. In one sense these disciplines refer to the same object, but in another sense they do not, for they transform the object they start with in two specific ways *that have no common model.*[13] And the object they start with is in itself so confused—in the sense in which Bachelard said that immediate experience is confused—that it is incapable of serving as a fixed point of identity where the two problematics might intersect. This place of inevitable confusion is called a sensation of pleasure in one language, an experience of jouissance in the other, inasmuch as the jouissance is produced on a body. This is the place Freud opens up when he raises questions about the relevance of a physiology of pleasure and when he dem-onstrates the inadequacy of the psychophysiological vocabulary to define erotogenic zones.

Where do we stand, then, with respect to hysteria? We have come very close. For when we think about the status of erotogenic zones, we confront the origin of hysterogenic zones. "A precisely analo-gous tendency to displacement is also found in the symptomatology of hysteria. In that neurosis repression affects most of all the actual

13. That is why all this research leads us to challenge Michel Serres's perspective on theoretical grounds: Serres imagines a cybernetic model of repression endowed, in any event, with ontological significance. See "Le point de vue de la bio-phy-sique," *Critique* 346 (March 1976): 265 ff.

genital zones and these transmit their susceptibility to stimulation to other erotogenic zones (normally neglected in adult life), which then behave exactly like genitals. But besides this, precisely as in the case of sucking, any other part of the body can acquire the same susceptiblity to stimulation as is possessed by the genitals and can become an erotogenic zone. Erotogenic and hysterogenic zones show the same characteristics" (*SE* 7:183–84). On this last point, Freud and Lacan make the same claim: erotogenic zones and hysterogenic zones are bound together, and the former can be understood by way of the latter. "It is precisely to the extent that adjoining connected zones are excluded that others take on their erogenous function and become specific sources for the drive" (*FFC*, p. 157). Thus we cannot deal with the formation of the erotogenic zones without mentioning a choice, a determination of the nature of *displacement* itself, which is at once the stylistic device of dreams and the formative mechanism of hysterical symptoms.

Concerning the order of the body involved, an order that Dr. Mathis's question invited him to define, Lacan responds by referring to the rimlike structure, that is, by invoking a topological notion implying a paradoxical space of the body, which nevertheless rejoins the common image of the body's boundaries playing the role of pleasure surface. Here Lacan stresses a direction that is present in Freud's own text: the idea is to reduce the obscurity of the notion of erotogenic body by viewing that body as a surface that can be cathected by language processes. The bodily surface presupposed by the organization of the erotogenic zones loses some of its mystery thanks to Freud's statement and one aspect of Lacan's reading of that statement: to understand how erotogeneity is inscribed on the body, we need to see how the repression of certain erotogenic zones designates other ones as primordial. Nothing in *this* discussion implies an energetistic interpretation of the notion of libido. Repression is a language process; and the surface-body involved in symbolization—in the accidents that mean certain erotogenic zones are chosen to the exclusion of others—is not an energetic machine: when the child traverses his body as pleasure-surface under precise signifying conditions, that is, conditions involved in the relation to the other, what is produced is an organization achieved by selection of certain erotogenic zones, that is, by an elimination of certain other zones by repression, by a perceptual scotomization of other parts of the body. *The notion of displacement of erotogeneity is not external to the theory of the erotogenic zones, since no erotogenic zones exist without a history of their selection.* That selection in turn represents the visible, positive side of a process of repression of other erotogenic zones; and in hysteria the repression bears upon the genital organs.

Between Freud and Lacan, nevertheless, we note a difference in the description of the erotogenic zones. *Lacan uses the term exclusion for the elimination of certain erotogenic zones that Freud designated by the ambiguous term "displacement of erotogeneity (Libidoverschiebung)."* Their respective readings of hysterical disgust differ as well. For Freud, that sexual sensations may be displaced and that certain organs are scotomized does not imply desexualization, whereas for Lacan, as we have seen, disgust is the sexual object that tilts toward reality. In the last analysis, the term "exclusion" has two different functions. It emphasizes that repression is a language process, and it turns hysterics into unwitting Lacanians: for these patients, in other words, the ultimate signified is the corpse. The ambiguity of Freud's expression of displacement of erotogeneity, which has not completely broken with an overly idealist notion of the body, is removed, but at the price of counting the body as "-1."

Can the interpretation of disgust as desexualization be separated from the idea that displacement of erotogeneity, and therefore repression, puts into play a language process and a body conceived as a pleasure-surface? That is what we shall presuppose in the pages that follow. We shall draw upon three theses that can be expressed as follows: (1) the notion of displacement is not ancillary but is essential to the conceptualization of the erotogenic zones; (2) this process, equivalent to a repression, does not presuppose any energetistic interpretation of the notion of libidinal displacement; (3) the hysterogenic zones are the continuation of the erotogenic zones (and they may use the same means). On the basis of these positions, we shall attempt to return to a clinical theory and to contrast the way Freud used the notion of *Libidoverschiebung* with the way first-generation analysts used it. If there is something left over, if we do not succeed in "reducing" the energetistic metaphors for the erotogenic body, we shall acknowledge this at the appropriate moment, after making a methodical effort to transpose them.

Displacements of Erotogeneity

First Example: Blushing according to Feldmann

In the process of erotogenic zone displacement that constitutes hysteria, nothing is displaced. The importance of defining the notion of *Libidoverschiebung* independently of any substantialist interpretation becomes clear when one reads certain studies in which ambiguities concerning that notion proliferate. Such is the case with the article by S. Feldmann we have already mentioned, for Feldmann's study represents a distancing from a dualist theory of conversion. Feldmann reflects on the way symptomatic blushing relates to exhibitionist scenarios and to his patient's onanist recollections. Thus his reference to the body always involves what we have been calling the pleasure-body, which is not to be confused with a physiological body. We never depart from what he calls scenarios of pleasure, whether we are dealing with narrated memories or with their actualization in the symptom of blushing.[14] Where the meaning of the erotogenic zone displacement is concerned, however, things become confused.

The displacement turns out to be defined in two ways whose relationship remains unclear. *How are we to understand the genitalization of Feldmann's patient's nose?* In two heterogenous ways, it seems. To be sure, a symbolic equivalence is involved, a displacement of the representations that substitute the patient's nose for his penis in his dreams, memories, and scenarios of pleasure. In childhood, as certain dreams indicate, his face played the role of a genital organ displaced upward. When the patient heard about storks for the first time, he believed that the stork's long nose gave it a very specific role. That belief took on concrete form in a dream the patient had when he was six years old. A giant bee equipped with a huge stinger was approaching him; the boy wanted to escape but could not. The bee caught him and stung him on the forehead. He thought that the stinger was stinging his mother on the forehead and that children came into the world this way. The patient insisted that at that age there was no way he could have known about Pallas Athena ("Über das Erröten," p. 22).

Let us recall briefly here that other dream in which he saw an

14. "Über das Erröten," *Internationale Zeitschrift für Psychoanalyse*, 1922, no. 1, pp. 14–34.

elephant whose trunk was long enough to touch his penis, and also the words of an uncle who had told him he would be a perfect child if only his nose were shorter. In this substitution of a representation of the nose for a representation of the penis, the prevalence of symbolic images, in the sense of visual analogy, is striking and seems to sum up what is covered by the term displacement.

Now the richness of the analogy is also found in the other language, which connects the physiological conditions of blushing to the physiological conditions of penile erection. "The symptoms chosen, the *form* in which blushing appeared as redness, warmth, tumescence, erection, shows that in the situation of blushing the face was genitalized through displacement from below, with the aid of the connection between the nose and the genitals. Blushing corresponds to an erection, which it replaces and represents [*vertreten*]" (p. 21).

The ambiguity of this passage depends on two things that are surely interrelated. A kind of rediscovered autonomy of the physiological seems to be present: this is because, physiologically, erections and blushing present certain common features that the unconscious, with a sort of mysterious physiological intuition, might substitute for each other, and this substitution would constitute the repression. A little further on Feldmann adds: "Blushing replaces a *repressed genital excitation* that is displaced in the *form* of blushing toward the upper regions and causes genital excitement to appear on the face in an *adequate* form" (p. 22).

We discussed the word "form" in chapter 1. Here it no longer designates the signifying constellation in which the symptom is produced, like the statement heard or dreamed by the patient telling him his nose was shiny; instead it designates an analogy or even a presumed identity with a physiological process that affects one of the organs in question. *The visual resemblance would then be like the common ground for the symbolic equivalence of nose and penis, and for the displacement of a physiological process belonging to one part of the body onto another.* But that does not explain how representations can pass into the physiological causal sequence instead of remaining representations. *The accumulation of imaginary data, the constant recourse to resemblance, is precisely what takes the place of explanation. But the explanation is imaginary* in that it does not resolve the heterogeneity of the two sequences: replacement of one representation by another in the dreams, replacement of one physiological process by another that would be identical with it.

Here the psychoanalyst, in his attempt at explanation, reduplicates the patient's imaginary by visualizing his body as a place where the phantasmic and the physiological can cancel out their difference, their heterogeneity. The resemblance and dreamed-of connection between nose and penis seem to come close, understandably, to the displacement onto the body of an influx of blood, because such an influx, being purely physiological, can also be seen—that is, can be known through the imagination by virtue of the features mentioned: blushing, heat, erection. In this view the unconscious is both an imagination based on symbols and an organic mechanism that knows and orders physiological transfers and transformations. Nothing indicates, however, that the physiological features identified are indeed the material of fantasies.

It is only by this reduction of the phantasmic to images and of the physiological to its perceived form that one can judge that the phenomenon has been explained and dream that a metonymic and metaphoric substitution of representations coincides with a transfer of something onto the body. At the same time,[15] this dreamed-of homogeneity would presuppose that knowledge of the phenomenon implies returning to the visual homogeneity it is made of, in other words implies reflecting the phenomenon. This is the particular illusion of idealism.

The notion of a transfer of something onto the body finds yet another expression: the illusory reduction of everything to the imaginary presupposes that something is displaced from one erotogenic zone to another. This "something" can be presumed to exist because it has a name: libido. For Feldmann there is no doubt that the nose is genitalized, that a sexual stimulus, an element of the libido, passes from the sex organ to the nose. We have seen with what reservations Freud spoke of sexual stimuli in *Three Essays,* doubting the possibility of constituting a physiology of sexuality, of pleasure. These reservations do not apply here: what Feldmann is looking for is a pleasure-substance that would be displaced both in

15. At this stage of our discussion, we are thus taking as our guide the critique of the conceptions of metaphor that would depend upon resemblance and are extending this critique to the discourse on knowledge. Cf. Octave Mannoni, "L'ellipse et la barre," in *Clefs pour l'imaginaire, ou L'autre scène* (Paris: Seuil, 1969), pp. 37–38.

the representations and in the organism. To make this perspective irrefutable, he invokes an evolutionary theory of the libido. In the end he views blushing, inflammation, and tumescence as regressive components in the phylogenetic and ontogenetic sense. If the patient puts his nose in the place of his penis in his dreams, it is because both organs can turn red; blushing corresponds to the return to a libidinal function that had been abandoned in the evolution of the species but that can always be reactivated.

The libido, here, is a general property of the species; it can regress in the symptoms of blushing, in the displacement of erotogenic zones onto an outmoded functioning of the epidermis. Libido is therefore something. It is the magical substance in which fantasy rejoins the organic and the individual rejoins the species, the night in which all cows are black.

One final remark. If in erotogenic zone displacements something is displaced, the repression of the libido that passes from the genital area to a regressive stimulus of the skin is also a biological process. This presupposes a model of development of the erotogenic zones that the subject would necessarily traverse and that, in displacements of erotogeneity, the subject might retraverse in the opposite direction. The repression of the penis in favor of the nose presupposes that, through a privilege arising from the achievements of evolution, the subject has an initial, natural access to genital libido and that he returns later to an older mode of functioning, shifting erotogenic zones by virtue of the identical physiological properties of these zones. The repression is imagined here more than it is defined, notwithstanding all the symbolic material contributed by Feldmann.

Here then the path opened up by Freud—the understanding of hysteria as the history of the repression of certain erotogenic zones—gives way to a substantialist and evolutionist theory of libido. What is important—and it can keep us from losing our bearings—is to identify the systematicity of this change of direction. Notwithstanding his perceptive auditory attention to what connects the hysterogenic zones with the erotogenic zones, Feldmann's argument breaks down when he privileges images in his search for a common ground between the fantasy and the organism; he goes on to act accordingly, by substantializing libido and biologizing repression. The problematic of the hysterical body as history of the repression of certain zones of the erotogenic body is thereby lost, as is some critical information about the history of the patient's jouissance. The patient does experience jouissance before his nose replaces his penis, as it were, but the experience indicates the possibility of such a replacement: he recalls that he had an orgasm one day when his mother was indisposed. The strength of the olfactory sensation, analogous to the burnt pudding smell in Miss Lucy's case, certainly connected his penis and his sense of smell—the olfactory sense more than the nose—but without there being any question of physiological coordinates that would establish a comparable link between these two erotogenic zones for an alert observer to see. How could this access to a genital jouissance, which the patient had somewhat audaciously attested by his behavior,[16] have been transformed into a symptomatic blushing? This is the order of question we must now confront.

When Dora meets Herr K. and feels his erect member pressing against her, why does she dismiss this perception from her memory? Why does she feel disgust, which represents an inversion of affect and a displacement of a genital sensation onto an oral one? Why does she keep as a memory of this intolerable jouissance a hallucination of pressure on the thorax that Freud designates as a secondary displacement of the erotogenic genital zone? How do these displacements differ from the phobic symptom that is established at the same time and manifested in the care Dora takes to avoid lovers who are conversing tenderly in the streets? We have to try to answer these questions by specifying what order of the body and what repression come into play here, instead of dissolving their specificity.

Second (Counter) Example: Dora

Up to this point, Dora's case has taught us just one thing: the consideration of erotogenic zone displacement has gained an advantage over conversion theory and over the importance of somatic compliance. Precisely what does the expression "displacement of erotogeneity" designate here? When Freud redefines hysteria by foregrounding the unpleasurable feeling that Dora had experienced

16. According to the expression that Lacan applies to the Wolf Man in "Réponse au commentaire de Jean Hyppolite sur la *Verneinung* de Freud," in *Ecrits*, p. 386.

on the occasion of her first seduction by Herr K. (*SE* 7:29), he speaks of a *displacement of sensation* (*Verschiebung der Empfindung*): in place of the genital sensation that "would certainly have been felt" in a normal young girl, an unpleasurable sensation was localized or experienced as localized in the oral zone. As we know, the terrain on which the notion of displacement is defined is that of dreams. In *The Interpretation of Dreams* the stylistic device of displacement is characterized rather briefly: if the thoughts that form a dream are compared with its content, we observe that the dream is differently centered, that its elements are organized around a center that is not the same as that of the dream thoughts. Since dreams use this device endlessly, it is not hard to find traces of it in Dora's dreams: thus in the fire dream the manifest content is organized around the theme of the fire from which Dora is saved by her father, whereas the thoughts that form the dream, those whose repression it lifts, have to do with enuresis and masturbation, which are just hinted at by the father's words, "my two children." The conjugation of the opposition between fire and water with the allusion to Dora's brother brings about the recentering of the dream on what was presented as a secondary detail. Through this reference to *The Interpretation of Dreams* we are not proposing to deal with the questions raised by the notion of displacement in themselves; we simply mean to recall that this notion applies to representations, so as to be able to compare displacement in general with the displacement of erotogenic zones or, more accurately, if we follow Dora's case, with the displacement of sensations.

In fact, to the idea that displacement in dreams involves elements of representations, it is appropriate to add that the structural over-determination of certain elements, which opens the way to the recentering of the dream thoughts on a different focus, may also be expression in energetistic or apparently energetistic terms: in the formation of the dream, the stressed elements of *intense* interest may be treated as if they were of little importance. The psychic intensity invoked here concerns the way the subject experiences his dream. A note specifies that it is a matter of sensory intensity (*sinnliche Intensität*, *SE* 4:306n.1) and that this consideration is borne entirely by the first, structural determination of displacement: the term intensity is introduced when Freud speaks of the imaginary—that is, sensory—impact of the representations for the dreamer. In this sense the consideration of displacements of intensity of the representations of the latent content onto the manifest content does not have complete autonomy with respect to the displacement of representations or signifiers. The so-called point of view of the affect and that of the representations are not in competition; to consider how the subject feels about his dream is to say how the subject experiences that organization of representations that has unfolded its structure through free association.

How then does the notion of displacement of sensation from the genital to the oral zone differ from the general meaning of displacement in dreams? Essentially it is through the localization of certain parts of the body that it presupposes. But then how is this local determination related to the signifying constellations in which it is produced? What are the conditions, determined but not yet spelled out in *Three Essays*, that make possible the sexual stimulus whose specificity does not stem essentially from the physiological viewpoint?

These conditions are clarified with the interconnections set up between Dora's symptoms, her experience of seduction, and the aspects of what she experiences in her body that are signified or presented (Darstellung) in her dreams. Let us recall Dora's symptoms, which are minor ones: nervous asthma, a cough, loss of voice, disenchantment with life. What Freud calls displacement of sensation or displacement of erotogeneity designates in fact the way the history of her desire is experienced through the body, in an imaginary geography whose meaning is explained by dreams. Dora's first dream, which we shall look at shortly, is really the promise made to what she experiences on her body, and to what has been incapable of elaboration in her encounters with Herr K. In the treatment narrative, the return of the repressed, the scotomization of Herr K.'s organ pressing against her, Dora's disgust, and the hallucinated pressure on her thorax remain unexplained at first. The true turning point in her treatment comes about when a lapsus on Dora's part refers her back precisely to her oral representation of the sexual relation, which had remained suspended in her loss of voice and in her latent disgust with food and sexuality. To talk about her "well-endowed" father, she uses the opposite term, one that, in German, also means "impotent": *unvermögend*. This term offers a true condensation of her symptoms and her dreams, of the way she

89

experiences in her body the impossible recognition of the difference between the sexes. When Freud points out to her that she cannot have it both ways, she cannot both accuse her father of having secret relations with Frau K. and tax him with impotence, Dora replies that a sexual relation can come about without the intermediary of the genital organs. Her persistence in reproaching her father suggests that there is indeed something she cannot "swallow," something that remains stuck in her throat, something she evokes in a repetitive and always relatively unconvincing way in her cough, her supposed nervous asthma, or her loss of voice. At the same time, her father's impotence becomes clearer in the series of dream associations showing that for Dora, enuresis and masturbation ended in disaster: "What is Papa doing to Mama? Anyway, he was out of breath, he doesn't make it, he's ill—sex is illness—I am ill" (cf. *SE* 7:82 ff.). The word *unvermögend* is thus a term of intersection, referring to two major significations of the symptom, oral and urethral—the very symptoms that the dream displays.

The fire in the dream also refers to Dora's oral cavity and her urethra. When she wakes up from the dream of fire, she smells smoke and associates this with Freud's statement that there is no smoke without fire. The importance of this orality that is constitutive of Dora's desire is borne out by the fact that she at first forgot the waking episode and reported it to Freud only later on. The smell of smoke reminds her, too, of Herr K.'s kiss and her own thumb-sucking past, which bound her to her father, since he was the one who had taken it upon himself to break her of the habit.

In one sense, what Dora's principal symptom betrays is an oral pleasure that dates back to her earliest childhood, to the time when a privileged relation of interdiction, but also of pleasure excluding any third party, bound her to her father. Now it is also by way of her mouth that she tries to present (*darstellen*)[17] her father's sexual relationship with Frau K., but she does not actually succeed in this: it can't be swallowed, it veers off into the symptoms of voicelessness. Dora experiences everything by way of her mouth. The unrepresentable encounter with Herr K., too, is transformed into something involving her mouth; precisely for that reason it turns out badly, ends in disgust.

Dora's mouth and throat are thus the theater where she tries to

17. And not *Vorstellen*, "represent," as French translations suggest.

articulate the way things are between the sexes. Yet precisely because everything goes by way of her mouth, this articulation seems to be impossible; if everything passes through the mouth, it seems to be because her thumb-sucking past, which linked her to her father and also to her brother in the screen memory mentioned earlier,[18] is for her an unsurpassable jouissance that catches or snags everything new, or different, that might come up in the order of jouissance. The fact that while exploiting every irritation of her throat or vocal cords she cultivates this irreplaceable pleasure is less astonishing when we understand, through the dream analysis, the meaning of the smell of smoke that Dora had at first forgotten as she recounted her dream.

Present in the symptom and in the dream, the oral pleasure that ties Dora to her father in a one-to-one relationship that is playful rather than prohibitory also sets the fundamental tone for her encounter with Herr K. The aspect of jouissance associated with the recognition of the other sex that might come to light here is immediately rejected in the name of an oral pleasure that is thus the place and the element in which nostalgia for the kiss is masked by disgust at the unacceptable penis. Discussing the oral component of Dora's disgust (not the only component involved here) and what remains of it—Dora's intermittent distaste for food and her feeling of suffocation—Freud speaks even here of repression of orality. Dora's nonencounter with Herr K. thus marks a reinforcement of the erotogenic zone that serves to imagine everything but that does not succeed in representing sexual difference. Dora manages to bury this difference under a jouissance that, seeking to bring everything back to itself, ends in an impasse.

We began with the fire represented in the first dream. That fire refers not only to the oral pleasure perpetuated and rejected in the symptom, but also to the experience of jouissance that the dream elaborates. Enuresis, the urethral and anal erotogenic zone—this too is a privileged terrain on which any possibility of symbolizing sexual difference runs aground. Fire, through its coupling with water, brings up first of all, for Freud, a memory of enuresis whose traces are dislocated in the dream narrative. This dislocation is in fact equivalent to omnipresence, since broadly speaking, without at

---

18. On the other dimension of this archaic orality, which Freud did not mention, see below, p. 131.

first knowing why, Dora is thinking about a quarrel between her parents over whether her brother would need to get up in the night. Their father's words of concern for his two children bring Dora's brother to mind, and Dora recalls her brother's bed-wetting before she remembers her own. One other element of the manifest content is also pertinent here. Dora's father, standing up, wakes her in the dream as he used to wake her up to prevent her from wetting the bed. This memory thus reproduces in the order of urethral eroticism Dora's relation of jouissance with her father, a dual relation that will block every attempt to elaborate a jouissance that would take sexual difference into account. This is what the element of the jewel case indicates in the manifest dream. Freud sees this element as the one that operates the most condensations and displacements in the dream. Lacan also sees it as the sharpest articulation of what Dora was able to symbolize of her desire:[19] Dora is quite willing to accept Herr K.'s hommage, the gift of a jewel case, but as for Herr K.'s own jewel, his sex organ, she refuses it, as she has suppressed the perception of it in Herr K.'s embrace, for she herself is the jewel. In her enuresis she needed no one, as it were, in order to experience jouissance. To be sure, her father was present, but her jouissance was not suppressed when she was awakened by her father in the middle of the night. The weaning role her father played here is more playful than prohibitory;[20] or rather, if it is threatening, it is in the sense in which Dora is seeking to take the place, in her dreamed omnipotence (an omnipotence realized, *dargestellt*, through masturbation), of an idealized father. The jewel case is inscribed in a synecdochic relation to Dora's genitals. The image of the vagina it calls up is conflated, through its associations, with the history of her masturbatory urethral jouissance, which prevented the success of an attempt at symbolizing a sexual relation between her parents: the jewel, in fact, brings her back to a gift her mother wished for, pearls in the form of drops she wanted to get from her husband. But here things start to get dirty, disgusting; what is played out in Dora's repression of her masturbatory experiences is the impossibility of signifying her own place with respect to her parents' jouissance.

19. Unpublished seminar, "L'envers de la psychanalyse," February 17, 1970.
20. It seems as though this game in which Dora takes herself to be a boy in an erotic relation to a man is recovering, remarking the terrain of a primal oral catastrophe in her relation to her mother.

Would Dora have wanted the jewel in the form of drops that her mother did not want to accept from her father? All the dream associations indicate to the contrary that she did not want that, for sexual difference is not only something that cannot be swallowed, something that remains stuck in her throat, it is also something that can never have become autonomous, has never distinguished itself from a venereal disease. Dora began to dream, during the treatment, just as she was wondering why she had fallen ill; in her dream she accused her father of causing an illness identified with sexuality, an ailment that he must have transmitted to his wife. Here, too, as at the moment of the lapsus concerning impotence, which took us back to orality, we have a word that opens up signifying pathways as it traces the geography of Dora's erotogenic body. Dora says that, like her mother, she is suffering from catarrh, a heavy head cold. She uses the same term to designate her father's sexual malady and his lung problems. What is called displacement of the erotogenic zones, from the lower to the upper realm, is thus produced on the basis of an effect of signification that itself depends upon the reduction of sexuality to something dirty and sick.

Once again the three levels we have distinguished—the symptom, the dream, and the return of the repressed—are in strict correspondence. The word "catarrh" refers first of all to the anal and urethral component of Dora's disgust. It was her distaste for life that convinced her father to bring her to Freud for treatment. This disgust had been clearly manifested in the seduction by Herr K., and in his discussion of that scene Freud is careful to point out at once that Dora did not distinguish clearly between genital sexuality and anality. Dredging up the old adage of the church fathers for the occasion, *inter urinas et faeces nascimur,* he pinpointed in this important episode of the history of the symptom the unbroken synecdochic connection that, for Dora, conflates sexual difference with uncleanliness. In the first dream, finally, what is thus played out signifies itself, since the jewels represented in the manifest content refer to the pearls in the form of drops whose significance as a gift from Dora's father to her mother is destroyed in the dirtiness of the illness that her father, owing to a sexual life defined a priori by that very token as dissolute, had passed on to her mother and herself. This explains the importance Dora attaches to the milky discharge from which she suffers and which seems to concretize for her the dirtiness of sex, as well as her own masturbatory responsibility in this shift from jouissance to curse. We shall soon discover that the origin of Dora's illness has to be sought in the process through which her masturbatory jouissance was repressed; put to the test of a transformation, it did not hold up when Dora had to represent to herself, with her own sex, some aspect of her parents' jouissance from which she found herself excluded. It was at this point, rather than for natural reasons, that the milky discharges associated with masturbation turned into filth, that the masturbatory jouissance was at once spoiled (like the thumb-sucking) and fixated as a symptom.

To the very extent that Dora's dreams, far from implying a lack of interest in the symptoms, allow them expression, it is appropriate, finally, to emphasize the extent to which their organization corresponds to that imaginary geography of Dora's body whose oral and anal-urethral functions enter into metonymic connection. Since the signifier *catarrh* associates her cough with the milky discharges and associates the element of sexual difference that remains stuck in her throat with filth—or worse, with a fateful and devastating illness—that is indeed what she experiences in the order of the imaginary, even though it is realized on her body and culminates in disgust. Disgust provides Dora's sensuality with an immediate passage from sex-as-filth to the oral jouissance that is also spoiled, turned rotten, by the approach of sexual difference. The first mechanism of symptom formation, the inversion of affect (*Affektverkehrung*), is thus not independent of erotogenic zone displacements: it is what puts them into play and indicates the order of reality from which they arise. Given the complexity of the history that left Dora disgusted with sex, it is understandable that the definition of this disgust can stem only from a physiology in which nervous reactions correspond to stimuli. We can grasp to what extent the expression "sexual stimulus" is metonymic when it purports to designate the order of jouissance, the unfolding displays of jouissance, although perhaps "metonymic," is not quite the right term, since it presupposes a homogeneity between two terms in syntagmatic relation, one of which represents the other. In our case, when the physiological aspect of jouissance is charged with representing its signifying aspect, these two terms are not homogeneous, since the construction of a physiology of the sexual stimulus is achieved at the expense of the determination of the specific conditions in which it is produced.

This study of the relation between dream and symptom suggests certain conclusions. When we speak of genitalization of an organ or of part of the hysteric's body, we have to be quite clear. Genitality is not a property, specific in nature or function, of a sexual substance that at certain points in human development would pass from one part of the body to another. For Dora the approach to genitality is the attempt to discover something about sexual difference, to inscribe something of it onto her own body, which is inhabited by an intense oral and urethral jouissance. In his article on blushing,[21] Feldmann spoke of a genitalization of the nose in the sense that the *proof* of penile repression was not only the nose-penis equivalence signified in the dream, but also the desertion by the sexual stimulus of a zone it ought to have cathected, the penis, in favor of another, the nose and face.

From this perspective there is no such thing, properly speaking, as a history of the erotogenic body. Jouissance has a path already laid out by the visible reality of the body: the genital organs are made to symbolize the problematic of sexual difference and to concretize a specific corresponding mode of excitation. Feldmann based his discussion on the analogy between the signs of the two physiological processes—heat, redness, tumescence, and erection of the penis and of the face in blushing, that is, natural qualities of certain parts of the body—in order to define the displacement of a stimulus. That is conceivable only if we recognize that everyone possesses a natural organization of the erotogenic zones suitable for representing, in turn, at various stages already prepared, different forms of relation to the other. *To say that there is genitalization of the erotogenic zone in Dora's case would be to presuppose that Dora ought to have had a normal genital sensitivity, since she had a vagina,* and that the processes of libidinal stimulation that unfold there have been secondarily transferred elsewhere for symbolic reasons. It is obvious that such a conception rests entirely on the idea of a libidinal stimulus that not only is specific in itself but also is differentiated by functional levels. Freud defined the erotogenic zones precisely in

21. See above, pp. 59–63, 83–87.

opposition to such an idea, while pointing out that their organization through repression and displacement was essential to the history of a pleasure-body.

If we follow Feldmann, indeed, displacement is a secondary derivation, a change of place of a sexual stimulus that had its natural place elsewhere.

The reading of Dora's body that we have undertaken seeks to show, on the contrary, that if a history is at stake it is because not everything is decided in advance. Dora uses oral and urethral jouissance to approach sexual difference, to attempt to inscribe something of this difference on her own body. There is no such thing, then, properly speaking, as genitalization, but there is failure on the part of oral and urethral jouissance—which binds Dora to her father, agent of weaning—to represent some aspect of a relation between her parents, because that relation could not be expressed without the representation of her own symbolic loss, without Dora's own exclusion being signified in it somewhere. Perhaps the representation of this loss necessarily falls within the order of oral jouissance: we may recall how Freud reconstructs the substitution of a cough for masturbation, at the point where the latter is being repressed. Dora tried to represent the sexual relation between her parents in the detail of heavy breathing, panting: she must have *heard* this relation, he tells us, and must have felt a stimulation that made her participate in it (*Miterregung*). The paradox in Dora's story is confirmed here: when she approaches a jouissance from which she herself is excluded, it is in the mode of fusion. What survives, then, in the symptom of the cough—which brings to mind, for example, her father's relations with Frau K.—is that attempt, always aborted but always available to be taken up again, as her dreams testify, to reinscribe differently something of sexual differentiation. What Dora's body expresses when it signifies itself in dreams is that failure experienced in her body, that abortive attempt at symbolization of a loss, that is fixated as a symptom. To speak of the *history* of the erotogenic body is thus to recognize that what is at stake is a symbolization suspended in the signs presented by the hysteric.

"Genitalization" designates nothing but the challenge that Dora never stops confronting, as we see from her constant and unexplained preoccupation with her father's relations with Frau K.; she approaches endlessly, in the element of oral jouissance, an experience of sexual difference that could be reported only if something of that oral jouissance were to be represented as lost. Instead, the approach of sexual differentiation "spoils" the oral jouissance itself, transforms it into disgust and a cough. It does not leave the jouissance intact, but it does not really redefine for Dora, either, the status of her body with regard to jouissance. It is clear that the term genitalization does not account very well for this whole process that is blocked in the symptom but that, at some point, is reopened in the treatment. There is no natural history of the pleasure-body, or else there would be no question of history. Erotogenic zone displacements presuppose no physiologically specified libidinal stimulus, nor any libidinal substance.

It is important, too, never to confuse erotogenic zone displacements with a causal connection between two phenomena in the organic body. Georg Groddeck, in an article published in 1926, thought he was defining erotogenic zone displacements by invoking a functional solidarity between two organic problems that would stem from the same mechanism as the displacement of representations in dreams: "As an example of displacement [I shall cite] the characteristic afflictions of the retina accompanying kidney inflammations or the articulatory inflammations of the knees associated with *blennorragie*."[22] If the *Verschiebung* is thus assimilated from the outset to a physiological causality, or even if one presupposes, however briefly, the possible identity of these two types of relationships, one can no longer divide up the field of hysteria between body-as-surface and language, the latter being the field where what is at stake for the body itself, which in the symptom functions as a sign, is access to jouissance at the price of a loss.

Displacement of Erotogeneity and Repression

Finally, if nothing is displaced in the erotogenic zone displacements that are constitutive of hysteria, it is because nothing is

---

22. "Traumarbeit und Arbeit des organischen Symptoms," *Internationale Zeitschrift für Psychoanalyse*, 1926, pp. 504–12. ("Travail du rêve et travail du symptôme organique," in *La maladie, l'art et le symbole*, trans. R. Lewinter [Paris: Gallimard, 1969]).

repressed, in the sense implied by the hydraulic metaphor. The pleasure-body, blocked in the symptom, meets an impasse in its effort to represent sexual difference in its own order, for that would mean representing a loss of jouissance. This concept of displacement, which we are attempting to clarify, implies that the status of repression is also determined in the "genitalization of the erotogenic zones." There is repression, a process of language, to be sure, but what process is in question here, exactly?

In erotogenic zone displacements, nothing is displaced; no substantive libido that alone would allow a sexual moment to be defined through the evidence of some physiological specificity. *Or rather, nothing is displaced, for the libido has no natural organization or way of acting on the body* with respect to which the approach to the problematic of sexual difference Dora experienced could be said to be secondarily displaced. In short, there is no zero degree of displacement; that would presuppose an evolution of jouissance marking itself on the body in the course of the body's development, whereas Dora's example brings a history to light.

Repression in the Cancellation of the Erotogenic Zones

As for the modalities of repression in displacements of erotogeneity, several points need to be clarified. Is the hysterical symptom the effect of a repression or of a foreclosure? Since there remains in the signifying chain an allusion to the scotomization of what Freud calls clitoral jouissance and of the perception of Herr K.'s sexuality, we find ourselves confronting a typical case of *Verdrängung*, for the repression involved cannot be distinguished from "the return of the repressed through the place where the subject screams out through all the pores of his being what he cannot speak about."[23]

This removal of a perception from the circuit of memory, to the extent that it constitutes a displacement, thus seems to stem from repression. But a remark in Freud's text (badly translated in the French edition) goes further: the sensation of replacement, the pressure on her thorax, derives "its excessive intensity from its repressed source" (*SE*7:30). Freud's French translators rendered the word *Quelle* (meaning source of the drive or instinct, that is, erot-

23. Lacan, "Réponse au commentaire de Jean Hyppolite," p. 386.

ogenic zone) by the word *pulsion*, referring to a "sensation that owed its exaggerated intensity to the repression of the drive." The error is instructive: influenced by the presence of the term "intensity," which naturally but wrongly inclined them toward an energetistic reading, the authors replace the relation Freud set up between a bodily surface and a symbolization—in the name of a jouissance that can give it reality in the subject's perceptions—with the idea that some force is repelled or flows back. This error confirms, to the contrary, our contention that to build a theory of hysteria we have to restrict ourselves rigorously to the idea of the body as the perceptual surface of jouissance, incapable of conceptualization on its own, without the processes of symbolization of desire being taken into account. We have all the more reason, then, not to dissolve this very specific terrain through energetistic images.

Such images are solicited here by the term *Intensität*. It is as if the presence of the word "intensity" in Freud's text provided an automatic authorization to summon up an energetics of drives. The specific text under consideration ought to dissuade us from making this mistake. What happens, then, in Dora's case? What is the real meaning of the excessive intensity of the sensations that affect part of her body? *Cannot the intensity of disgust or of the suffocating sensation be conceptualized as the feeling of uncanniness* that arises in the reality of our body or the world without having been symbolized? *The notion of intensity refers to violence; but this violence is the violence of the hallucinatory itself.* Freud specifies that the pressure on Dora's thorax was a sensory hallucination that she experienced from time to time. The perception of Herr K.'s sexuality and of her own *shocked* Dora; she could not stand it. The violence of that experience, far from calling for an energetistic representation of the body, more closely resembles the disruptive nature of the Wolf Man's experience: after his seduction by his sister, the Wolf Man's libido "shattered to bits."

Another indication that this reading is relevant, and that the body involved in the formation of the hysterical symptom on this body surface inhabited by language is limited, is provided by the other, phobic symptom established at the same moment. By avoiding lovers who were engaged in intimate conversation and who might therefore manifest the somatic sign of male sexual arousal, Dora

cast over the world around her a symbolic net that made her scoto-
mize certain of its circumstances or that impelled her to remove
herself from certain situations.

The hallucinatory pressure on her thorax involves the symbolic
saturation of the only part of her body she is willing, or able, to
recognize and whose signification, in the history of her oral jouissance, is now spoiled, since it has been transformed into disgust.
Sensoriality in hysteria can play such a role because it is the register
in which thought, through symbolization of jouissance, allows or
forbids the subject access to her body and to the world. Such is
Freud's thesis, moreover, when he recalls, in the text on negation,
that it is from the sensory extremities of the psychic apparatus,
from sensory perceptions, that the ego first learns to explore the
world, to undertake or refuse to work on primordial representations that are still neutral with respect to any judgment of reality,
the only work on which such a judgment can be based.

Hysterical Disgust as Projection

Yet if we accept such an interpretation for the notion of intensity
of the displaced sensation, we must then specify how the scotomization first designated simply by the term repression differs from
foreclosure. How does the uncanny that is exorcised by the hysterical symptom differ from the Wolf Man's libidinal shattering? It
differs essentially through the projective character of the violence
that protects Dora from sexual difference by throwing over the
world a defensive net woven of all her hatred. This global rejection
accounts for the sharpness of her views on the history of the sexual
ailments affecting her parents. And the relation of her disgust to her
defensive construction of a world system has all the appearances of a
seed of paranoia, such as is regularly found at the root of hysterical
conversion, signaling the proximity between hysterical traumas
and traumas that feed delusions of homosexual jealousy. For the
acuity of knowledge that Dora develops about others is fragile:
according to Felix Deutsch, who saw her again in New York in
1922, she spent her life accusing her husband of infidelities. Hatred,
in hysteria, blocks the threat of being ravished by another woman;
the other woman fascinates through the power to swallow up the

patient's entire existence, a power attributed to her,[24] when she "steals" from the patient the heterosexual object of her desire.[25]

Some aspect of Dora's body, then, lacks existence for her, for want of symbolization in the history of her jouissance. This scotomization arises from Dora's partial absence to herself and from a negative hallucination involving certain objects that are not integrated into the work of her desire.

In this sense we need to specify that the somatic compliance through which hysteria is defined depends upon the hysteric's absence to her own body. The hysteric has no body: Breuer's earliest research was directed along these very lines. Among Anna O.'s symptoms were her absences. These may be described equally well as a way of ceasing to answer to her own identity or as a way of ceasing to recognize people, in particular the doctors in attendance. The symbolic mainspring of these negative hallucinations was particularly clear in her case, since the presence of her visitors was abolished for Anna solely by the loss of meaning of the words they spoke. Anna no longer spoke nor understood the language of her own people.

When Dora's earliest symptoms set in, first of all her cough at the age of eight, such a process of nonsymbolization has to be recognized. This alone accounts for the subsequent appearance of positive phenomena such as the sensory hallucination of pressure on her thorax or the hallucinatory smell of smoke that, cut off from the symbolic chain, returns in reality at the limit of her body and the world. Freud questions the modalities of this nonsymbolization again and again: he enumerates the favorable circumstances, emphasizing that what is at stake is something quite different from the influence of external events. How is it that Dora's experience of masturbatory jouissance was repressed?

Dora's cough, which replaced that experience, appeared at the time of one of her father's first trips away from home, while he himself was recovering from illness. According to Freud's recon-

24. Sigmund Freud, Letter to Wilhelm Fliess, December 9, 1899 (no. 125), *SE* 1:280. See also "Some Neurotic Mechanisms in Jealousy, Paranoia and Homosexuality," *SE* 18:223.
25. On the absence produced by such a ravishing, see Marguerite Duras, *The Ravishing of Lol Stein*, trans. Richard Seaver (New York: Grove Press, 1967).

struction, what blocked masturbation was Dora's intolerable over-hearing (*Belauschen*) of an act of sexual intercourse between her parents. What was Dora listening with? With her throat, with her breathing, as much as with her ears. Dora, whose orality turned out to be invested with a jouissance involving her father, found herself confronting the impossible task of transforming that same jouis-sance, without loss, into a three-way jouissance. Dora's overhear-ing her father's labored breathing during intercourse was a sort of desperate attempt to participate, with the means available to her own jouissance, in her parents' sexual relationship, which excluded her: Freud speaks of *Miterregung*, of arousal concomitant with her overhearing of her parents' heavy breathing. That was what caused Dora's jouissance to be transformed into a nervous asthma; al-though her need to do so was unquestionable, it was impossible for her to symbolize her own loss of jouissance implied by the recogni-tion of her parents' sexual relation. This attempt at participation in an experience from which she is necessarily excluded represents, as it were, the fixation point that comes back over and over in symp-toms: her cough, her loss of voice, her asthma. All the "objective" proofs she used as pretexts, first of all her father's illness (shortness of breath), are only the signifiers of the refusal that constituted her. Shortly after this unfortunate attempt to grasp by way of her own masturbatory jouissance something of a sexual difference that called herself into question in an access of anxiety, the little girl must have had nostalgic thoughts of her absent father; and the impossible return of the earlier masturbatory satisfaction involving him, along with the anguished passion of rediscovering this overhearing of an unheard-of relation, must have transformed her jouissance into asthma.

The thoughts that accompanied the reversal of the child's sex-uality involve everything she could come up with in the environ-ment and the circumstances of the time, to support her denial of a loss of jouissance. The respiratory difficulty she experienced pro-vided an occasion for thinking again about her father, whose role vis-à-vis her mother she criticized by saying that he was always short of breath, whether he was hiking in the mountains or with her mother, and what is more he must have worn himself out that night. Dora drew upon everything at hand to transfer onto an order of things independent of her own suffering what she was experiencing as intolerable.

Her subsequent history is nourished with everything that might accredit the idea that men are always found wanting, that they all lead dissolute lives. Moreover, her father had not only a lung problem, but a mysterious sexual malady that had contaminated everybody, herself included, since her former jouissance had been spoiled. The origin of Dora's disgust with life, of the scotomization of the other sex that she experienced with Herr K., of the hallucinatory return of her feelings of being crushed, can be found in the impassioned edification of this world system that could set aside any representation of its own exclusion of a jouissance that threatened it. What is lived in an imaginary fashion as disgust is precisely that defensive symbolic net thrown over the world to safeguard a realm of satisfaction that had, however, become unlivable, *lost*. In the text on negation, Freud writes: "It is evident that a precondition for the setting up of reality-testing is that objects shall have been lost which once brought real satisfaction" (*SE* 19:238). Here is the origin of Dora's problem: the representation of such a loss of her earlier positions was intolerable to her, so she constructed a sort of delusion involving sex and illness to protect herself. Freud does not fail to note, in her disgust with men, the primitive mechanism of projection, for this disgust was in the last analysis what she experienced when she had her own milky discharges, assimilating her sexual existence to an illness. Disgust in hysteria exhibits, at the heart of the conversion symptom, a passionate denial of sexual difference that seeks to attribute to the other a kind of responsibility for having "spoiled" sexuality.

The paradoxes of hysterical conversion all refer to this denial. We have observed repeatedly that the hysteric has no body, owing to a lack, in her history, of symbolization of the body. Yet at the same time, he (or she) has too much body: it is as though, in constituting this evidence of her loss of jouissance, Dora was freezing up and attempting to enclose within her own body as a totality, without any residual formations, everything having to do with her own jouissance. The exclusion imposed on her by her parents' sexual relation is experienced as absolute, not limited, and it is not representable; and at that moment, just as the delusion about genital filthiness is being established, just as disgust is being actualized, every experience of jouissance is locked onto the urethral and (especially) the oral erotogenic zones. Every sexual experience is precipitated onto these places in the body, in that register of jouissance, so as to exorcise any experience of anguish that might be felt as a sort of disagregation of these erotogenic zones.

From this viewpoint, a hysteric (male or female) suffers not from a lack of body, but from an omnipresence of body. There are only erotogenic zones where no disarticulated being [*désêtre*] is inscribed, and the subject is frozen out of any attempt at reorganization; thus any limitation of the erotogenic zones is precluded. Concerning the attention Elisabeth paid to her pains, we have already remarked the precipitation of all pleasurable experience onto privileged places in the body, which thereby make other erotogenic cathexes impossible and remain there so that other cathexes continue to be impossible. In this impossible reorganization of the hysterical body, the subject basically rejects any change in the status of her body: she refuses to acknowledge that an erotogenic zone may represent the impossibility of contenting herself with oral jouissance, for example, with that complicity with her father for which Dora the thumb-sucker remains nostalgic.

So that no part of the body has to represent an absent portion of jouissance, a missing portion, this jouissance has to be present, *dargestellt* and not *vorgestellt*: hysterical conversion as precipitation of the subject's entire existence in attacks that privilege certain erotogenic zones in an attempt to totalize the body, to ensure that nothing has to be represented as lost. This comes about in experiences that demand imperiously that the subject be situated in her ascendency and constitute herself as desiring by symbolizing the exclusion that confronts her in her parents' sexual relation.

If the nucleus of conversion lies in this desperate presentification [*présentification*] of jouissance, in this precipitation that acts as though no aspect of the subject's body could escape it, must we not reexamine the idea of passage into corporal innervation? This would summon up such an obnubilation by way of the body.

Chapter 3

The Actualization of Instincts in Hysterical Symptoms

"A hysterical attack is not a discharge, but an *action*; it retains the original character of every action—of being a means to the reproduction of pleasure," writes Freud to Fliess (*SE* 1:239, letter 52).

In all the clinical work we have consulted, hysterical symptoms appear as enactments of fantasies that short-circuit speech during treatment. Elisabeth's pains and her motor inhibitions maintain a disjunctive relation with narratives of erotic scenes whose elaboration had remained as if suspended in her symptoms. In Feldmann's patient, blushing takes the place of what is formulated during treatment as exhibitionist scenarios and as the history of his body in relation to masturbatory experiences that have established its erotogenic configuration.

We propose to use the term "actualization of instincts" to designate the regime of desire that hysterical symptoms exhibit. This expression points to problems that remain to be solved. After a preliminary investigation, it becomes self-evident that the expression refers to something unambiguously distinct from what Freud designated as "actual" neurosis, for the act whose status with respect to hysteria remains to be clarified is defined through a specific relation of the body's imaginary cathexis by movements taken not in a physiological sense but in the popular sense. The hysterical symptom often "moves"; it involves movements as well as sensory disturbances. What does this mean? From this particular viewpoint, the Freudian notion of conversion as diversion into bodily innervation is hard to separate from a physiological construction of the body that can be of no use to us in specifying what actualization of instincts is involved in hysteria. Insofar as it concerns discharge and bodily innervation, Freud's language seems in spite of everything to indicate a homogeneity between actual neuroses and hysterical enactments. This appearance of homogeneity has to be dissolved.

The precipitation of a desire that is quelled in a scenario enacted by the body, while setting forth the limits of what we should like to clarify, also distinguishes itself from the bodily order whose characteristic features Pierre Fédida identifies in his study of hypochondria.[1] The dream body is defined by projection, and projection permits a reevalution of the somatic that designates a different bodily register. It will be useful to attempt to distinguish the two orders of projection on the one hand and visible action on the other, so as to understand finally how they can intersect and interact with each other clinically. In each case bodily visibility comes into play; but the dreamer's egoism[2] uses this visibility to elaborate the relation of jouissance to suffering and pathos, whereas the hysteric's appeal to sight enacts a rigidified demand for an impossible completeness of the pleasure-body that has more to do with narcissism than with the solidary egoism of projection.[3]

We need to clarify, too, the actualization of instincts in hysteria with respect to all forms of short-circuiting in symbolic elaboration, forms whose coordinates often remain confused. There is no point in speaking of enactment unless we are prepared to confront the act in question with the Freudian notions of discharge, specific action, obsessional acts; we must be prepared to unravel the metaphors of motion and energetics that Freud often uses to identify the act's various registers. The metaphor of discharge, for example, makes it possible to deal with widely differing phenomena: the model of regression that Freud elaborates in his letters to Fliess and presents in *The Interpretation of Dreams* makes the distinction between dreaming, sleepwalking, and diversion into action inconceivable. If the psychic apparatus is traversed by a current that

1. See in particular "L'anatomie dans la psychanalyse," in *Nouvelle Revue de Psychanalyse* 3 (1971), and "L'hypocondrie du rêve," *Nouvelle Revue de Psychanalyse* 5 (1972).

2. "L'hypocondrie du rêve," pp. 227–28.

3. Our stated intention (see above, p. 18, note 1) to differentiate, as Freud did, between the orders of hysteria and hypochondria thus begins to be realized explicitly only in the present chapter.

passes from perception to motion, one could readily imagine a reversal of the current in order to explain that the signal of consciousness is switched on in dreams. Yet such a schema is useless for a theory of the modes of actualization of instincts, for despite its surrealist overtones, the image of the act that it proposes remains immobilized in a linear and reflexological representation.

Has the notion of discharge ever been freed from its grounding in the theory of regression? Even if that theory, like the notion of primary judgment, indicates that some hallucinatory element always remains in any object cathexis (since such a cathexis aims at a rediscovery), even if the theory indicates that every action is first of all a way of procuring pleasure, the fact remains that being a somnambulist, having hysterical crises, passing into action, masturbating, painting, making love, all these are still modes of discharge that involve "acts," to be sure, but that are not differentiated by the acts in question. It is ultimately the place of the hysterical symptom among these modes of realization of instincts that we are seeking to delineate; and we speak of actualization to prejudge its specificity among all these acts. The question now becomes more pointed as we move on from discharge to motion.

A Hysterical Attack Is Not a Discharge

From the time of the Fliess correspondence, two approaches to this actualization intersect in Freud's writings. The first situates it among all other forms of act and discharge; the second relates it to onanism.

An abrupt diversion into bodily innervation is conceived as a caricature of the adequate act: in any search for pleasure that conforms to the requirements of the secondary process, motor and intellectual acts guaranteeing a rediscovery of the object have as their goal the specific act to which passion is bound (*SE* 1:200). The adequacy of this reflex act consists in its timeliness, and the discharge is split into two movements: cathexis of the image of the object and cathexis of the motor image, which represents in pleasure that fusion of the subject's body with the reality of the desired object. Since this dual cathexis, representational and motor, exists in every perception,[4] it is present a fortiori in the experience of pleasure.

In relation to this model of the "normal" sexual act, hysterical attacks short-circuit not the reflex but the work involved in relocating the object. Instincts are not absolutely objectless, in symptoms or attacks, but their object is the subject's own body. We have taken the text quoted at the beginning of this chapter as Freud's most specific attempt (although he did not pursue it further) to situate the actualization of instincts.

That hysterical attacks do not constitute a discharge means that discharge is only one phase of the action that leads to the achievement of sexual pleasure. This action, inasmuch as it has the subject's body as its terrain and object, is distinguished from the montage realized in the "normal" sexual act.

In no other text does Freud distinguish so clearly between a conversion from the psychic to the somatic and the passage into somatic innervation, as a narcissistic cathexis connecting with a dimension of movement.[5] The bodily innervation here is not the physiological aspect of pleasure, as Felix Deutsch thought when he made hysterical manifestations and emotions homogeneous; it refers to a different conception of bodies and acts. Freud said so himself, moreover: "Attacks never seem to occur as an 'intensified expression of emotion'" (*SE* 1:239).

To the best of our knowledge this separation between the problematic of the act imposed by hysteria and the metaphor of discharge, as well as the explicit disentangling of the hysteric and the psychosomatic, is an apex of sorts in Freud's work. He did not so much answer the question as avoid it.

When the theory of hysteria changes register, in 1908, Freud amalgamates his physiological images and his reference to onanism without further explanation. To be sure, in his 1908 texts "Hysterical Phantasies and Their Relation to Bisexuality" (*SE* 9:159–66) and "Some General Remarks on Hysterical Attacks" (*SE* 9:229–34) he is no longer feeling his way. These texts no longer seek to distinguish organic elements from psychic elements in conversion,

---

4. "Project," *SE* 1:333. We shall return to the theme of motion as the moment of thought that elaborates jouissance.

5. This articulation between narcissism and movement seems to us to be the core of hysteria.

and they scarcely mention somatic compliance: the hysterical symptoms or attacks "are nothing else but phantasies translated into the motor sphere, projected on to motility and portrayed [*dargestellt*] in pantomime" (*SE* 9:229). And in Freud's summary, motor innervations are clearly related to the masturbatory experiences of which they are parts or segments.

The fact remains that the subtle but important distinction between discharge and hysterical attack is not taken up again, still less pursued in depth: the relation between hysterical attacks and the actualization at stake in masturbation is once again conflated with the physiological aspect of the sexual act, whether onanist or not; it is conflated with discharge. "What points the way for the motor discharge of the repressed libido in a hysterical attack is the reflex mechanism of the act of coition—a mechanism which is ready to hand in everybody, including women, and which we see coming into manifest operation when an unrestrained surrender is made to sexual activity."[6] No traces remain of the impressive precision of 1896, except perhaps a certain hesitation and a substitution of terms: the two texts quoted express a reservation concerning the somatic nature of hysterical problems. On the one hand, Freud writes, "hysterical symptoms are nothing other than . . ." (*SE* 9:162), "these attacks are nothing else but . . ." (*SE* 9:229). On the other hand, "*in so far as the symptoms are somatic ones*, they are often enough taken from the circle of the same sexual sensations and *motor innervations* as those which had originally accompanied the phantasy when it was still conscious" (*SE* 9:162; emphasis added).

In place of the distinction between hysterical attacks and discharge—which opened up a reflection on action, masturbation, and hysterical symptoms—we see a shift from corporal to motor, and we remain uncertain about the somatic nature of these innervations. Finally, if we read the text as if we were listening to a patient's discourse, the problem of the body that comes up in onanism and in hysterical symptoms is not purely and simply eliminated. This problem brings into play the transformations of the texts' manifest content; and for this passage the allusive presence of the repressed question even draws upon the resources of overdetermination.

6. "Some General Remarks on Hysterical Attacks," *SE* 9:234. The reference to women repeats almost word for word the passage in draft G on the adequate act.

This reworking of Freud's thought produces a result, as well as a task to take up again. Why "motor" rather than "corporal"? And what is the action that is accomplished in hysterical symptoms, as a reminder of masturbation?

What Does Darstellung *Mean?*

Presence and Figurability

By actualization of instincts in hysterical symptoms, we mean the enactment that the symptom attempts and the presence of the object it lays claim to. The observation that this claim is made in vain and constitutes the impasse of hysteria deserves some clarification. In "actualization" there is at once the dimension of movement—of motion, in Freud's terminology—and the dimension of presence: the hysterical symptom is not a representation (*Vorstellung*), it is a presentation, or a presentification (*Darstellung*). The hysteric posits the object of her desire in the element of presence—as if it were there—whereas the eccentric behavior of the obsessional neurotic is rather a caricature of Vorstellung, of what is necessarily marked with the sign of absence in the object. The obsessional neurotic, to be sure, returns unceasingly to this dimension of absence associated with a symbolization of desire, but his incessant return is produced within the element of representation, that is, of meaning. The obsessional neurotic attempts, through his symptoms, to turn the symbolic back on itself; he forms a thought that represents the object of his desire, consenting to use a language that acknowledges the object's absence—a truly symbolic language in the sense in which the word kills the thing.[7] But this eroticized murder takes on real, that is, magical, value for the obsessional neurotic, and through his contradictory rituals he tries to cancel out that element of symbolization in which his thoughts and acts continue, however, to circulate. Obsessive representations and actions attempt to reveal that the symbolic—perhaps, even so, there is some doubt—is not as symbolic as it is thought to be, but in the process of forming such representations and performing such acts the obsessional neurotic resorts to the means of the symbolic while remaining within the element of Vorstellung, of words that have acknowledged the ele-

7. Jacques Lacan, "Function and Field of Speech and Language," in *Ecrits: A Selection*, trans. Alan Sheridan (New York: W. W. Norton, 1977), p. 65.

ment of absence in the desired object, the missing piece in every elaboration of jouissance. The obsessional neurotic never stops trying to undo this, to act as if it were not the case, but his efforts can only end in frustration, for the means he uses in his thinking—motor symbolisms (*SE* 20:119–21) and contradictory representations—belong to the symbolic order and presuppose the recognition of what he is struggling not to recognize.

The hysterical Darstellung effects a totally different compromise. In hysterical symptoms and attacks, the subject uses plastic and figurative thought to try to achieve the presence of the desired object and to achieve a jouissance in which nothing will have to be represented—that is, acknowledged as absent. The problems encountered in translating Darstellung—too often rendered "representation"—are well known. To be sure, the term Darstellung may be used in the general sense of "means of expression" and "means of representation"; however, Freud generally reserves it for dreams, onanism, and hysterical symptoms. In the chapter of *The Interpretation of Dreams* devoted to dreamwork, the notion of Darstellung comes up again and again. Freud's French translators often chose to emphasize the reference to figurative language, especially in the translation of essay titles. "Die Darstellungsmittel des Traumes" comes out in French as "Les procédés de figuration dans le rêve" (in English, "The Means of Representation in Dreams," *SE* 4:310) and the title of the following passage, "Die Rücksicht auf Darstellbarkeit" as "La prise en considération de la figurabilité" ("Considerations of Representability," *SE* 4:339). It is unquestionably difficult, in a translation, to bring all the overtones of a term into play; for our purposes, however, it is indispensable to make some careful distinctions. What is involved here is not only representability, but also presentification. If we fail to perceive this, we risk misunderstanding: thus, when Freud states that "dreams have no means at their disposal for representing these logical relations between dream thoughts" (*SE* 4:312), the significance of the relation he has just established with the languages of the pictorial and plastic arts is canceled out if we say, as the French translation does, that these relations "are not given any separate representation in dreams."

If we look at the translation of a later text, the case study of the "Rat Man," we can locate an identical sidestepping of the precise meaning of Darstellung, and this time with regard to masturbation, onanist scenes in which the Rat Man evokes his dead father, at night. The French version says simply: "On oublie qu'elle [la masturbation] sert à la décharge des composantes sexuelles les plus diverses" (It is forgotten that masturbation serves to discharge the most varied sexual components), where Freud was connecting the question of the act with that of discharge, as he did in 1896. Something has indeed been forgotten: "Dass sie die Abfuhr der verschiedenartigsten Sexualkomponenten . . . darstellt" (That it can represent [present and figure] the discharge of every variety of sexual component [*SE* 10:202]). We are not subjecting these texts to such close scrutiny merely for the sake of proposing a few corrections to the French translators; the point is rather that these errors hinder us, for they make us lose sight of a problem. What is there that is homogeneous between unconscious thought in dreams, masturbation, and hysterical symptoms that would justify the use of the same term in each case?

Perhaps the question was never answered, even for Freud himself, especially insofar as the relation between the first term, dreams, and the two others is concerned. Since, as we have seen, the schemas of regression preclude any distinction between visual and motor modalities of actualization of instincts, there is no reason to be astonished that a single term should designate the presence of images and forms in dreams, the theatricalization of masturbatory scenarios, and the work of transformation that a hysteric accomplishes on his or her own body, work through which fantasies are "portrayed in pantomime" (*SE* 9:229).

Darstellung Adrift in Freud's Texts

We may be able to derive a few insights from this Freudian muddle. In *The Interpretation of Dreams*, the chapters devoted to Darstellung follow an astonishing course. We begin by examining images, and we gradually reach sensations of inhibition in dreams— that is, precisely the aspect of dreams that articulates them with hysterical symptoms.[8] Freud starts by examining the semiotic system in dreams; he analyzes its elements—images that presentify and represent or figure things—and its rules of formation, comparing

8. It will become evident that this moment plays a decisive role in Dora's second dream. In it Dora experiences all the anxiety that her symptoms smother.

the sequences dreams produce with other languages. Next he confronts the question of the intensity of dream images, the feeling of reality the dreamer sometimes experiences. It sometimes happens that a dream thought is realized *by the material of the dream rather than by its context*. And Freud's examples are the same ones we examined in Elisabeth's case: "Man will gehen und kommt nicht von der Stelle" (One tries to move forward but finds oneself glued to the spot [*SE* 4:336]). The stylistic turn of phrase in dreams coincides here with hysterical conversion: owing to a metaphor, an element of the dream content passes into the body; we might almost say it "leaps into the organic." The Darstellung changes register, as if, when the content of an image becomes a hallucination in a dream, the object's presence is at its height, projected in sensations and motor impressions. As we know, such dream events often lead to waking and anxiety. The imminence of the object that is presentified in the body, no longer merely transposed into a language of images, perhaps requires us to reconsider the idea that dreams are realizations of a desire. Does not the dream keep what it presents at a distance? Does not the counterevidence of the feelings of inhibited movement, in this experience that is defined by an unfelt motor inhibition, bring to light a higher degree of realization of desire or of actualization of instincts that would signify a catastrophe for the subject?

Freud does not formulate the question. He avoids it by positing a reciprocal equivalence of voluntary thought and motor innervations,[9] which of course simply replaces a problem with an image and so resolves nothing.

Nevertheless he indicates that this is in any event an important difference in the style of dreams, a difference surely associated with a change in the regime or organization of desire in the sense that, as Freud puts it in the "Wolf Man" text, a dream is truly a psychic event, a moment in which something is organized, is produced for a subject. Freud wonders "why . . . we are not perpetually dreaming of these inhibited movements"; he goes on to suggest that "it is reasonable to suppose that this sensation, though one which can be summoned up at any moment during sleep, serves to facilitate some particular kind of representation, and is only aroused when the

9. *SE* 4:337: "An impulse transmitted along the motor paths is nothing other than a volition."

material of the dream-thoughts needs to be represented in that way" (*SE* 4:336).

There are as many organizations of unconscious desire as there are styles of thought, turns of phrase in dreams. In dreams themselves, perhaps not everything arises from the same degree of actualization of desire; perhaps the regression linked to visualization does not have the same character of imminent presence as the cathexis of the body induced by a metaphor in hysterical conversion or its dream model: the sensations of inhibited movement.

This stylistic modification in dream thoughts might be expressed as follows. In dream images, to be sure, an object is represented, is outlined, but to the extent that these images are organized in a syntax that refers to a spoken language, they do not lose all relation to the element of Vorstellung. If Freud can say that dreams retain representations of things, it is perhaps because as a signifying organization the dream keeps the thing at a distance; the dreamwork thus would consist in elaborating that distancing, that removal. In the hysterical Darstellung, or in the Darstellungen of the feelings of inhibited movement in dreams, does not that distancing stop abruptly when a wordplay crashes into the body? Wordplays and metaphors: they certainly exist in dreams and in neuroses, but in the cases that concern us, what is involved is a metaphor battered by movements that fix and isolate the play of signifiers. Freud referred in 1895 to "a separate psychical group" (*SE* 2:157). What allows wordplays to designate objects is the system of possible substitutions and the fact that the signifiers slide over the signifieds.

In hysterical symptoms, inasmuch as they are induced by a very specific metaphoric play, language is fixated; it precipitates onto the body instead of continuing to play in the element of the signifiers. It is as if, all at once, the words covered a thing, a portion of the body, whose otherness with respect to the words that designate it is no longer apparent. What is called hallucination consists in an obliteration of things by words, by certain words, that solidify in fixing themselves onto a thing. This thing, by the same token, loses its quality as object, as remainder of judgment, as residue of a loss taken into account by language, to become a thing, *the Thing*, too present, not sufficiently lost. Is not the diversion from fantasy into bodily innervation, in hysterical conversion, the imminence of jouissance when it is presentified by a material that, in fact, belongs neither to the order of words nor to the order of things properly speaking? It is a material made up of feelings and bodily movements.

Masturbation and Hysterical Symptoms

From 1908 on, Freud makes the connection between hysterical symptoms and masturbation the axis of his new approach. What can this juxtaposition contribute to the study of Darstellung? Does it help us understand what links the hysteric's concentration on the body's visibility with the presentification of the body image that that concentration attempts to guarantee by way of the patient's motor problems?

Masturbation offers first of all a model of enactment, of actualization of instincts on a terrain that clearly differentiates the instinct in question from a behavior, a discharge, or a psychic repercussion of the physiological difficulties connected with the sexual act. That is the conclusion that can be drawn from the proceedings of the colloquium on onanism held in Vienna in 1912. Sandor Ferenczi saw masturbation as the cause of "neurasthenia" (what we call neurosis today). His point of view is not directly challenged, but it is sidestepped by way of a noncausal conception of the act for which expressions such as *exekutiver Akt* (Sadger) and *Exekution den Phantasie* (Freud) are first proposed[10] (the latter expression resonates with all the more brilliance in that it remains largely unargued). The situation is reminiscent of 1896, when Freud put forward the idea that a hysterical attack is not a discharge but an action whose status remained to be clarified; these new terms are bandied about in Vienna in a similar way. Other questions have priority in the fray, however. In 1912 the psychoanalysts were fighting on several fronts. They all agreed in their critique of the old idea that masturbation is harmful in a purely physiological sense. Masturbation by itself does not make anyone ill. But very few analysts agreed with Wilhelm Stekel's contention that if children were let alone, if their

10. *Die Onanie: Vierzehn Beiträge zu einer Diskussion der psychoanalytischen Vereinigung* (Wiesbaden: J. F. Bergmann, 1913), pp. 11, 22. Freud's concluding remarks appear in the *Standard Edition* as "Contributions to a Discussion on Masturbation," *SE* 12:243–54.

masturbation were no longer repressed, all would be well, since their sexual tensions would be discharged. Against Stekel's optimisic approach, Freud suggests that masturbation correctly understood makes it possible to comprehend the pathogenic aspects of sexuality itself. Thus Freud does not propose to treat masturbation as a clinical entity; he is seeking to grasp the import of an impasse in sexual development that no subject can avoid. "If you admit that the sexual urges have a pathogenic effect, you should no longer deny a similar significance to masturbation, which after all only consists in carrying out such sexual instinctual impulses. . . . Masturbation . . . is sexual activity subject to certain limiting conditions. Thus it also remains possible that it is precisely these peculiarities of masturbatory activity which are the vehicles of its pathogenic effects" (*SE*12:251). When the hysteric shows the doctor that she is ill, is she not situated precisely at that point of the ordeal where she is stuck, even as she states the enigma?

The second front is defended brilliantly by Ferenczi, who reworks the hypothesis of a pathogeny tied to quantitative and qualitative problems in the sexual discharge of masturbation.

In these circumstances, anyone seeking to consider the issue from a standpoint other than that of what today are called neuroses is compelled to emphasize the importance of the so-called psychical factors in masturbation or, better yet, to say that masturbation is first and foremost a psychical affair, which is assimilated to "a fantasy affair."

Sadger himself does not exploit his own formula, *exekutiver Akt*. On the contrary, he declares that actions count less than thoughts in masturbation. It no longer seems to matter that thoughts themselves are actions, and the question is conflated with another: Might there be such a thing as a purely somatic masturbation? The genetic approach, harking back to attempts to generate thought on the basis of the body, now comes into its own: is it possible that, at the very onset of masturbatory activity, either in infancy or in the case of premature seduction, its enactment might concern the body (*Körper*) alone? This hypothesis is related to a clinical observation. Very often the patients that Hitschmann, Ferenczi, Sadger, and Tausk discuss have in fact stopped masturbating, even though masturbatory fantasies continue to organize their desire. The most serious neuroses are indeed those in which the patient has abstained from any actual masturbation. It cannot be denied, then, that the moment at which the masturbatory act is repressed is important for the theory of onanism. On the contrary: the modalities of this repression of the act may well determine the fate of the neurosis. Does not hysteria attempt to bear witness to what is at stake in the act, whereas obsessional neurosis, giving up the attempt to actualize that impossible jouissance, would continue to elaborate nostalgia for it by imagining the prohibitions that weigh upon incestuous desires with a cruelty that is all the greater in that the subject has not accepted the prohibition? On this point, all the participants in the colloquium on masturbation grant theoretical priority to the obsessional over the hysterical.

Doctors of an earlier era were right to say that masturbation was much more serious in thought than in bodily practice.[11] Thus we need to analyze the patient's guilt, which for its part is incontestably psychical, rather than the act itself. But is it correct to say that guilt marks the psychical nature of "true" masturbation? In what sense would incestuous fantasies accompanied by imaginary representations of taboos or obsessional symptoms be more psychical than masturbatory acts? Two intertwined problems have to be distinguished here. What is the significance of fantasies with respect to masturbatory acts? Is guilt always associated with masturbation, whether imagined or enacted, and is it associated in the same way in both cases?

Rereading Dora's Case with Tausk

Although Tausk is not interested in masturbatory acts as such, his contribution (*Die Onanie*, pp. 48–68) avoids Sadger's muddled alternative between fantasy and body. Tausk does not attempt to find out when masturbation becomes fantasy, but he identifies the place of masturbatory crises in the history of a child's autoerotic practices. For him there is no need to investigate masturbation as an act (he does not use the word). But during the sexual activity of early childhood (*Betätigung*), the way the child's caretakers handle his body conditions that body for pleasure. No purely corporal stage of eroticism needs to be identified since, as Serge Leclaire

11. Ibid., p. 16; the assertion is Sadger's.

117

would say, adults are needed to open up "gaps of jouissance."[12] To the full extent that the secondary sexual zones are left unrestricted and unsuspected as sexual, they bring the child pleasure; they allow an exchange of love and the discharge of sexual stimulation through the tender caresses proffered during contacts with other human beings. In autoeroticism there is not yet any object of desire, but bodily activity and pleasure are caught up in symbolic relationships. When the child, dependent upon the jouissance introduced by others, seems to say to himself while sucking, "It's a pity I can't kiss myself" (*SE*7:182), his pleasure is not purely somatic (*rein somatisch*), as Sadger sought to argue. It is certain, however, that this pleasure, implicated in the symbolic element from the start, is a partial pleasure that is not linked to any object love, to love of the totalizing form of another body. Between the erotic and symbolizing presence of others and the configuration of the child's own pleasures, no form introduces a stable connection.

The situation is indeed unstable and threatened by its disproportion with the unknowable Other to whom the child is beholden for his jouissance—a jouissance that is moreover quite solipsistic.

Tausk does not address the problem of form or object. He merely mentions that this pathway for discharge never suffices, cannot satisfy. The child's sexual need becomes insistent, leading him to discover a primary erotogenic zone that ensures him *the greatest and most perfect pleasure*. Here is where the conflict with adults arises.

Unquestionably, something still remains unclear in the development of the child, who is presumed to discover his own genitals quite naturally. But according to Tausk, what counts is the child's need for excess, his demand for the greatest, most perfect pleasure. Is sexual activity not exacerbated in what would be its masturbatory and hysterical actualization? The sex act would thus belong to the all-or-nothing category, requiring a perfect and complete jouissance. Our first glance back at Dora in fact made reference to something along those lines: when Dora, the bed-wetting thumb-sucker, *overhears* her parents' sexual relation, she wants to participate in that higher jouissance (*Miterregung*), and for an increase in pleasure—that is, without any loss, in particular without the loss of her oral or urethral pleasures. Her passionate desire for all there is of jouissance means that, for her, masturbation represents a confron-

12. *Psychanalyser* (Paris: Seuil, 1968), p. 72.

tation with the *impossible*. She is condemned in advance to remain excluded from what she wants to approach, but it is out of the question for her to give up this passionate desire for total pleasure, to acknowledge that she is being deprived of it. The new forms of pleasure that awaken in Dora's body as she listens to her parents' bodies are, at that point, condemned to remain unsatisfied. But she refuses to recognize this, and her hope for a perfect, untrammeled jouissance uses the means at hand to try to become a reality nevertheless, or at least to announce that hope is not lost. The means available are those of oral gratification (and this is precisely when Dora becomes asthmatic, through her reworking of an orality laden with the undisillusioned passion for a greater jouissance) and urethral gratification. Dora's fall on the stairs and the false step of her second dream remind us that she preferred to suppress the existence of a vaginal appeal to pleasure in favor of what she does not want to lose, enuresis; and at this point, charged with the impossible, enuresis becomes disgusting. Thus her oral pleasure turns into asthma, her urethral pleasure turns into disgust with sex: these transformations are produced as retroactive reinforcements of autoeroticism. Retroactive, that is, situated after the confrontation with the desire for total jouissance that she has never relinquished and with respect to which she cannot conceive of what she lacks. What makes her a hysteric is the recathexis of the infantile erotogenic zones that she does not want to give up but to which she confides the hope of realizing all the jouissance that escapes her in her parents' sexual relation.

About Dora's childhood masturbation, about the specificity of its form, as Wilhelm Reich would put it, we have very little information. But the importance of Dora's recathexis of her pregenital erotogenic zones—which recall her passionate rejection of sexual difference in the masturbatory *act* and in her symptoms—might incline us to modify Joyce McDougall's assertions about man and his masturbation.[13] Conceiving of the *act* as of a piece with genital eroticism, and contrasting it with the fantasies she sees as confined to pregenitality, McDougall concludes that in the masturbatory act the hand plays the role of the Other's genitals, takes the place of the sex organ in the sense in which the spool takes the mother's place in

13. "L'idéal hermaphrodite et ses avatars," *Nouvelle Revue de Psychanalyse* 7 (1973): 263 ff.

the game of Fort-Da. McDougall's thesis is based on a study showing that the healthy patients in her sample had practiced active
masturbation in childhood and thus demonstrated their genitality;
another group had merely played with excrement, while the least
healthy ones had confined themselves to masturbatory fantasies.

This perspective does not account very well for what McDougall
had asserted shortly before, that active masturbation has as its aim a
bisexual illusion that represents less a symbolization of the difference
between the sexes than the rejection of that difference, inasmuch as
the difference implies emptiness. Does not the masturbatory act, at
least as fixated in hysterical symptoms and in certain dreams, aim
more at actualization than at ludic activities? Not all forms of these
acts are on the same level, it seems, nor are all objects. The hand is
not an object in the same way as the spool is: the hand is less
detachable. To play at the mother's absence is to transform into
action an insufficiency in enjoyment of the object that is accepted as
real; such play creates absence in order to render it conceivable.
Masturbation, on the contrary, amounts to clinging to the impossible presence of the object; playing at bisexual jouissance amounts to
wishing to actualize what is unactualizable.

Proceeding on the logic of her own assertions, Joyce McDougall
recalls the "famous congress" (*sic*) on onanism and in the process
dedramatizes the Freudian thesis. Freud, in fact, clung firmly to the
idea that masturbation is the revealing agent in the test of what
pathogenic elements there may be in the sexual order. All those
writers who, like Sadger or McDougall, raise the question of masturbation, retaining as relevant the distinction between its performance as act and its performance as fantasy (only the latter being
construed as pathogenic) perhaps fail to grasp the specificity of the
masturbatory act played out on and by the body, as well as the
allure of catastrophe that it has for the subjects Wilhelm Reich
discussed in his article on specific forms of masturbation.[14] It has
such an allure for Dora as well; her hysterical symptoms perpetuate
this onanist impasse. Rather than situate the Fort-Da game and
masturbatory acts on the same plane, let us attempt to get at the
truth underlying that impasse. That masturbation can be produced
only as an act means that, in his approach to sexual difference, the

14. "Über Spezifität der Onanieformen," *Internationale Zeitschrift für Psychoanalyse*, 1922, pp. 333–37; see below pp. 138–141.

subject involved lacks a representation of himself. If the masturbator plays several characters at once, it is because he himself is part of his own body. His hand is not so much the representative of the Other's genitals as the organ that is attempting to enclose the unrepresentable of which the subject, in this respect, is constituted. The subject figures in the scenario as an element of what is unrepresentable; he is caught up in an act that lacks the status of a game; or if it is a game, the subject plays less at symbolizing an absence than at "imaginarizing" the absence so as to avoid its symbolization.

Dora even tries to stitch her pleasure-body together by a term that would bring the poles of her erotic configuration into communication: her sex, having become disgusting, rejoins her throat and mouth, where an act of oral coitus is evoked through the word *catarrh.* In this way something is sewn up, something attempts to unify itself in Dora's body, at the cost of the visceral pleasure that had been taking shape in her. She eradicates that pleasure because she cannot stand having some aspect of herself, of her own body, remain in suspension, in waiting, unrealized. Tausk offers a precise description of this reorganization of the erotogenic body at the time of the masturbatory crisis or the masturbatory experiences that necessarily become a crisis (*Die Onanie,* p. 53). What is important in masturbation—and this is never played out in advance—is the way it is resolved, the way it persists after the ordeal of the parental prohibitions. Masturbation always regresses, as it were, to pregenital scenarios. To the extent that genital sexual representation succeeds in being repressed outside of consciousness, the energies thus liberated turn in other directions. One portion of these energies is sublimated, transformed into an intellectual interest in the objective world. But another portion cathects the secondary sexual zones and takes on activity as specific sexual gratification without genital representation. This regression of masturbation to pregenital scenarios, laden with a portion of the genital libido to which satisfaction is forbidden, conditions the subject's eroticism and determines what he or she will desire in the bodies of others.

The secondary zones become perceptible through the objects of satisfaction that suit them; a child's desires and disgusts draw upon precisely the same modes of erotic reaction as do those of adults. Body odor, hair color, the shape of organs, personal affection determine the position the child will take with respect to others.

And as it happens—Tausk does not explain clearly enough how—
some secondary zones become hypersensitive and are in constant
activity: the child picks his nose, licks his lips, bites his nails, sniffs
out strong smells, and so on. Among the regions of the body whose
autoerotic activity sustains the ordeal of the first object experience,
we should also mention, where Dora is concerned, that she clears
her throat, grows hoarse, is irritated by the milky discharge she
discovers in a region of her body whose contours disgust her, and
so on.

In this persistent sexual activity (*Betätigung*), in these bad habits
(*Unarten*), Tausk recognizes the quality of authentic masturbatory
acts (*echte onanistische Akte*), infantile precursors of perversions. And
he notes that in certain cases this regression to autoeroticism is held
together by a metaphorometonymic device. Thus, in German,
bitten-down fingernails are called *Neidwurzeln*, roots of desire. We
are dealing with metaphor here, for to bite one's nails is to "select" a
specific bodily act as the substitute terrain for the prohibitions one is
rejecting, the metaphor being the play between one register and
another, between representing and presentifying. And metonymy
is also involved, in that when one segment of an erotic scene is
fixated in a symptom, one part of the body monopolizes the jouissance.

Why the term *act*, which Tausk uses here for the first time? We do
not know. Let us therefore consent to remain in the dark a little
longer even as we note its sudden appearance.

As soon as this term disappears, interest is displaced onto an
aspect of those bad habits to which Tausk attributes a very special
importance in the fate of masturbation, namely the sadomasochistic
components of sexuality. For Tausk these components represent a
compromise between the genital activity conserved in fantasy and
the confrontation with prohibitions. Conserved in fantasy? In fact
here Tausk is not clear, since at the same time he recognizes that for
the child the fantasies are connected with unambiguous genital
stimuli. When the child "makes himself" hurt, cultivates pain, hits
or scratches or bites himself, these pleasures come so close to genital
sensations that one hesitates to say that through them the child is
giving up the presentification of what is at stake in his masturbatory
jouissance. It is as if the child's punishment fantasies were in league
with the repression of the act. In the last analysis, this is indeed the
decisive moment for differentiation between hysteria, perversion,

and obsessional neurosis; however, these itineraries are very closely related. When fantasy truly wins out over action, when incestuous desires are fully maintained by the imaginary elaboration of guilt, masturbation is transformed into obsessional neurosis; and Tausk gives priority to this path in the remainder of his contribution. As soon as the fantasy is sufficiently well developed, it becomes a conscious accompaniment of the masturbatory act. Then it can function as the act's moment of resolution, the act being sublimated in reading, conversation, or glances that punctuate cutaneous or sexual secondary stimuli; thus we enter into psychical masturbation, *represented* masturbation.

When, owing to the tenacity of painful pleasures, fantasy joins forces with action without representing it, remaining fixated on scenarios that connect the genital and secondary erotogenic zones through pain, placing them at the same level (this corresponds, in the fantasy, more to the sexualization of punishment than to precipitation into guilt), masturbation has perversion as its outcome. Perversion thus colludes with representation, succeeds in bringing it into play in such a way that it does not have a castrating function.

When guilt is not truly installed, when the hope of incest is maintained, when incest *is thought of as impossible rather than as prohibited*, the ordeal of masturbation continues to be played out, repeated in hysteric symptoms. It is not represented; it attempts endlessly to presentify itself. The hysteric does not give up the presence of jouissance as she desired it when the object relation was established for her for the first time. That is why the thought of her desire uses the resources of the figurative and plastic arts, of the image and movement that shape that element of the object's presence. This is not to say that desire is elaborated *identically* in the plastic arts and in the hysteric symptom, but rather that the plastic arts succeed where the hysteric achieves a semifailure.[15]

Dora's Second Dream: From "Darstellung" to the "Vorstellung" of Desire

Let us try to test the consistency of what we have just been saying by returning to Dora. Up to now we have referred much more

15. On this question, see below, chapter 4; Imre Hermann, "Organlibido und Begabung," *Internationale Zeitschrift für Psychoanalyse*, 1923, no. 2, pp. 297–310; P. Racamier, "Hystérie et théâtre," in *L'évolution psychiatrique* (1952).

frequently to her first dream than to her second. This is because Dora's first dream seems to constitute an explanation of her masturbatory experiences. The Darstellung of desire recalls what was at stake in these masturbatory experiences without really breaking with their enactment or with the hope of a fully present jouissance. The dream images and narrative construct a sort of *insignia* of the masturbatory experience fixated in Dora's symptoms.

The second dream, on the contrary, reorganizes an essential aspect of her desire; or rather, her desire is for the first time *signified* in it, in the element of Vorstellung and no longer in Darstellung. Words and letters suddenly operate in an entirely new way. Let us recall the story line of this second dream. Dora walks alone in an unfamiliar city, following a route that leads to a train station. She discovers, in deliberate isolation, an adorable Madonna[16] who captures her gaze. She pursues the quest, too, for the nature of woman's sex, as signified by the linguistic plays that carefully weave a web unifying the city, the station, the forest, and the genitals. A condition of possibility for this exploration is finally mentioned. For Dora to be able to acquire knowledge about sex, or to accede to sex inasmuch as it has to do with knowledge, her father needs to be dead. All these elements open up a new field for investigation. The solitude of the first dream consisted in a dismissal, a demolition of everything that could bring to mind sexual difference as opposed to masturbation, that is, as opposed to the pleasures in which Dora, even though her father served as her accomplice, finally experienced her jouissance alone. The solitude of the first dream is really the solitude of autoeroticism. Or rather, the first dream makes present the continuing impasse in Dora's sexual development: the approach of the object relation. Any encounter with sexual difference is immediately converted into a strengthened autoeroticism. Contrary to Freud's insistence on the importance of Dora's desire for Herr K., the analysis of the key terms of this dream—"catarrh," "jewel case"—indicates that Dora denies all sexual difference. Freud locates the dream's formative desire quite precisely: Dora does desire to save herself from Herr K. so as to rejoin her father (*SE* 7:85–88). But it is essential to be clear: rejoining her father certainly does not mean running toward her father as toward someone who loves her and her alone, in the sense of a heterosexual object relation.

16. This essential element does not belong to the manifest content.

It means relocating the oral and urethral forms of a pleasure in which Dora thinks of herself rather as a companion in erotic games with her father as accomplice. It is not so he can protect her virginity but because sex disgusts her that she appeals to her father against Herr K. Tausk provides a good description of this type of experience, in which the—necessary—presence of another serves the solitude of a jouissance; and this is possible even when the subject's autoeroticism is burdened with the unresolved masturbatory crisis. Heterosexuality does not appear in the latent content of the first dream.

In the second dream Dora's solitude takes on a different meaning. Her father is no longer the homosexual accomplice of her games; he is dead. Thus she can usurp his place, *not so as to continue to masturbate but so as to explore the sexual order.* We do not mean to suggest that from this moment on everything is clear and that at last she discovers and accepts sexual difference. In the second dream, too, she refuses the presence of men, whether a suitor or Herr K. is involved. But this rejection and the desire to chart her own course—or else to be a guide for the others who are exploring the city—lead her toward other shores where what remained enclosed in localized masturbatory realizations can for the first time be formulated, represented. Dora is no longer merely an enuretic little boy; she is a being fascinated by the image of a woman's body that may finally close up on itself, because it is there *to be seen*, and looking at it may finally bring a jouissance that is fulfilling, that brings liberation from the conflict and violence inherent in the autoerotic solution. In place of sexual difference and autoeroticism, we ultimately need that beauty, that calm, and perhaps that death. This solution to the crisis is conceived only in the element of form, gaze, and immobility: paintings, a statue.

Freud underlines the importance of this theme: the photo album, the Dresden paintings, the pictures seen the day before at an exhibition. Dora's fascination with woman's form evokes quite precisely her desire for the death of desire, since the associations concerning the album suddenly remind her of a monument, a stone body, that stood in the square of the deserted city (*SE* 7:96). In the first dream Dora recalls the solitude of the masturbatory realizations that have been fixated in her symptoms. In the second this solitude dares to say what it consists of, and thus the dream is no longer a decoding of masturbation but a release from its grip.

This is even more true for the other directions pursued by Dora's desire. For although Dora may spend two long hours in front of the Madonna, nevertheless she does not remain absolutely fixed there. Some part of herself goes on walking and elaborates other outcomes for the masturbatory impasse. Dora, whose symptoms served to prevent anxiety from coming into being, suddenly experiences anxiety along with the impression of being unable to escape it ("I had the usual feeling of anxiety that one has in dreams when one cannot move forward" [p. 94]). The feeling of motor inhibition is produced in the dream when the facade of her desire suddenly cracks. This dream event stems from the regression that Lacan defines, in his discussion of Irma's dream, as the moment when the imaginary comes undone.[17] We might first list the paths of Dora's desire at the level of their meaning, their content. She dreams she is a young man discovering a woman's body. Freud, attentive to the dreamwork that is making a metonymic allusion to a woman's sex, emphasizes the violence that colors this fantasy of defloration. To this is juxtaposed, without any possibility of further commentary, what is most repressed: the desire to know and the history of her womb. The dream staircase that Dora suddenly evokes stimulates an infantile desire for pregnancy that was replayed at the edge of the lake with Herr K. and that was followed, in each case, by a sore foot. With this false step, Freud recognizes his good fortune in identifying a "true hysterical symptom" (p. 201). What does this mean? It is undeniable that what arises here is a desire involving Dora as a woman: her desire for a child is no longer conflated with disgust and the catarrh. It is expressed quite differently, as a stomachache, and the genital nature of this ailment is not ruled out by the dream, since the encyclopedia alludes both to Dora's investigation of her cousin's appendicitis and to the scholarly term *Vorhof*, which designates a part of the female genitals in the German medical lexicon. This dream expresses both Dora's curiosity—for she would in fact like to deflower a woman—and the shape of an infantile genital desire whose addressee, as we shall see, remains indeterminate throughout, although that addressee subsequently becomes Herr K. Dora's heterosexuality has few overt manifestations. What leads us to declare that we are now facing a desire for a man, however, is that for the first time guilt is signified in the

17. *The Seminar of Jacques Lacan*, Book 2, p. 165.

126

treatment material. This confirms one of our hypotheses: in the hysterical Darstellung, incest is experienced as *impossible* and not as *forbidden*. Its role is not to express itself, but to actualize itself as impossible. It is in this sense that the first dream became the sign of masturbation, as though the dream's images were simply reflecting masturbation without forbidding it. Sex can be filthy, Dora can be disgusted, without implying that participation in the sex act is forbidden. Disgust is the last recourse of actualization for a subject who conceives of this actualization as unrealizable but for whom the terrain of this impossibility is not defined as symbolic, that is, as identical with an *interdiction*. Dora can speak of her false step, on the contrary, only after laborious efforts along a circuitous path. As long as she imagines castration as a real loss of her body, the subject stiffens up to ward off the intolerable through attacks and symptoms. Dora's disgust, her asthma, and her loss of voice are at once sensory and motor symptoms. Does not Freud's repeated reference to the diversion into bodily innervation and to the figuration of fantasies projected onto motility ultimately refer to the hysteric's *inability to conceive of any reality but that of her own body*, with the result that she uses this ground to express her refusal of an unrepresentable incompleteness?

The second dream opens up that field of expression, allowing a certain guilt finally to be signified, and thereby limited.[18] This is perhaps the essential element of what is at stake at this point in Dora's treatment. And our emphasis, so far, on the content of the dream thoughts should have prepared the way for a study of the dream syntax. Octave Mannoni writes that even if an analyst uses symbolizing interpretations in a treatment, the fertile moments of his own expression, like those of his patient's history, can be elaborated only through the resources proper to the signifier.[19] Freud said just this when he announced the tenor of his discovery: "A dream is a picture-puzzle . . . and our predecessors in the field of dream-interpretation have made the mistake of treating the rebus as a pictorial composition" (*SE* 4:278). The study of Dora's dreams

18. As Melanie Klein shows, guilt is not first of all Oedipal; it refers to the difficulty inherent in existing as separated. In hysteria, this inability to desire or this desire for the death of desire is revealed in fantasies of homosexual jealousy.

19. "L'ellipse et la barre," in *Clefs pour l'imaginaire, ou L'autre scène* (Paris: Seuil, 1969), p. 45.

leads us to add that certain dreams are dominated by a metaphorical style and are perhaps more inclined to resemble drawings. As we have seen, the catarrh and the jewel case, the elements of Dora's first dream that collect the greatest number of condensations, turn out to be the insignia of the symptom without breaking with the instinctual actualization of the masturbatory crisis. Other dreams shape their material like a rebus: instead of reflecting the symptoms in images and symbols, they renew the history of a desire.

When Dora evokes the train station of her dream, Freud first reassures himself by seeing it as a repetition of the box in the first dream. This station is awkward for the symbolism: "A box and a woman: the notions begin to agree better" (*SE* 7:97). But this attempt to place the two dreams on the same level in the search for symbols does not hold up. The station is not a repetition of the box; moreover, the box does not necessarily designate Dora's sex, but perhaps represents her whole person, as Jacques Lacan suggests.

With the station, we are dealing with something else entirely. The *Bahnhof-Friedhof* series contains a missing third term, but one whose absence is represented by the memory of the nymphs seen the night before in the background of a painting, owing to the double meaning of the word *Vorhof*, which also designates a part of the female genitals. If Dora's sex is in question in this passage, it is not because she is dreaming of a thick forest resembling one seen in a painting and the one she crossed at L. Or rather, if there were nothing more to it, nothing crucial for Dora would be happening in this dream—nothing compromising enough to make her interrupt her analysis. In fact, the image of the forest is framed by metonymies, in the specific sense that Lacan gives to this term in "The Agency of the Letter": "It is the connexion between signifier and signifier that permits the elision in which the signifier installs the lack-of-being in the object relation, using the value of 'reference back' possessed by the signification in order to invest it with the desire aimed at the very lack it supports."[20] Lacan's algebra gives the following notation: $f(S \ldots S')\ S \cong S\ (-)\ s$; or, in the case in point:

$$f(\textit{Vorhof} \ldots \textit{Bahnhof, Friedhof}) \cong \frac{\textit{Bahnhof, Friedhof} / \textit{Vorhof}}{\text{woman's genitalia}}.$$

20. *Ecrits: A Selection*, p. 164.

Whatever the import of this writing may be, one thing is certain: it is no accident that the first time Dora alludes to genital sexuality, the first time she insists on an answer to her question ("Am I a man or a woman, and what does that mean?"), she is guided by the resources of a signifying latency, of turn of phrase or rather a syntactic organization that inscribes her sex as marked by an absence. What is decisive in the fact of passing through the structure of the signifier is that it introduces lack into the signified and it puts on stage the barred subject, $. This may be translated into a different language: it is only when Dora passes through the structure of the signifier that she exits from the *Darstellung* of her desire; only then can she play with her suffering. (But since Freud did not recognize this exit, it was "converted" into another, an enactment that constituted the termination of Dora's analysis.)

We mentioned earlier a double metonymy, with reference to the term *Bahnhof* (station), whose connection with *Verkehr*, that is, with traffic and with sexual relations, evokes, along with *Nymphen*, the third term of the series of words ending in *-hof*. The identification of these wordplays opens up another interpretation of Dora's dreams that takes as the guiding thread their syntax rather than the content of the dream thoughts. Although Freud identified this syntactic dreamwork, he did not carry his analysis beyond a juxtaposition of desires. Dora adores the Madonna–Frau K.; she explores the city as a young man explores the body of a woman; she also alludes to her desire for knowledge about sex in connection with an imaginary pregnancy. The metonymy seems to indicate, on the near side of the content of the dreamer's desires, the moment in the dreamwork when the one desire spills over into the other. The alliterations that evoke the genitals come into play in the recital of the walk during which Dora in effect deflowers a woman. But through metonymy this thought comes undone like a setting that is changed at the theater, or like the surface appearance of a drawing that conceals another scene, one not immediately visible. When Dora's genitals are designated in the mode of absence, her own are indeed the ones in question, without the detour of this investigation of woman through identification with an other. As proof, the remainder of the dream, remembered because Freud identifies the *Vorhof* as lacking, puts Dora herself onstage: the big book and the stairs refer to the history of her womb and to her desires for pregnancy. The articulation of Dora's desires is thus produced at the level of the dream syntax, not at the level of the content of the dream thoughts; and the element that brings the heterosexual dimension to light is the metonymy of sex. We may well ask whether Dora is not succeeding here where she had previously failed when she overheard her parents engaging in sexual intercourse: she now finds the words, the letters to represent her exclusion from this relation, so she no longer has to presentify it endlessly, in symptoms.

The paradoxical relation between the hysteric and her body has become clearer: in a sense, the hysteric lacks a body. From the beginning of this study, we have seen that the insistent symptoms that guided medical observation on Dora's body pointed to the wrong path. Correctly understood, her negative hallucinations and her erotogenic zone displacements allow us to comprehend that, for a hysteric (male or female), certain zones of the erotogenic body— those whose symbolization refers to the first constitution of an object relation—are in fact condemned to nonexistence. But another aspect of the paradox comes to light here: if the hysteric lacks an erotogenic body, it is because he or she passionately rejects the lack, dreams of a perfect erotic body that could display itself as a whole.

In a third reversal, we find that the repetition of masturbation in the symptoms constitutes a desperate declaration that there is nothing but body and that "that lacks body" must be disallowed at all costs. There is obliteration of the subject by a body that could be figured as a whole and adored as Dora adores the Madonna or Frau K., through her gaze. Dora's second dream makes clear what lay behind the attention she had paid to her pains. And the correlation is better established now between the passion for form and the enactment that together make up the hysterical symptom as *Darstellung*. This enactment—which Freud represents as figuration of the fantasy through projection onto motility (cf. *SE* 9:229)—is the hysteric's inability, at the height of the ordeal during which her desire is constituted, to make part of her own body the symbol or rather the signifier of a lack, of a determinate absence to herself. Better to repress that aspect of her body that is summoned up to be lacking, as it were, through overhearing her parents' sexual relations, at the risk of remaining fixated in this demand for presence, for actualization, for totality.

The hysteric suffers in that she considers the body the only reality, or rather in that she is unable to know—through unconscious knowledge—that the order of language also has a form of existence of which her body is capable.[21] When the resources of the symbolic order take into account the void that inhabits a body, they do not suppress it; they give it limits, as does Dora's second dream. Because she was unable to symbolize this lack of being, Dora becomes passionate about the form of an adorable body on which her desire is fixated, as the dream monument indicates; and her own body has no configuration, no limit. If we reflect, indeed, on the crucial importance of orality for Dora, we may well wonder whether that erotogenic zone does not function for her like a sort of abyss that serves to represent everything (*SE* 7:83): the sexual relation in which she identifies with Frau K., the filthiness of sexual secretions that flow like those in her throat, her desire for a man and her father's complicity in her perverse games. One erotogenic zone swallows up Dora's desire in the same mode of all or nothing as the adoration of the Madonna. Paradoxically, her passion for form prevents her body from taking on an erotic configuration. Perhaps the nature of this orality bound up with passion for form has not been adequately emphasized. Jacques Lacan follows Freud's lead here when he points out, in the Dresden Madonna, the one who "knows how to sustain [Dora's] desire for the idealized father but also to *contain* if I may say so and at the same time deprive Dora of the counterpart that turns out thus to be doubly excluded from her grasp."[22]

The figure *contains*, certainly, but also it transports desire just as Dora's mouth does, swallowing up everything sexual that comes its way. In Dora's oral identification with Frau K., pointed out by Freud, must we not see a struggle of the all-or-nothing type, in which no body succeeds in finding its limits? Dora's orality and the specific way her passion for seeing comes into play perhaps allude to what binds a woman to her mother and is so difficult to symbolize.

21. It would be appropriate to investigate the "hysterical structure of the object" in modern philosophy since Descartes. Do not Cartesian extensivity, Kantian objectivity, and perhaps even the Bachelardian superobject all seek to continue to posit a real that is immune from language or from the transcendental or phenomenotechnical procedures that apprehend it?

22. Unpublished seminar, "L'envers de la psychanalyse," February 10, 1970; emphasis added.

What does Dora risk losing, or what loss is to be symbolized? Beyond any doubt, certain parts of her body involved in urethral and oral eroticism may come to represent a weaning of jouissance, of which she has never known anything but a caricature. But it may be that her passionate interest in the form of another woman's body, along with her voracious orality, manifests a woman's need to symbolize differently the experience of emptiness that her separation from her mother's body entails. And we know that, in the remainder of her story, that inclusion in her mother is indeed what Dora faces. She has identified with the only feature Freud picks up concerning her mother: the housewife psychosis.

We have been investigating the modalities of symbolization of a lack or void not in and for themselves, but only insofar as they mark the resolution of the hysterical and masturbatory Darstellung. In describing the relation of a subject to her body in hysteria and its masturbatory prototype, to avoid confusion one needs to distinguish between two types of unification of the erotogenic body: on the one hand, the totalization dreamed in a form produced by motion, on the other hand, the metonymic configuration of sex as body excluded from itself or body of which a part is missing. Through this process that constitutes the desiring subject, her body acquires limits. This distinction may clarify certain remarks made in the course of the colloquium on onanism. Sadger, Ferenczi, and Tausk keep coming back to the question of the body, total or partial, of masturbators. Ferenczi and Tausk agree on a description of what the sexual act is for an onanist. In his own particular terminology, Ferenczi articulates a paradoxical thesis: a masturbator who makes love is not in his own body, has no body. He is entirely caught up in his own fantasy, whereas in normal coitus there would be no fantasy, but only bodies, and whole bodies. Normal orgasm is conceived as the sum of all the preparatory pleasures that would arise in the erotogenic body. "I do not think," Ferenczi declares, "that the preparatory pleasure is a purely psychological process. When one looks at a satisfying sexual object, touches it, hugs and kisses it, a violent stimulation of the optical, tactile, oral, and muscular erotogenic zones is produced; these zones *automatically* abandon a part of the stimulation to the genital zone. The process takes place first of all in the sense organs, the sensory centers, and the fantasy participates only secondarily in passion, more precisely in joy" (p. 8; emphasis added). The mention of an automatism here conflates the configuration of an erotogenic body with a reflex montage, in the absence of a conceptualization of how a body is unified, how it comes into existence for the subject, something that does not stem from any automatism. This term automatism connotes a naturalist residue, also present in Tausk, which presupposes that autoeroticism necessarily turns into masturbation because the child, in part unsatisfied, arrives at the genital excitations from which he hopes to get great pleasure. In both cases, this natural history of the libido short-circuits the history of the erotogenic body, whose configuration is formed not through a libidinal increase but through a metonymy.

All this notwithstanding, Ferenczi's contribution indicates admirably the sense in which the masturbator—like the hysteric—lacks a body. Tausk specifies that it is because the masturbator has too much body (*Die Onanie*, pp. 63–64): what inhibits the onanist in the choice of sexual object is that every reality has to be measured against the perfection of a phantasmic representation. The notation that is evoked, for example, by Dora's adoration of Frau K. also displaces the decisive opposition that Ferenczi established between body and fantasy. The body's obliteration by fantasy is instead extended in the subject's inability to acknowledge an object that is not the reflection of her perfectionism. And the quest for perfection has the role of preventing lack: "When an onanist has a love object, he is intolerant in the face of the irremediable lack of its body." The impossibility of metonymizing the sex organ leads to the result Ferenczi described: there is no preparatory pleasure, because only the genitals are attractive to a masturbator. Tausk cites the cases of certain patients who expect a woman to cure them. Analysis always reveals that it is the woman's genitals they are looking for, not "a woman as a whole." Moreover, the same patients end up expressing the return of a repressed homosexuality: with their "enormous interest" in genitals, they desire to see someone else's organs in order to assure themselves that their own are more imposing and that their anxiety is baseless.

This obliteration is responsible for the fact that in sexual relations masturbators no longer dispose of the autoerotic and homosexual pleasure fixated in fantasy. "They cannot be led into preliminary play. They cannot take on the role of the one who brings about a beginning of pleasure; they cannot transfer the sum of stimulation that arises from these pleasures to the accomplishment of the sexual act." What Tausk called "a woman as a whole"—as opposed to "seeing a whole woman as a sex organ"—corresponds to what we are calling the "configuration of an erotogenic body." Failure to distinguish between the two leads to the conflation of the erotogenic body with a natural body.

All these remarks tend to confirm our contention that it is indeed with respect to the genitals that the subject's absence to herself is signified or challenged, but also that the configuration (in the active sense) of the erotogenic body is undertaken at the risk of all or nothing.

Chapter 4

Is a Metapsychology of
Movement Possible?

As our study progresses, we see more and more clearly how difficult it is to conceptualize the dimension of movement that is involved in hysterical symptoms and in onanism. The unending twists and turns of this theme can be spotted in diverse texts. The dimension of movement is hinted at in expressions like *executiver Akt* or *Execution der Phantasie*, yet Tausk, Sadger, and Freud seem to have been unable to get a firm grip on that dimension; they did not succeed in pinning it down or working it through. Whether we follow Ferenczi's energetics of pleasure or recenter the investigation, with Tausk, on the interwoven fantasies of masturbation and guilt, we lose the moment proper to movement itself, as a cathexis of the body charged with bringing forth jouissance. It is hardly our intention to stand apart from these authors and criticize them, however, for the very difficulty they encountered runs through our own work as well. Our efforts to clarify the presentifying function of the hysterical symptom was a way of announcing that that form-giving activity was situated at the point where the dimensions of sight and movement converge, and that the specificity of hysteria depended on this articulation. Yet when we returned to Dora's case, the dimension of movement vanished. Its disappearance may perhaps be attributed to the dynamics of the second dream, which symbolizes what remained in suspension and in motion in the oral and urethral symptoms that the first dream recalled. But it is no accident that we have hastened to reach the point where the phenomenon to be studied offers thought a better grasp because the dimension of movement is suppressed in it. This shift in focus may recall Tausk's: he began by studying the cathexis of the body in autoeroticism, but he recentered his interest on guilt and prohibition as soon as he arrived at the masturbatory crisis. The outcome of the crisis as he saw it was one we find again in obsessional neurosis rather than in hysteria, where jouissance is conceived as impossible rather than as prohibited. At this point a question arises: Is this refocusing of the analysis inevitable? Better yet, is it necessary? Is it legitimate, is it even possible, to seek to grasp the meaning of the dimension of movement in hysteria? And if we set out along this path, are we not falling into step, in theory, with the symptom? Movement in hysteria does seem to indicate in some way a limit of the conceptualizable; the problem is rather like that of conceiving of original repression. And this accounts for the ease with which the narcissistic act is confused with movements conceived according to a behavioral schema, whether energetistic or biological. Furthermore, the context of the questions that traverse our study perhaps situates the unconscious meaning of this investigation: to justify the hysterical symptom in some respect "no matter what," and to pursue what presents itself as almost impossible to conceptualize. What can we do, then, except acknowledge that in fact a theoretical discourse can be analyzed like a dream, that the subject is not foreclosed from it in a simple and uniform way?

On quite another plane, our efforts may produce excellent theoretical justifications that constitute an equal number of secondary rationalizations. How are we to distinguish among the forms in which bodily movements come into play in various configurations of the unconscious? From infantile motor excitation through somnambulism, obsessional rituals, and movements in the sexual act to the plastic arts, from masturbation to hysterical attacks and tics, how are the various orders of bodily movements implied by the organization of the sexual impulse? No doubt this question is motivated by a desire to rehabilitate something that is at work in hysteria. Its elaboration and the search for an answer will perhaps lead to lateral clarifications concerning the conjoined elaboration of a desire to know and the content of a knowledge.

The Motor Order at the Limits of the Analyzable: Two Examples

To return to the fleeting, recalcitrant question of the dimension of movement proper to hysteria, let us attempt to pinpoint the articulation of instinctual and motor elements that needs to be spelled out. Movement is not limited to hysteria. With reference to obsessional rituals, Freud speaks of *motor symbolisms*, behaviors intended to cancel out what has happened through motor activity. Hysteria presents itself quite differently, since the subject is unable to modify the external world in view of her own pleasure and thus can only modify her own body; this comes about in her attacks and symptoms (*SE* 20:94–95, 119–20). What does it accomplish, exactly, to contrast alloplastic and autoplastic movements? Does this not presuppose an unjustified coincidence between the object relation and the orientation of a behavior toward the outside, whereas hysteria and onanism would present autoplastic movements coinciding with an autoerotic turning back of the object libido? On this coincidence between observed movements and instinctual organization, Freud offers very little explanation. Can it truly be said that the object relation, the objectality of a relation of desire, is proved by the fact that the subject acts on the external world in order to attain the desired object and that, on the contrary, when the subject moves independently, it is because he is in a state of autoeroticism or narcissism? This position is not a viable one, and we may recall Ferenczi's insistence that a sexual act carried out with another person could constitute an act of masturbation.[1] Some subjects masturbate in their partners' vaginas, he declared. The homology between the instinctual topology and the observation of movements indeed seems to constitute both an almost natural development and a misleading imagination. Perhaps its charms can be dispelled if we frame the question as follows: What aspects of movement are involved, respectively, in hysterical actualization and in obsessional rituals? And what does "aspect" mean here? In a discussion about psychosomatics and hysteria with François Perrier,[2] Jacques Lacan raised an analogous problem: What organs may come into play in the narcissistic relation, that imaginary relation with the other in which the ego is formed? And he responded with the example of the eye, the organ that is involved in the narcissistic relation and that plays a structuring role in the function that is the specular image. It is a matter not of finding a criterion in the organs themselves, but of noting that certain organs may be involved in a relation that arises

1. *Die Onanie: Vierzehn Beiträge zu einer Diskussion der psychoanalytischen Vereinigung* (Wiesbaden: J. F. Bergmann, 1931), p. 7.
2. *The Seminar of Jacques Lacan*, Book 2, pp. 95–96.

from an entirely different order, the narcissistic relation. With regard to the Freudian references to motor symbolism in obsessional rituals and to autoplastic movements in hysterical attacks, the difficulty can be formulated as a question: Are the same movements involved in both symptomatic formations? That is, can movement as it is perceived or understood in behavioral models be articulated equally well with different instinctual "trajectories," or are differing aspects of movement respectively involved in the diversion into action, obsessional canceling-out rituals and hysterical attacks? By examining the contributions of Reich, Sadger, and Landauer, we shall try to determine whether a metapsychology of motion can be established; next we shall investigate the status of movement in hysteria and obsessional neurosis, focusing on a limit, a frontier between these two symptomatic devices—namely, tics—and on what we have learned on this subject from Ferenczi, Karl Abraham, and Melanie Klein. Finally, looking at hysterical movements from a different angle, we shall try to conceive of them as the blocked metaphor of a loss of body, or of a body's fall. This impels a confrontation between the activity of the hysterical symptom and the activity of a painter's hand as he creates a picture by dribbling splashes of color on a canvas.

First Example: Reich

In a brief article published in 1922, Wilhelm Reich returns to the discussions of the colloquium on onanism that had taken place ten years before.[3] Sadger had insisted that actions matter less than thoughts in masturbation; and most participants in the colloquium pointed to the incestuous fantasies typical of masturbation, the feeling of guilt connected with the resulting imagination of castration. In 1922 Reich argues that these considerations fail to take into account the clinical and therapeutic importance of the *forms* of onanism: in several of the cases cited, the repression was lifted not when the patient merely said that he masturbated, but when the apparently ancillary details of the scenario were clarified. Here Reich is interested in movements insofar as their observable specificity alone opens the way to the aspect of an instinctual motion that

3. "Über Spezifität der Onanieformen," *Internationale Zeitschrift für Psychoanalyse*, 1922, p. 333.

is actualized. The *exekutiver Akt*, the enactment of the fantasy, as Freud said, has the same status in analysis as the manifest content of a dream. *The natural connection among bodily movements must be broken, and the defunctionalized fragments of these movements must be analysed.* Little by little, one of Reich's patients reveals the meaning of the movements manifest in his masturbatory experiences: he masturbates lying on his bed, his body bent way back, his penis held straight up, one foot outside the bed. Shortly before ejaculation he grabs the pillow, in theory so as not to dirty the bed. He uses only three fingers for masturbation and in particular the fingertips, in such a way that the index finger and the little finger can adhere to the external surface of the penis. These gestures on the patient's part refer to a precise symbolic configuration. His bent posture recalls the story of the sacrifice of Isaac, for in the illustration with which the patient was familiar, Isaac was in just that position, with his father standing above him holding his knife. The patient's desire for castration by his father and his masochistic orientation are expressed in this scene. His foot, held outside the bed, represents escape in the face of this same threat, or in the face of the *impossibility*[4] of the scenario in its totality. For the patient here is acting out a drama with several characters; the pillow into which he ejaculates takes him back to a very old desire—he wanted his mother to fish out his penis and hold onto it to get him to urinate. "In my masturbation," he said, "I am playing both mother and child."

These details clarify what is at stake in masturbation as an act. Just as Dora's throat, mouth, vocal cords, and catarrh served all her purposes, allowed her to presentify what was unactualizable, so here the patient's movements indicate that the subject is playing out his identity symbolically on his own body, but not only in representation. He is doing so, rather, in the element of Darstellung. We still need to identify the game involved. It is a tragic game, for actualization through movement presentifies the loss of the subject in this primordial fantasy that he is attempting to enact upon himself and that constitutes the key to his jouissance. Is there not a relation between the fact that the subject is caught up in what he presentifies, that he can bring himself into being only as a piece or

4. We are emphasizing the term common to the problematic of onanism and that of hysteria.

part of his own body, and the instrument of that scene, at once substance and decor—namely, movement? That the subject moves, in masturbation, designates the act's nature as an impasse: an untenable attempt to lodge symbolic markers within one's own body, markers that cause the body, however, to *lose hold* of itself. The movements of the defunctionalized body take the place of the lack of a signifier that would allow the subject to be identified with his body. The element of masturbation is a motor element, to precisely the extent that the subject cannot bring himself to be present to himself. It is by way of the place where he escapes himself that he moves in masturbation. The same thing happened when Dora converted the impossible representation of her sexual identity as absence of self to self into oral erotic activity. Movements thus seem to be a form of thought, the only one, as it happens, that can designate the subject in the place where he loses himself, in the operation of the primary repression.

Reich does not say this himself, of course. Yet his observations are important in that they clearly differentiate the dimension of masturbatory movement from any motor discharge. The "actual" character of the instinct represented in the scenario does not by nature have anything to do with the metaphor of pleasure as a sensation of discharge. The order of movement, which involves unconscious work or in which the unconscious is engaged insofar as "that" works in it, is not movement in its physiological nature. The aspect of movement that stems from the physiological perhaps also calls forth meaning, if only lack of meaning, the point whereby meaning is lacking to itself. Even for psychoanalysts, it is not self-evident that movement should require interpretation. Toward the end of his article, Reich reveals how difficult it is to hold this position. After clearly situating the importance of the movements that have to be analyzed as elements of a dream, he plunges into the strange enterprise of classifying the forms of masturbation for both sexes on the basis of observation (pp. 336–37). The word "form" no longer designates anything but what one sees and no longer evokes relations of movement and loss. Thus we have to differentiate subjects who masturbate while lying on their stomachs, using an improvised vulva (bedcover, cushion, or hand) from those who prefer to be lying on their backs, localizing their activity in the hand while the torso remains passive. For the first group the prognosis is good: since they are inventing a vulva, they have some chance of acceding to heterosexuality. The others remain fixated in an entrenched feminine position. To be sure, Reich establishes these correlations on the basis of experience. But by what criteria experience allows itself to be invaded! This ought to suffice to demonstrate that, psychoanalytically speaking, the effort to pass directly, even in summary, from a description of movements and positions to a classification of instinctual outcomes leads to an impasse.

At the least, this shift in focus shows in what sense the dimension of movement in the unconscious constitutes a limit of the interpretable. Because a modality of the unconscious resists interpretation—and in a principial fashion, no doubt—analysts hasten to act as if that modality were no longer at all related to the unconscious, thus repeating the undertaking of Cartesian philosophy, which can conceive of movement only as a radical elsewhere of thought.

Nevertheless, Reich's attempt makes it possible to point to a path: it is a question of conceptualizing the articulated play of parts of the body as an instinctual montage whose organization requires a spatial dimension. The threat to the Reichian enterprise consists in confusing the requisite spatiality with a classical perceptual space, the one that an observer of habitual actions can perceive. Such a proposition thus turns quickly to caricature by presupposing a reversibility between the order of perceived movements and the order of psychoanalytically conceived movements. But this caricature can be justified by what remains unthought in the Freudian theory of the specific action that procures pleasure by triggering a signal for discharge after modification of the external world. Reich's weakness here is that he manipulates that opposition between inside and outside less skillfully than Freud.

Second Example: Sadger

Numerous other clinical studies attest in a different way to the difficulty of conceptualizing the dimension of movement without leaving the field of the unconscious. In a 1914 article on tics, Sadger likewise fails to get at the heart of the matter.[5] A tic is indeed an action that should make it possible to see whether the opposition between external and internal behaviors has any relevance. Sadger's discussion of tics entails a certain confusion, however. It is not so

---

5. "Ein Beitrag zum Verständnis des Tic," *Internationale Zeitschrift für Psychoanalyse*, 1914, pp. 354–66.

much that he identifies the internal-external schema with the distinction between autoeroticism and objectality as that he conflates movement with a biologically inherited predisposition to which he gives the mysterious name "heightened muscular erotogeneity." One of Sadger's patients was a seamstress, a young woman of twenty-three afflicted with tremors in her eyelids, forehead, mouth, nose, arms, and hands. These motor symptoms were particularly pronounced when she got angry, when her brother treated her roughly, or when she was worried about her mother. The symptoms appeared when her father died suddenly at the age of forty-nine. From then on the young woman was in a state of constant worry about her mother, who had respiratory problems. The patient was frightened of police cars, which made her think her mother had been rushed to the hospital; she was also afraid of fire, "for her youngest brother, her mother's favorite, was very careless with lamps." All such incidents triggered violent tremors. Sadger then accounts for the patient's motor instability by depicting her as caught in the middle between her parents, endlessly running back and forth from one to the other. Moreover, when the patient was a child her mother dragged her from one hospital to another in search of treatment, convinced that her daughter's state was worsening because the doctors did not exert themselves on her behalf. This practice provoked quarrels between the parents, who kept passing the blame back and forth, as they did between themselves and their daughter: "My father said that I was crazy, that I was only imagining things; and my mother took me under her protection. I grew more and more attached to her, which made my father furious." As the child was tossed back and forth there was particular provocation on her father's side. She identified with him: her mother had always told her she was the spitting image of her father, and she herself liked to recognize that she belonged to a family of stubborn, hot-tempered, though not mean-spirited individuals. Her father, who worked for foreign firms, drank a good deal as he traveled about, though he had little tolerance for alcohol. When he was in good spirits he played with his daughter, tossed her about playfully, and took her off with him in his wanderings while the others stayed home. This provoked renewed tremors.

The patient remained fond of the wandering life (she herself went from one house to another with great frequency, feeling at home everywhere except at home); she retained a fondness for her father's forms of playfulness as well, for her greatest pleasure lay in pinching and shaking her fellow workers and friends, as her father used to do, until her mother raised her voice in protest.

In his discussion of this material, Sadger interprets it as a tableau of hysteria. The young woman's excessive demand for love makes her identify with her father; even her stubborness presumably grew out of her love for him. Sadger thus links the identification with the symptom: muscular eroticism leads to the expression of affection through pinching, and by the same token the tic repeats a scenario of pleasure and anger that comes from the father. Why did this patient, who presents a specific disposition toward hysteria, not simply become neurotic? Why did her illness settle in her muscles, thus creating the tic and the tremors? "There is no explanation to offer but a particular organic condition, in other words a heightened muscular eroticism" (p. 362) that she had inherited from her father.

The appeal to muscular pleasure here plays the same role as the sleep-inducing virtue of poppies. And if, despite the details cited, Sadger does not take his analysis of this case beyond an organicist, psychologizing, event-oriented point of view, it is because he appeals to the confusing evidence of movements that have to be understood without further explanation as pleasure producing. Because the symptom the young woman gets from her father is a complex of movements, it need not be viewed as arising from a specific instinctual montage; it is perfectly clear that the symptom is transferred from father to daughter through their destabilizing games. The appearance of that transfer is stamped and sealed under the label of predisposition. Sadger brings analytic thought to a much more radical halt here than Freud does in his *Studies on Hysteria*, where the history of desire suddenly comes a cropper before a primary organic problem.[6] Only the misleading evidence of motor symptoms makes the comparison possible.

Real and Imaginary Spatiality of the Drive

It is noteworthy, then, that a problem that can vanish completely from view is taken up again in Karl Landauer's article—published in 1926, the same year as "Inhibitions, Symptoms, and Anxiety"—

6. On this point, see the first chapter of the present work.

on "motor excitation in the child."[7] The question we are raising—whether a metapsychology of the dimension of movement is legitimate and possible—receives the beginning of an answer here.

The Defunctionalized Motor Order

According to Landauer, psychoanalysts often come across motor excitation. In most of our patients, reactions are produced that can be classified according to established medical categories: athetiform, choreiform, myokloniform movements; twisting motions of the face, the torso, the entire body or its extremities. These are transferential manifestations of affect, processes of satisfaction, repetitions of an ambivalent situation in a return of the repressed.

If these symptoms can be appropriately related to the motor storm of the very first moments of life, if it is not absurd—Freud and Otto Rank agreed about this time that it was not—to imagine the existence of a close relationship between anxiety and the order of movement by considering birth as a primal experience in which such a relation is established, this still does not imply that we have to be satisfied with a physiology of anxiety (*SE* 20:133).

In "Inhibitions, Symptoms, and Anxiety," Freud used the term "anxiety" to designate a set of features that included the following: "(1) a specific character of unpleasure, (2) acts of discharge and (3) perceptions of those acts" (*SE* 20:132–33). Are physiological data really involved here, or do the acts of discharge rather point us to the imaginary physiology of the "Project for a Scientific Psychology"? In that earlier text, Freud undertook to acknowledge the physiological foundation of anxiety, even while asserting that true anxiety is conceivable only as the defunctionalization of that foundation. Anxiety transforms what is at first merely a movement into a signal; this prepares the psychic apparatus for other ordeals of loss, separation, or castration.

Karl Landauer also takes the defunctionalization of movements, observable in newborns, as his point of departure. He applies to movement the same type of analysis Freud applied to autoeroticism in *Three Essays*. It is not a matter of observing an empirical derivation of the instinctual dimension from the biological, but of conceptualizing the copresence of these two dimensions that find them-

7. "Die kindliche Bewegungsunruhe," *Internationale Zeitschrift für Psychoanalyse*, 1926, pp. 379–90.

selves articulated in the motor storm of birth. In contradistinction to what is required by a functionalist conception like that of Moro and Bernfeld, the motor excitation of the newborn is not organized in its totality to ward off a danger. Landauer goes beyond Freud here, for he posits a parcelization of movements from the outset. This fragmentation perhaps stems from some sort of autoerotic regression of a function that would seem to organize the organism for action with respect to the environment. Doctors do not know whether motor excitation results from excessive blood flow to the brain stem or, on the contrary, from a sanguinary stasis; they do not know whether excitation manifests some physical damage caused by the birth event or whether it grows out of a mode of being specific to the intact infantile organism. Landauer concludes that this problem "does not count" for his own research. What matters for him is the observation that at all events stimulations overwhelm the newborn: the respiratory process begins, the ambient temperature changes, new tactile impressions abound. This observation suffices to bring to light the presence of a defunctionalized, afunctional order of existence—that of unpleasure.

Motor excitation, or at least one of its component parts (*Teil*), consists in the expression of such an unpleasure. Just as that first human unpleasure is exemplary for those that follow, its expression is the expression par excellence (*Katexochen*) of unpleasure. Noncoordination thus functions as a functional indicator of an instinctual configuration, the motor modalities of which can be observed in an adult's body and in language. The specific motor patterns that a subject deploys in every experience of pain are not adaptive behaviors of self-defense or flight, but a continuation of that motor autoeroticism. The same is true of the externalization (*Äusserung*) of all the affects—inarticulate vociferations on the part of the ill tempered, voice tremors on the part of the anxious. *These defunctionalized movements are not purely and simply behaviors adapted to a displaced and symbolic goal.* The biological element begins to function as a signal, to be sure; but that is not all. We are not dealing solely with an attempt at intimidation, with a demand for pity or a symbol of inanition. These manifestations are incoherent, and in their incoherence they indicate a space, an instinctual topology that belongs *neither to the biological nor to the signifying.*

In their very incoherence, the movements that are discernible in the newborn and that organize themselves in the course of a subject's history indicate a spatiality of the body, where pleasure and unpleasure occur. This spatiality is not the perceptual space considered by the observer or by the subject himself,[8] nor is it physiological space. The space promoted by motor autoeroticism is articulated very precisely with the symbolic order, with the definition of symbolic goals. It is undeniable that the infant's cry becomes the signal of every moral motif, as Freud wrote as early as 1895. But it is not a pure symbol; the material of the signifier does not have the same status as the component parts of a language-generating machine. Its materiality is not assimilated (*aufgehoben*) like the inner workings of a computer, pure parts of a signifying machine. A certain level of motor noncoordination remains active, tracing in perceptible reality the limits of an imaginary body.

The articulation of this spatiality with language, at once real and imaginary, effectual and autoerotic, is produced by signifying nodes whose precision Landauer notes. The newborn's motor excitation survives and lives on not only in the subject's body but also in language. The German term for anger, *Grimm*, belongs to the same family as "worry" (*krümmen, zusammendrücken*) and "cramp" (*Krampf*). Without invoking hysteria or symbolizing conversion, which is perhaps one of its avatars, Landauer designates at once the *distinction* and the *articulation* of movements of anxiety as signifiers and promoters of a particular space in the body for pleasure and pain.

How can this articulation be spelled out? Is it an effect of spatialization of jouissance produced by the subject's engagement in the symbolic? Would we not do better to say, with Michèle Montrelay, that "the body wipes out language"?[9] To settle the question, we need to specify what is involved in this instinctual topology whose index is the persistent noncoordination of movements.

The Plastic Organization of Movements: First Castration

Landauer's second proposition consists in circumscribing the unconscious work accomplished in motion, the intermeshing of un-

---

8. That is why the notion of body image, too caught up in theories of perception in Schilder, for example, strikes us as ill suited to account for the topology of the drive. See Paul Schilder, *L'image du corps*, trans. F. Gantheret and P. Truffert (Paris: Gallimard, 1968). On the other hand, our effort to conceptualize movements "within" the unconscious encounters the Lacanian enterprise of an instinctual topology, particularly as presented in *FFC*, pp. 174 ff.

9. *L'ombre et le nom* (Paris: Editions de Minuit, 1977), p. 49.

pleasure and pleasure that constitutes its apparent incoherence. Movements serve as symbolic expressions of pain, signaling non-biological dangers; but they also serve to actualize a jouissance, a release that brings pleasure to its pinnacle (*lustvolle Entäusserung*). How is that expression to be understood? Landauer's use of it comes a year after Freud's text on negation appeared (*SE* 19:235–39). What "outside" is thus in question in motor judgment, which traces something like a first imaginary exterior via the movements of the body? It is certainly related to the judgment of attribution rather than the judgment of existence, for the distinction between the pleasure principle and the reality principle is not present at the outset in the motor noncoordination of anxiety states. Landauer posits that *this very terrain is where the reality principle can take shape*, through a self-limitation of the uncoordinated movements. These are first produced as an interweaving of unpleasure and pleasure in which the subject's release in the trajectory of the drive arises from a catastrophic jouissance. But the *rhythm* of the uncoordinated movements organized in the newborn gives a relatively stable configuration to the imaginary space in which this jouissance is accomplished. The autoerotic reversal of the drive is produced in the body through the installation of a topology of movements. As Landauer writes: "Every mother has seen instances in which her child makes a great effort to keep the breast in his mouth, but instead of sucking . . . he loses the nipple by tossing his head from side to side while pursing his lips, moving his tongue, or pushing away his mother's breast with his arms. Often some force or artifice is needed to stop the sucking reflex: thus the disturbing stimulation is withdrawn through recourse to oral activity itself."[10] The exercise of the oral drive itself limits motor excitation in a process that Landauer calls inhibition. This creates some confusion, since he shows precisely that movement is not suppressed; instead, it changes scale and becomes rhythmic, allowing the subject to abandon a first form of hallucinatory jouissance *that uses itself to calm itself.*

Jouissance thus changes its regime owing to a structuration by the rhythm of movements in orality. Let us now look at some other motor phenomena. In a little girl suffering at birth from an athetosis localized in her left arm in particular, the right palm was rapidly and with increasing rigidity kept in a fixed position near her mouth and became a replacement for the breast. At first her left arm was tossed

10. "Die kindliche Bewegungsunruhe," p. 382.

back into the air; about the fourteenth day, it finally found a resting place in her hair. The infant began to twist her hair between her palm and her fingers while bending and straightening the joints. To this was added a monotone sound like "reireirei" (at the age of two and a half, this whole set of behaviors was still activated in periods of fatigue and in situations of unpleasure). When she was three months old, if someone playfully took her right palm in his mouth, the child began to twist that person's hair. In discussing this gesture, Landauer suggests that it was no longer possible to find an action, but only a surrogate. In particular, in the passage from the athetosic movements to that outline of a masturbatory scenario, he identifies the passage from one hallucinatory jouissance, uniquely governed by the pleasure principle, to another that retains something of the initial aim of the drive even while proving to be compatible with the reality principle.

"Up to now," he notes,

we have followed the development of infantile motor excitation up to a certain point and have discovered that the excited limbs often *find*[11] an object of autoerotic or symbolic love on which they fixate in such a way that the love object is, as an erotogenic zone, the subject of another pleasure. The quest for this other pleasure allows the hand involved to limit its own motor excitation and thus to give up, in part, the motor pleasure that it had itself attained. To the extent that the motor pleasure contradicts those demands of reality that stress the lack of food, and especially thirst—for example, by preventing silence, by undoing clothing, by bringing about an expenditure of strength—the pleasure that the love object draws from the erotogenic zone is in harmony with the ego (oral eroticism, sadism, anal eroticism, genital onanism and its substitutes). Motor pleasure thereby succumbs easily to repression. The process is now accomplished by complicating itself, through the intermediary of an often quite complicated mechanism that we can reconstruct if we let ourselves be guided by observations of athetosic adults who express themselves very well in speech.[12]

The body of every subject is thus formed by movements, positions, arrests of motor excitation, which the instincts have shaped and are continuing to shape.

11. In the sense, no doubt, in which Jacques Lacan shows that *a* objects are "found."

12. "Die kindliche Bewegungsunruhe," p. 386.

Thus what is called bodily expression is the result and the always active ground of that definition of jouissance in motion. If this work of jouissance on and through the body is designated with reference to "expression" or "expressivity," this is not because its course should be determined by some essence of beauty that would be the aim of art. The process has to be reversed: ordinary language makes it clear that art is nothing but the continuation of this elaboration of the body in a modeling of movement that forms rhythms and circumscribes places. The thought that is in play here has no *aim*, either in art or in the motor history of a subject's jouissance; it corresponds rather to the same type of necessity that allows the pleasure principle to bend itself into a reality principle. How is this latter instituted on the basis of the former? Freud sometimes answers, in the text on negation for instance, with lessons drawn from experience. The subject would learn to limit jouissance, would learn not to trigger the signal for discharge as long as the fantasized object has not been relocated in reality. It is not hard to see that this presupposes what one is looking for as a given, since it is a matter of knowing how an event manages to constitute an experience. The issue is perhaps clarified when the history in which the jouissance of a body is elaborated is compared with the way a painting, a statue, or a musical composition is constructed: it is a matter of imprinting on movements a configuration that outlines an object around which the melody of perspective turns, even though that object is not truly lodged in those contours, even though the movements, which are self-limiting in the rhythms and forms in which they become audible and visible, do not come to rest definitively in the objects they support.

And this activity is without conscious aim. It is the work of thought, but it is work that, like writing, does not have as its end the development of a program of ideas. It responds to the imperious necessity of elaborating a primary catastrophic jouissance, of removing the threat of a *lustvolle Entäusserung*, even as it draws from that source and stabilizes it in objects, which are the provisional configurations of the rhythm that is born as these movements are limited by bending.

Lacking in intellectual aims, the thought in question does not lack a goal, all the same, in the sense in which the sexual instinct has a goal, one that Freud calls discharge. The subject certainly lacks any specific sense of reality that would lead him to abandon, in favor of

149

perceived objects, the imaginary objects constituted by instinctual space. And the reality principle would never govern the formation of the superego if the superego did not have as its goal satisfaction on the very terrain where thought is struggling with the shaping of a jouissance. The pleasure principle reshapes itself into a reality principle because the rhythm, the forms, the limitations of the motor excitation that constitute a human infant are discovered by her or him as so many resources to deploy against a jouissance in which to lose oneself without remainder. It is perhaps time to embark upon the elaboration of remainders.

Lacan with Landauer?

To our initial question, whether a metapsychology of the dimension of movement is possible and legitimate, a comparison between Reich's method and Landauer's allows us to reply in the affirmative. We need to specify, however, the way the relations between the instinctual topology and perceived and observed motion are to be conceptualized.

Landauer's method avoids both the pitfall of description and the pitfall of psychologization of the fantasy by conceptualizing a structuration of the instinctual space. Reich related observed movements to incest fantasies in such a way as to disarticulate the instinctual, which lies between the order of the visible and the order of the represented in the usual sense of the term. Landauer stops short of relating his patient's motor habits to fantasies whose psychical motifs could be discovered, and yet he avoids empiricism: the movements he describes are the ground and the instrument of the exercise of a drive whose montage he locates in a space that is not perceptual. In his seminar on the ego, Jacques Lacan posited that "the notion that there is a kind of pleasure proper to activity, pleasure in play, for instance, cripples the very categories of our thinking."[13] Psychoanalysis indeed has nothing to do with a pedagogy of bodily exercises. To offer such an interpretation of Freud's emphasis on motility, his emphasis on the modifications of the external world that the libido carries out in order to discharge itself adequately, would amount to turning one's back on analytic research. Motor pleasure can no longer be taken as a self-evident

13. *The Seminar of Jacques Lacan*, Book 2, p. 84.

point of departure, as it was by Sadger, if we remain attentive to the paradoxes of the pleasure principle. Motion is not the exemplary terrain of discharge in the sense that the libido consists in the pursuit of motor pleasure. The Lacanian position on this point is clear: nothing is said about orgasm, analytically speaking, when the term "discharge" is bandied about. This is a paradoxical theme in Freud: people do not seek their pleasure, since what is sought is the cessation of pleasure. Pleasure thus constitutes "something which in the pleasure principle tends to its own end." This theme, present from the start in Freud's work, plugs pleasure "into" what will be called the death drive. For a subject, the reality principle consists in limiting her pleasures—those pleasures whose nature it is to cease—and in finding ways for pleasure to *renew itself.* This Lacanian expression rejoins in part Karl Landauer's approach to motor excitation: when Landauer asserts that the child's first pleasure is a motor pleasure, he does not base this assertion on any evidence, but he spells out the modalities of the *renewal* of pleasure of which Lacan also speaks. The pleasure in the pleasure principle tends to its own limitation; Landauer indicates this by showing how the *lustvolle Entäusserung* that is the point of departure, and in which suffering and pleasure can scarcely be distinguished, manages to stabilize itself by limiting itself. But we still have not found a specific determination of what Lacan himself calls the "dimension of movement" in the unconscious and about which he says little, in the seminar on anxiety, even though he introduces that expression there.[14]

To avoid prejudging motion and to conceptualize the essential relation that links it to the structuration of jouissance, Landauer distinguishes poles in the trajectory of the drive, in the structuration of movements through self-limitation, feedback or constitution of embedded chains of motor sequences. From earliest childhood the erotogenic zone of the musculature has to be viewed as a subject of love, the movement of athetosic form as a sexual aim; in the case presented above, hair has to be recognized as a love object. The object here is the pole whose discovery allows movement to redirect itself—since at first the young patient's left arm was thrust out into space—and thus to renew itself. Hair serves as a relay here. The order of jouissance is presented at its origin as catastrophic in that its dependence upon a need induces the absence of object, that

14. Unpublished "Séminaire sur l'angoisse," November 14, 1962.

is, a catastrophic release of the subject confronted with nothing. The poles where instincts are organized in autoeroticism make it possible to play with this nothing, to surround it with space—that is, with body. The newborn seems to say: "It's a pity I can't kiss myself." To do so would allow him to retain something of himself in the experience of the void. And in sucking, if the imaginary object (the lips) is to take shape, real movements are required. Oral anticipation, threatened by the void, finds in sucking an initial pleasure wrenched from jouissance when the erotogenic zone outlines a scenario. Instead of that opening onto absolute nothingness, there is an autoerotic movement, that is, a body creating an imaginary space for itself. The movements of the infant's mouth correspond to those of the hand in the hair in Landauer's little patient. For that arm initially thrust out into empty space, she finds an object that, by inflecting the arm's movement, will allow that movement to be renewed and will keep her body from being lost.[15] The poles seem more distinct here than in the newborn, whose mouth is both subject and object of love, if we accept Landauer's categories. In this play with the palm that twists the hair, however, the body that is constituted is just as imaginary as the one the newborn dreams of. Imaginary, that is to say, not unreal or dereistic (*FFC*, p. 23), not unrealized either—in the sense in which Lacan proposed the term to designate another level of elaboration of desire—but unactualizable in the sense in which the relation of a subject to his body is marked by an inherent inadequacy.

In specifying the object's function here, we recognize that the topology of the sexual instinct does not arise from visible movements, even though those two spaces may occasionally intersect. If we say that the instinct is curved back on the object, we are designating one of those points where the two spaces coincide. This does not mean they are identical, for the change of regime of jouissance cannot be observed. And if we posit the function of an unactualizable object—the lips that seek to touch themselves from some other place so that they may come into existence, that absolute elsewhere toward which the little girl's left hand first flies and that succeeds in finding an image in her hair that allows the elsewhere to be enclosed—the traces, the movements we are talking about arise from

15. Lacan writes that "the object is simply the presence of a hollow, a void" (*FFC*, p. 180); we are suggesting rather that the object is won against the void.

an order of visibility that has to be constructed. That is how we can avoid Reich's error, for he was counting on a natural motor space, and he thus naturalized the drive by classifying subjects according to their masturbatory gestures.

Landauer's categories call for further discussion, for they do not coincide precisely with the ones Freud defined in "Instincts and Their Vicissitudes." The change of regime of jouissance through the structuration of an instinctual topology may be summarized as follows: The love object becomes the subject of another pleasure. The term "subject" thus links the source and the instinct. This elimination of reference to the economic order of a demand for work[16] goes hand in hand, perhaps, with the new way of conceptualizing the dimension of movement: a topological representation seems more appropriate for describing actual movements and symbolic trajectories, for describing that space, at once imaginary and real, in which jouissance is structured. An energetistic model could not indicate its metaphorical character except by multiplying the paradoxes, and even so the paradoxes would not succeed in distinguishing what is different.[17]

The Pleasure Principle and the Reality Principle Redefined

To return to the problem of hysterical conversion by identifying it as a certain moment in the history of motor excitation, we shall emphasize what may be the most crucial point in Landauer's article: the passage from the pleasure principle to the reality principle cannot be understood without an analytical description of the order of movement and the unconscious thought that is structured in it. Here again, Landauer needs clarification when he characterizes the autoerotic scenarios described by the drive as sadistic or occasionally as fetishistic: the role of the object is decisive in the self-limitation of movements not because of its fixity but because of its precarious presence. In the case most recently cited, Landauer hesi-

16. Cf. Jean Laplanche, *Life and Death in Psychoanalysis*, trans. Jeffrey Mehlman (Baltimore: Johns Hopkins University Press, 1976), p. 10.

17. It will be recalled that the schemas of regression do not allow us to distinguish dreams from sleepwalking, or sleepwalking from hysterical symptoms.

tates before identifying the object: Does it consist in the palm of the hand and the fingers that twist the hair or in the relation between the two? Moreover, he recognizes that it is not always as easy to determine the initial object of the drive as it is here. And even here, the passage from the first object, the mouth, to the second, the hair, comes about only by way of a detour: while the palm of her hand was playing with her mouth, the little girl imprinted small movements on her fingers, which were free to move about, and on her elbow and shoulder joints. When her mouth was busy elsewhere, with the maternal breast or later with food, she scratched the outside surface of her right thigh and bottom with small athetosic movements, injuring herself in the process. Landauer speaks here of autosadism or rather of a sadism of the right hand directed against the thigh and buttocks.

The importance of the type of object relation that structures movement becomes even clearer when Landauer refers to certain montages as *fetishism* rather than autoeroticism. One eight-week-old infant habitually used his left hand for athetosic play with the corner of a pillow while he was sucking his right hand. When the child was four years old, the corner of a handkerchief sticking out of his pocket replaced the pillow. Landauer doubts that this is an instance of objectless pleasure activity.[18] But what status does the object have for him, if he can call this inflection of movements fetishistic? In the other case he describes, the object implies a change of regime of the instinct, by the self-limitation that instigates rhythms; some jouissance is lost, and the object, far from recovering it, allows it to be lost. The object allows this removal of jouissance by circumscribing a loss. In this sense the object in the organization of movement allows the reality principle to be instituted. The void does not swallow up the subject; the void has a configuration, but the presence of the object presupposes that it is not denied. The fetishist plays with the reality principle by expecting the object not to give some configuration to the void but to replace in reality the lost jouissance. As Serge Leclaire indicates, for example, the object always has an ambiguous status in the organization of desire.[19] In one sense, the object makes it possible to give up some jouissance; it is the instrument of a loss. In another sense, it

18. "Die kindliche Bewegungsunruhe," p. 384.
19. *Psychanalyser* (Paris: Seuil, 1968), chap. 5, pp. 79 ff.

seals off the very process of that loss. In the fetishism of the example cited, the moment of the object is the moment in which movement congeals, in which it attempts to deny—in a motor judgment, as Freud would say—what there is by way of loss in the transformation of the *lustvolle Entäusserung*. Once again, the phenomenon of fetishism, a perversion of the objectal function, clarifies the so-called normal process in its ambiguity. Every rhythmic movement and every erotic scenario bears the mark of a charmed-away threat of loss of self; the object arrests and circumscribes the uprooting that is never lacking in experiences of jouissance, especially in the sexual act, where the plasticity of movements may represent a refined elaboration of this release of the subject. If we relate this example to the example of art, we find confirmation that in art too an arrangement is set up between the pleasure principle and the reality principle on the terrain of modeling, of movements. In "Formulations on the Two Principles of Mental Functioning" (*SE* 12:218–26), Freud designates in art a way for the subject to develop his own delusion even as he constitutes a language work in which others will be able to see themselves, a work that exorcises insanity, somewhat as the fetishist does. By conniving with the reality principle, the fetishist copes better than the neurotic does, since he manages to turn his symptom into an instrument of speech that can be addressed to others instead of being consumed in an unending solitary jouissance. Now art is indeed the terrain of a thought of the body, in the sense in which eroticism elaborates a thought of the body.

Landauer's remark on the fetishism of certain instinctual montages—the object at any price, the derisory and absurd object— sheds some light on Freud's text on negation. The passage from the pleasure principle to the reality principle remains quite obscure, in fact, in Freud's study, as long as it is not related to the terrain on which it operates, on which that structuration of judgment can concern the subject: the order of movement. We can thus understand the strange paragraph in which Freud, who held on to an intellectualist conception of judgments of attribution and existence at the cost of a certain obscurity, jumps suddenly into motion—a curious leap into the organic: "Judging is the intellectual action which decides the choice of motor action, which puts an end to the postponement due to thought and which leads over from thinking to action. . . . It is to be regarded as an experimental action, a motor palpating, with small expenditure of discharge. Let us consider where the ego has used a similar kind of palpating before, at what place it learnt the technique which it now applies in its processes of thought. It happened at the sensory end of the mental apparatus, in connection with sense perceptions. For, on our hypothesis, perception is not a purely passive process. The ego periodically sends out small amounts of cathexis into the perceptual system, by means of which it samples the external stimuli, and then after every such tentative advance it draws back again" (*SE* 19:238).

Thought and perception, from the analytic viewpoint, are thus never anything but ways of experimenting, "palpating," groping. This is not intended as a witticism, or rather it is indeed a witticism, but one that brings to the surface the true terrain of the unconscious in any work of thought. If, instead of applying physiological schemata to the motor order, we identify the dimension of movement in the unconscious, we shall find that, in any intellectual work, in every work of language, there is elaborated, "under" the meaning or the logical content of the discourse, an instinctual space, a topology of the body that supports these thoughts and makes it necessary for a subject to produce them.

If we follow the Lacanian interpretation[20] of the process of negation, *Verneinung*, we discover something unclear in Freud's text. The passage from the pleasure principle to the reality principle is not achieved, for the exterior constituted on the basis of the judgment of attribution, the *Entäusserung*, the *Ausstossung aus sich* does not prepare the second exterior, the exterior of reality in which the object elaborated in fantasy is sought (so as not to be found again, so as to be able to elaborate itself as a lost object). How do the two exteriors come to coincide, to be identified with each other, given that in Freud's analysis they remain heterogeneous and their identity is required, not demonstrated?

It is probably fair to reply as follows: A specific operation of the subject must recreate absence. It is not enough for absence to *be*, as in the judgment of attribution; absence has to be symbolized. In the field of primary affirmation and exteriorization, everything holds steady: presence and absence stem only from the order of fact. That

20. "Réponse au commentaire de Jean Hyppolite," in *Ecrits* (Paris: Seuil, 1966), pp. 387–89.

is why presence, like emptiness, is so threatening; that is why pleasure is almost confused with pain, as Landauer said of the *lustvolle* Entäusserung. Unless the subject is to remain without recourse, an operation is required that creates absence outside and inside the subject, in an outside and an inside that are not yet the solidary objective and subjective entities of the judgment of existence. The operation that changes the status of the outside, thus of lack, would be the primary repression: where the subject symbolizes absence, not creating it, since it is there, but constituting himself as if not knowing, the real lack of signifier in reality is transmuted into symbolic lack. Be that as it may. Analysis does indicate that the place of castration is the forbidden, is language. But analysis does not say how the subject's body is related to that place. Freud's text, up to the passage on thinking as experimenting and palpating, had intellectualist accents—it was not clear how jouissance is involved in judgment. The Lacanian reading allows us to advance only if we designate the terrain of the subject's involvement by the symbolization of lack, which gives him not a guarantee, as the fetishist believes, but a recourse. This terrain is that of the topographical structuration of the drive in what Landauer describes: the self-limitation of movements that create a space in which to circumscribe jouissance, to construct a body. Motor judgment is the symbolic operation in which the subject accedes to the signifier of the lack of signifier.

To be sure, the subject is constituted by being "split open again by the signifier," but this would not come about for the subject by virtue of the pure logical necessity of the operation. That the subject has a part to play in the operation in question presupposes that a space of his jouissance exists in which that resplitting takes effect, that there is some material of which the jouissance is made. Lacking this, the opening of the erotogenic zones, the formation of gaps of pleasure by the letter-bearing finger,[21] instead of introducing the subject to the vivacity of pleasure, would remain dead letters.

This space of jouissance corresponds to what Freud designates by his repeated references to motion, whether he is alluding to motor innervation in hysteria or to motor symbolism in obsessional neurosis. To say that the reality principle is a modification of the pleasure principle, that it limits pleasure even while serving it, is

21. See Serge Leclaire's formulations in *Psychanalyser*, p. 72.

conceivable only if there exists a place where that self-limitation can be carried out. And this place must be a place produced by movements, since, as Serge Leclaire says, jouissance can exist only in a body. But although he shows clearly how that body is determined by the signifiers of a jouissance that comes from the Other, Leclaire does not adequately set forth the coordinates and proprieties of the bodily space in question.

To designate that space or place is not to fail to recognize that the subject is formed in the place of the Other. Landauer indicates in his article that the first movement of the left hand is organized, finds a rhythm, when a neologism resembling a cry—"Reireirei"—is constituted. This meaningless cry attests that the self-limitation of motor excitation is the terrain where the body begins to symbolize itself and to structure itself as imaginary space; the complex relations of meaning and nonmeaning are conjointly elaborated in the later organization of movements. Landauer describes the role of the people who play with the child as decisive for the instinct's change of object and for the transformation of the little girl's first speech sounds (*muss mal reien*) into a sentence. The Lacanian recommencement of psychoanalysis, which starts from the symbolic order for its understanding of the way a subject is formed, makes it possible for us to stop confusing the dimension of movement with the physiological dimension. In a second stage, it behooves us to take a different sort of look at movement and to reread the Freudian energetics in another way: in essence, we shall be reading a discourse on jouissance and the body as Reality.

Body and Language in Symptom Formations

While Landauer makes fairly clear the sense in which infantile motor excitation designates the terrain of jouissance, he also wants this to be the model for every unconscious organization of the motor order. Now the exemplarity of this model is not self-evident. If we were to go along with Landauer, we would readily yield to the illusions that are attendant upon the consideration of origins in psychoanalysis, where the elements that make it possible to understand the structuration in question are all given in advance. Landauer sees all forms of motor excitation that can be identified in the adult as *vestiges* of a primordial anxiety; favorite postures, bearing, the specific movements of each subject in daily life and in his or her erotic practices, symptoms, and tics—all these appear as so many repetitions of the inaugural moment, although it is hard to see how they reorganize it. Not that Landauer neglects that question, for he asks himself at what point the love objects of a playful hand— hair (in the case cited), a pillow, a handkerchief, a watch chain, a nose—acquire genital signification. They symbolize the penis; Freud says so.[22] But Landauer fails to answer his own question. How might it be restated?

If jouissance is initially structured by the formation of a spatial compromise between the void onto which the drive opens and the dream of an object that would fill it, does this first structuration survive, without supplement and uniformly, in everything that Landauer cited pell-mell? In particular, what does it become in the formation of the hysterical symptom, in obsessional motor symptoms, and in tics? How does the creation of a body space come to be articulated with the Oedipal prohibitions? How does a verbal construction determine that space? It seems that, especially in these three cases, the status of the body is not identical, if we use the term body for the spatiality described by motor excitation. One may infer from Landauer's work that the imaginary in the Lacanian sense refers not only to a seizing by the image, but also to the plastic elaboration that gives a configuration to a subject's jouissance. Nevertheless, does this field where the logic of desire "takes" have the same importance in the outcome of every neurosis? Does its reality weigh as heavily in the hysterical Darstellung, which seems to "go too far" on the terrain of movements, and in obsessional cancellations, which on the contrary attempt to free themselves hastily from that motor imaginary? Our hypothesis holds hysteria to be a plastic suspension [*obstination*] of the erotic body, and obsessional neurosis to be an awkwardness that eradicates, in the name of the demands of the symbolic, the terrain where the symbols are exercised.

Outcome of Motor Excitation in Guilt

As these outcomes are sorted out, the determining moment is decidedly that of prohibition. It is as if motor excitation faced certain tests: that of its own structuration by self-limitation, and

22. Landauer, "Die kindliche Bewegungsunruhe," p. 385.

that of another limitation that, far from instituting a space defined by rhythms, demands the bracketing of the rhythmic exercises. It is no longer a question here of a ruse internal to the dimension of movement and of the imaginary, but of an order that commands that dimension—the dimension elaborated with such difficulty—to cease functioning in some measure. In this sense symbolic castration is an actual loss of jouissance: the prohibitions require that something disappear from this jouissance, which is unsatisfying in the end, but which did find a terrain. Through castration, the body changes status. Tausk sheds light upon this when he posits that *guilt in the masturbatory crisis is formed on the terrain of anxiety.* "Anxiety, at first a floating feeling of insecurity and oppression, is rationalized, that is, linked to a representation of which the anxiety-producing signification is valid for the judging consciousness. This representation is borrowed from the punishment complex and it maintains *a direct relation* with the experiences of early childhood, determined by the sadistic exteriorizations of the child. Anxiety thus linked is guilt [1912]."[23]

That we regularly find incestuous desires "underneath" guilt signifies that motor excitation, the terrain of jouissance, is also that of guilt. This constitutes the articulation of body and language whose modalities we have been seeking to pin down from the beginning of our study. Starting from the onset of autoeroticism, anxiety is the apprehension of a bodily incompleteness with respect to jouissance, to motor excitation associated with individuation and with the absence of a truly satisfying object. During the entire period known as pre-Oedipal, the instinctual organization elaborates this anxiety but does not suppress it. Tausk said that the masturbatory crisis comes from an excess of anxiety in relation to what may be calmed by it. Castration transforms into prohibition the lack of satisfaction linked to motor excitation. Anxiety then consists in the apprehension of a prohibition of being, bearing upon something in the body.

This moment that structures desire is not, as Sadger would have it, the one in which masturbation, at first purely somatic, would become psychical, for the creation of an imaginary and real space for the drive does not stem from the physical or the physiological, these terms being equivalent here to "somatic," since they are

23. *Die Onanie*, p. 61; emphasis added.

opposed to "psychical." The lack in autoeroticism consists in the subject's persistent lack of satisfaction; desire is as if suspended, waiting for something that will transform it, for it lacks the resources to undertake to transform itself; desire is not physical. And *since the terrain on which guilt is elaborated is anxiety itself, in castration we do not pass from the corporal to the mental.* It is important to note how Freud's thought here exceeds the categories of metaphysics, for this is not always self-evident: the imaginary and the symbolic are not body and soul.

The only grain of truth in the idea of a passage from corporal masturbation to psychical masturbation is that a change of regime of jouissance is produced. In a sense, to understand castration we have to start with the body and show that anxiety is the terrain of guilt that otherwise would never "take," would not involve the subject. In another sense, however, it is indeed from the symbolic, from the prohibited that we have to start, since desire does not really exist without the prohibition that offers it another terrain, that lets go and displaces the terrain of the instinctual topology where desire vegetates in autoeroticism. The trick of the symbolic is to extort, to draw out of motor excitation an actual loss of jouissance. The object of castration is real, since the motor imaginary of the drive is imbued with jouissance. But at the same time this transposition of anxiety into guilt makes it change register. From the motor imaginary, guilt passes into the symbolic; the symbolic transforms the dimension of movement.

This grasping of the order of movement in the symbolic constitutes the operation of primary repression inasmuch as the subject is constituted by the jouissance that escapes it in the process. From this viewpoint, the prohibition is what produces the loss of jouissance; and the fact that the body is determined by the signifier presupposes that the appearance of the subject is correlative of a nonknowledge. Tausk too suggested this: "The content of guilt is an actual [*wirklich*] fault against an unconscious demand." We must be dealing here with the unknown, the unconscious, since the demand that transforms the child's anxiety comes only from the resources proper to his own autoerotic jouissance. This jouissance finds itself put in another place, *aufgehoben*, as Hegel would say; in Lacanian terms, it is resplit in the advent of the subject.

During the masturbatory crisis, motor excitation becomes hysteria or obsessional neurosis, depending on whether or not the anxiety is transposed into the tissue of guilt—the effects of the prohibition.

What characterizes obsessional neurosis is severance from the instinctual source, whose prohibited portion is transferred elsewhere. To be sure, the subject continues to experience enjoyment in her own body, but under the influence of the prohibition her erotogenic zones emigrate into certain fields of reality that they colonize.

Transformation of motor excitation into guilt and metaphorization of the erotogenic zones go hand in hand;[24] Freud shows in detail that, in his masturbatory experiences, the Rat Man is seeking the paternal interdiction, taking the risk of playing at transgression. The structural element common to such varied occasions is even what induced him to masturbate (*SE* 10:211–12). The element of obsessional neurosis is not the figuration of an impossible incest, but the crossing of the threshold of its prohibition. Jouissance here seeks to limit itself according to the second modality defined, by turning the erotogenic zones into forbidden places of immediate jouissance. Anal eroticism continues to be the place of a horrible jouissance unknown to the patient himself. But along with a return of the repressed, the "rat complex" is an attempt to delay jouissance, to turn it aside.

Signifying games ensure the incorporation of the anal erotogenic zone into the paternal tradition. The place of the body turns out to be concerned in a specific way with the symbolic, at the very time when, even though it remains an erotogenic zone, it is released by jouissance, as it were. Freud thus describes how, through the captain's narrative of the rat torture, the tradition is articulated with the instinctual circuit: "The presumption was that it was a question of 'complexive sensitiveness,' and that the speeches had jarred upon certain hyperaesthetic spots in his unconscious" (*SE* 10:210). The metonymic substitution of *Rate* and *Spielratte* for *Ratte* does not originate the day the captain tells his tale; it activates what already remained in suspension in the relation of the anal zone to the patient's history. And this is so because this scenario rejoins the

24. We are using the term *metaphor* here in the most general sense of symbolic transposition. It then becomes necessary to spell out the modalities of this passage of the body into the symbolic order.

structure by putting the theme of prohibition, of punishment, into play: what gives the patient jouissance as he listens to his captain is that torture and punishment (*Strafe*) are involved (pp. 166, 213) in that remote practice; the crime that provoked it, moreover, is not known—an ignorance that corresponds also to the position of the subject caught up, without knowing how, in his father's unpaid debt—nor is it known just how far the debt extends. This seizure of an erotogenic zone in a prohibition corresponds exactly to Tausk's description: the content of the guilty consciousness is an actual, authentic failure to comply with an unknown (*unbewusst*) demand. The identification with a demand that is impossible to pin down and that perpetuates the child's love for his parents can come to consciousness only as desire; it is precisely as an imperative coming from the parents that it is unconscious. Thus the Rat Man may find again, in fragmentary memories and in transference, his desire and his hatred for his father: his father is the one he calls for, after the latter's death, to show him how he is obeying him in preparing for examinations, so as to please him, that very father whose anger he is at the same time courting by exposing his penis to his father's gaze.

The recent masturbatory scenario is not unrelated to the anal complex, since the patient's misconduct and rudeness toward his father had begun on the occasion of a memorable physical punishment. Anality and the equivalence of penis, rats, and children, identified by Freud as one of the directions of the complex, have the function of forming scar tissue over what remains unresolved in the masturbation the patient addressed to his father. But that appeal to the forbidden is aggravated as it gets caught up in the unpayable debt that the father himself had contracted. Nothing has been really settled in this erotic appeal to the father, who observed merely that he must never repeat that physical punishment: surprised by his son's great violence, he judged it better for everyone that what was at stake be left in obscurity (*SE* 10:205). In the son's story, anal eroticism is indeed, as Tausk said, laden with the unresolved phallic problematic.

The articulation of that problematic with the infantile erotogenic zones differs from what is found in hysteria, however. We would do well to compare the syntax and semantics of the symptom in the two cases. Dora had learned at a very early stage to use the term catarrh for the disgust with sexual genitality that had spilled over onto the order of her earlier oral jouissance: very early, which is to say at the time of her stay at Franzensbad with her mother, who was suffering from a sexual disorder. Dora's repudiation of sex, that filthy illness, had crystallized in the term catarrh, which is thus the analogue of the series *Ratte-Spielratte-Hofrat* for the Rat Man.

Toward a Syntactic and Semantic Analysis of the Motor Order

But the articulation of language with the erotogenic body is produced in two syntactically different ways in the two cases, and the symptom cannot uniformly be said to be metaphoric in nature. In Dora's case the word "catarrh" alludes to sperm, immediately identified with the flow from infectious genital ailments that, through her father, also afflicted her mother. The learned term "catarrh," a metaphor for flow, allows the registers of sperm, genitality-illness, and orality to be confused and finally to be crushed under the jouissance of the dominant oral symptom. The term operates what is called displacement from the lower to the upper regions, by concentrating all of Dora's erotic life in her mouth and throat—her stomach, her sex organs, and even her urethra are condemned to nonexistence. The metaphor here reorganizes places in the body; it represses some of them and transforms the other into an abyss for jouissance, but it does not, according to the expression we have proposed, cause certain erotogenic zones to emigrate into fields of reality. Hysteria here uses the signifier's resources even as it contests them, in such a way that language does not have a castrating, prohibiting function.[25] Tausk says almost nothing about this case, since in the sole outcome of masturbation that he describes the forbidden is articulated with the body. If, in hysteria, symptoms are metaphors, is it not in the sense in which metaphor eludes the prohibitory function of language? Metaphor, or a certain type of metaphor. To be sure, there are metaphors in the organization of the Rat Man's symptom, but it seems as though the symbolization of the erotogenic zones in that case first follows a metonymic line in the double sense that may be accorded that term: according to Maurice Le Guern,[26] metonymy is the linguistic transcription of a substitution involving the referent. And in psychoanalysis the entire

25. This question is taken up again in the Conclusion.
26. Maurice Le Guern, *Sémantique de la métaphore et de la métonymie* (Paris: Larousse Université, 1973), pp. 23 ff.

problematic of support can be based on this conception of meto-nymy.[27] The second meaning of metonymy, to which we referred in analyzing Dora's second dream, makes it an intralinguistic pro-cess, on the contrary, and an intrasymbolic one, in the sense that only a letter game opens up the proper space for expressing the lack,[28] a space that is not a referential space, but the space of a body that traverses the second transformation described, the one in which unsatisfaction is changed into prohibition. To bring out the differ-ence between hysterical metaphorization and castrating metonymy, one might imagine that, if Dora had not interrupted her analysis with Freud after the second dream, she would have become inter-ested in meetings in intersections of stations and cemeteries, or in novels that use these sites as settings.

Specificity of the Metaphor in Hysterical Conversion

This weak theoretical fiction has as its aim the reformulation of what Freud says about motion in hysteria and obsessional neurosis, by considering the syntax and semantics of symptoms: "In thus degrading a process of satisfaction to a symptom, repression dis-plays its power in a further respect. The substitutive process is prevented, if possible, from finding discharge through motility; and even if this cannot be done, the process is forced to expend itself in making alterations in the subject's own body and is not permitted to impinge upon the external world. It must not be transformed into action" (*SE* 20:95).

That conception of adequate action, in which modification of the external world would allow a timely discharge, confuses the spa-tiality of the drive with an elementary biological schema and with the naive perception of inside and outside. It is difficult, in this framework, not to imagine motion, in short, as turned toward the inside of the body in hysteria and toward the outside, toward the "word," in the object relation or in obsessional neurosis. Yet this precludes an analytic conception of the dimension of movement. Expressions of autoplastic activity and alloplastic activity often partake of the same confusion.[29] If, on the contrary, the motor

27. See especially Laplanche, *Life and Death in Psychoanalysis*, pp. 8–24.
28. See above, pp. 136–138.
29. See, for example, Melitta Sperling, "Conversion Hysteria and Conversion Symptoms: A Revision of Classification and Concepts," in Index Medicus, *American Journal of Psychoanalysis*, pp. 745–70.

order is conceived metapsychologically, as we have tried to do in rereading Landauer's article, it is possible to determine by what specific semantic and syntactic plays the motor excitation of the erotogenic zones is shaped at the end of the masturbatory crisis. It is this approach that leads us back to metonymy and metaphor: Is there really, in hysteria, representation of anxiety? The operant metaphor of catarrh, here, by achieving an extreme condensation of Dora's erotic life, invents in language a formula that avoids the dangers of expressing jouissance. Perhaps it would be appropriate to wonder whether that use of the metaphor does not characterize the relation of hysterics to discourse in a more general fashion, their competence at discounting the signifier, even when—especially when—they are exploiting its resources. We would have to go back to what Michèle Montrelay says about the regular cancellation of the name of the father that rhythmically marks the discourse of her patient Cécile.[30] The hysterical use of metaphor perhaps also accounts, at least in part, for a common feminine attitude that consists in adopting the rigor and demands of philosophy only to shed them at certain discursive moments by using stylistic figures that organize the mockery of these features, figures whose syntax and semantics merit study. Hysterical theatricalization, the conversion of the conceptual into a display by way of a linguistic pirouette that suddenly subjectivizes the "rigor" of a development, would be one version of hysterical metaphor, in the field of discursive practices. As far as the symptom is concerned, it is formed by the caricature of what may be the grasping of an erotogenic zone in the symbolic order. It is important to note that in fact the hysteric maintains close proximity to the castration she is avoiding.

Her terrain is not that of motor excitation in general. It is frequently argued that there is no regression in hysteria. In hysteria, in any event, there is no sadistic-anal regression, and the intense oral cathexis is always developed in phallic significations: Dora's treatment begins with the analysis of the oral figuration of coitus betrayed by her lapsus concerning her father's impotence, which she confirms to Freud by pointing out that one can make love in nongenital ways. One might even say that, by seeking the impossible, by seeking to represent sexual difference and thus spending her life wondering if he (or she) is a man or a woman, a hysteric is

30. *L'ombre et le nom*, p. 32.

"closer" to castration than an obsessional patient, who displaces the specific question of difference toward the question of hierarchy and aggression. Freud first differentiated hysterics and obsessionals[31] by positing that the obsessional symptom represented the reality of a sexual experience and its prohibition, whereas hysteria would be limited to a rejection of jouissance in the mode of disgust. If that radical refusal were not as close as possible to what it excludes, it would be hard to understand why Freud added that the hysterical symptom is also self-punishment.

It seems that the catarrh metaphor and the extreme overdetermination of the oral symptom reveal the syntacticosemantic device that forms the paradoxical exclusion of sexual difference, which does not leave the terrain of that metaphor. That metaphor alone allows the *Miterregung*, Dora's overhearing of her parents' intercourse, to be absorbed by the archaic orality whose paternal signification is all we perceive in Freud's text, but which also plunges its roots into a catastrophic relation to the mother. That everything may be indistinct, that oral pleasure may be the same in the relation to the father and to the mother—in the way the illness that comes from the father contaminated the mother by effacing the distinction between sex roles, confusing the roles in the filthiness of what drips and flows—such is the order Dora assigned to her body, in the style of a mockery of the prohibition. Far from making the infantile erotogenic zones pass into the symbolic, far from drawing from them a loss of jouissance, metaphoric games in hysteria confirm these zones in their role of abyss for jouissance.

Freud wrote in 1905 that the formation of hysterogenic zones does not follow a course different from that of the erotogenic zones in general, since, in polymorphous perversity, the genitalization of certain places in the body and the exclusion of other zones is commonplace.[32] Freud was targeting here the modifications of innervation and sensations of which an erotogenic zone is the impact point, and he gave erection as a model. This formulation reinforces the

---

31. Letter to Wilhelm Fliess, October 8, 1895, in *The Complete Letters of Sigmund Freud to Wilhelm Fliess, 1887–1904*, trans. and ed. Jeffrey Moussaieff Masson (Cambridge, Mass., Belknap Press, 1985), pp. 140–42.

32. *SE* 7:168. Lacan takes up this idea in *Four Fundamental Concepts*, and in the unpublished "Séminaire sur l'angoisse," December 19, 1962, where he shows, in a discussion of Ferenczi, that the genital organs themselves, paradoxically, have the status of hysterogenic zones.

mysteries pertaining to the theory of conversion, if we take at face value the exemplarity of erection with regard to all phenomena of erotogenization. It is exemplary with this proviso: that erection is a model of erotogeneity only if one seeks to define motor excitation by visual evidence. On the contrary, when one conceptualizes the activity of erotogenic zones on the basis of the motor structuration of instincts, under the confused notion of innervation must be understood the imaginary figuration described by the motor arrangements of the parts of the body involved. Erection is the exclusive model for erotogeneity only if the spatiality of the drive is confused with what one sees. Some spatial organizations cannot be defined by simple perceptual markers; the erotogenic body is one of these.

No doubt that does not mean *any visual order* may simply be excluded from the representation of castration. To conceptualize hysterical conversion implies, on the contrary, the determination of another space of visibility of the body and of the genitals. And nothing says that hysteria sums up in itself every modality of intervention of the body and of seeing in the unconscious; the orders of spatiality doubtless have to be multiplied to account for various phenomena. Thus Pierre Fédida suggests confronting hysteria with "the sort of verbal hallucination of the organ in speech" that is specific to the hypochondriacal position.[33] And the value he accords the genital model subverts what we have been calling simple perceptual markers. Penile erection takes on an exemplary function only for the internal projection, akin, in hypochondria, to the screen lacking in surface and depth of the dream, where the somatic finds its interpretation. In hysteria, the visibility of the body concerns less that internal screen—where the hypochondriac confronts his own death and the "archaic body of his terror and his distress" (p. 230)—than a sort of external screen that is built by motor excitation and on which the subject attempts to represent himself as total body. It is remarkable that in Dora's case projection is not associated with the Darstellung of desire. We had used the term projection for Dora's interpretation of sexual relations in terms of filth and illness, an interpretation that allows her to avoid having to express her own place in that genealogy. Her passion for seeing,

33. "L'hypocondrie du rêve," *Nouvelle Revue de Psychanalyse* 5 (1972): 232–36.

which nourishes her love for the adorable Dresden Madonna, is exercised in a direction other than the construction of a projective defensive system: the moment of the picture or the statue is the moment when the dimension of movement finds its goal and fixates itself in an image of the death of desire that also constitutes an approach to death different from that of the hypochondriac.

It is appropriate, then, to distinguish screen function from figuration; and as a condition for doing so, we must dissipate the confusion that identifies instinctual spatiality not only with that of ordinary vision, but also with the body space constructed by physiology. The notion of innervation in Freud arises from the epistemological confusion that, in turn, prevents an understanding of the relation that the erotogenic zones maintain with the hysterogenic zones.

To be sure, the body of every subject is formed historically through the cathexis of certain bodily sites and the exclusion of other sites: this phenomenon is obvious in hysteria. But if we pursue the argument of this study, we find the following:

1. The cathexis of certain sites consists in the symbolization of these sites, by their real and imaginary figuration in movements of *self-limitation* and by their capture within the order of the forbidden and of absence. The positive term of cathexis thus corresponds to the fact that a given site comes to exist for the subject, is "cathected," in order to limit anxiety plastically and to signify a place of the body as lacking in jouissance. We cannot be certain, under these conditions, that erection remains uniquely exemplary, even in the paradoxical mode of representing the limited reality of the penis. The example of Dora's second dream suggests that there are other ways of signifying lack besides representing it in a plenitude marked with the seal of castration. Why is symbolic castration more "itself" when it is seen? Affirming this perhaps denotes "the small trait of hysteria which is regularly to be found" (*SE* 17:75)[34] in masculine discourse on castration.

2. Conversely, the exclusion, the repression of certain areas of the body can, in fact, be translated by the omnipresence and the omni-functionality of certain others, which serve as abysses for jouissance.

34. Freud's expression for the Wolf Man's constipation.

Counterproof: The Problem of Tics

Now that these details have been spelled out, we need to indicate the specific way the erotogenic body is formed in hysteria. We shall continue to pursue the contrast between hysteria and obsessional neurosis by considering an extreme case that gave rise to important discussions among Ferenczi, Abraham, and Melanie Klein:[35] the case of tics.

Tics are intuitively classified as motor symptoms: an erotic activity played out on and by way of the body, a tic seems to have the same status as an autoplastic hysterical symptom. Obsessional acts such as the Rat Man's hesitations are, on the other hand, called alloplastic; they are oriented toward objects external to the body. The repetitive stereotype of tics, however, relates them to obsessional compulsions rather than to the course of hysterical symptoms, which are more fixated in "illnesses" and more dependent upon crises or attacks. If we do not go beyond the bounds of this description, we shall have difficulty settling the question. We might well ask how the authors we have cited handled it.

In view of the fact that tics involve the body and that they are not subject to the same analysis as the other symptoms, Ferenczi identified them as narcissistic affections plugged directly into an organic shock, since he found no psychic trauma associated with the symptom, unlike what is observed in hysteria. Throughout this first elaboration, the biological body and the unconscious body are continually confused. Although he cites Dora's case, Ferenczi does not allow for the redefinition of motion that we are seeking on the basis of the syntax of the symptom. The catarrh figures in his text as an expression associated with a nervous cough, at first coincidentally. This view loses sight of the progress Freud made when he inverted the order of factors—instead of seeing the symptom of conversion grafted onto a preexisting organic problem, Freud saw functional difficulties like the catarrh persevering because they reactivate the infantile erotogenic zones. Furthermore, the association-

35. Sandor Ferenczi, "Psychoanalytische Betrachtungen über den Tic," *Internationale Zeitschrift für Psychoanalyse*, 1921, pp. 33–62; Karl Abraham, "Erörterung über den Tic," *Internationale Zeitschrift für Psychoanalyse*, 1921; Melanie Klein, "Zur Genese des Tics," *Internationale Zeitschrift für Psychoanalyse*, 1925, pp. 332–49, translated as "A Contribution to the Psychogenesis of Tics," in *Contributions to Psycho-Analysis, 1921–1945* (London: Hogarth Press, 1948), pp. 117–39.

ist notion of conversion fails to illuminate the metaphorical device
of hysteria.

A year later (1922), Karl Abraham countered Ferenczi with the
argument that tics stem not from narcissism but from the sadistic-
anal object relation; Melanie Klein pursued the same argument in
1925.

A tic is a "conversive symptom at the sadistic-anal level," Abraham suggests; and when Melanie Klein takes up the same thesis she
specifies that it is unanalyzable only as long as it remains unanalyzed. She also insists that tics are inscribed in a different narcissism from that of the psychoses, the one with which Ferenczi
conflated it. This notation would suffice to call up a confrontation
with hysteria if Abraham's astonishing formula had not already
done so: if conversion at the sadistic-anal stage exists, must we not
give up characterizing hysterical neurosis by conversion as we have
done from the start? By insisting on redefining conversion as a
precipitation of jouissance in a motor figuration where a body is
fixated at the point of wanting to enclose sexual difference, we are
positing the homogeneity of content and form in the symptom.
One does not choose conversion to elaborate any aspect of desire
whatever, any more than the plastic arts can claim to produce the
same type of thought as spoken language. In the chapter of *The
Interpretation of Dreams* where Freud states this principle,[36] he also
confronts the issue of the feelings of inhibition felt in dreams.
Instead of the dream content's expressing anxiety, here the dream
material takes it over. This should tell us something about the desire
that is expressed in that form: depending on whether anxiety figures
in the dream content or in the dream material, a different psychic
action is produced. Otherwise how could we account for the fact
that we do not always have the impression of "not managing"
when we dream? For the same reason, conversion is not a mechanism that would be indifferent to its content and that could change
register. What are called form and content in the plastic arts correspond to material and content in dreams and symptoms. The for-
mal material that the hysteric uses—*movements that can describe a
scene that is on display*—are the same thing as the content of the
symptom: thinking of incest as impossible, wanting to actualize
sexual difference in a spatial order, and through the body, so as to

36. On this point, and on this text we have already quoted, see above, p. 113.

171

avoid having to express it. The figuration of fantasies by projection onto motility is at the service of the effort to relegate the prohibition to the unactualizable of which the subject has become the actor.

Abraham's refinement raises a real question for this conception of hysteria: if the tic is a conversive symptom at the sadistic-anal level, one may also say that hysteria is a genital tic. Any fantasy in its content could borrow any symptomatic material whatever, and it would indeed be a matter of borrowing, since the form would not be the content itself.

Where does this leave the tic? It seems first of all that for Felix, Melanie Klein's patient, the tic attempts such a motor figuration and that, just like the hysteric symptom, it is a continuation of masturbation by other means. The tic had appeared a few months before the analysis, when Felix was thirteen, and it included three phases. "At the beginning, Felix had a feeling as though the depression in his neck, under the back of his head, were being torn. In consequence of this feeling he felt constrained first to throw his head back and then to rotate it from right to left. The second movement was accompanied by a feeling that something was cracking loudly. The concluding phase consisted of a third movement in which the chin was pressed as deeply as possible downwards."

This tic alludes directly to his overhearing an instance of parental intercourse. In its three phases, and in the repetition that led him to produce the tic three times in a row, Melanie Klein identifies the realization of three sexual positions: the passive role of the mother, the passive role of Felix's own ego, and the active role of the father. "The passive roles were represented predominantly by the first two movements; though in the feeling of 'cracking' was contained also the sadistic element representing the active role of the father, an element which came to fuller expression in the third movement, that of drilling into something."

In one sense it is hard to imagine a better bisexual realization, which should thus allude to a hysterical fantasy, according to the terms Freud adopted in 1908. These three roles refer to three identificatory directions; Felix takes his mother's place with respect to his father. The fantasy is dissimulated in the ambiguity of the second movement, which realizes an active homosexual attitude in which Felix chooses himself as love object. Finally, the third movement reveals a heterosexual fantasy, in an original identification with the father. These correspondences are established through the results of association: the third identification had been manifested by a precocious love of singing, which imitated the father's sounds during intercourse. This love of singing had succumbed to repression, under the influence of a castration anxiety activated by the father's return after the war and by an operation on the foreskin, which had oriented the narcissistic development of homosexuality (the second phase of the tic). Melanie Klein is actually less specific as to the identification with the mother that is realized by the first phase of the tic; and the picture does not stress bisexuality properly speaking so much as a conflict between a narcissistic homosexuality and the heterosexuality that was submerged early on.

This tic, which takes place in a region quite close to the one that Dora's desire cathects, does not constitute an oral symptom and does not function like what we have called an abyss for jouissance. Through associations, the tic appears as the congealing of anal fantasies that do not "adhere" to the upper body with the same fastness as hysteric orality, *that is*, they do not conflate the circuit of the drives with the body by virtue of metaphors, like Dora's catarrh. Let us clear the ground here: Melanie Klein does indicate that Felix had felt "thrown backward" [*rejeté en arrière*] by his father and by his classmates, but she does not present the relationship between this "tossing away" or rejection and that of his shoulders as the axis of a motor expression of rejection. It must be noted, however, that here the metaphor does not go very far. The movement of the shoulders presentifies a popular expression, but without much stylistic affectation, without any plastic ingenuity; and in particular this presentified rejection does not serve to express everything, to represent everything, as does the hysteric symptom, which condenses numerous metaphors. This is one more difference in style, then, and one that serves a different syntactic arrangement of the symptom in Felix's case. The stylistic devices are brilliant, but differently so.

The poverty of metaphoric condensation onto the symptom of conversion goes hand in hand with the emigration of the anal erotogenic zone in the field of music. The metonymic formation of the symptom deploys extreme virtuosity there, as it does in obsessional neurosis. We had pointed out the love of singing by which

Felix had precociously made his own the sounds produced by his father during lovemaking. From his parents' bed to a black grand piano, to the love of concerts, including conductors who set the rhythm and musical scores that represent, according to Melanie Klein, the mother's genitals, this cathexis developed in counterpoint with the sounds of which the anal zone is capable. The prohibition of castration experienced through a surgical operation did suppress the cathexis of the vocal cords, but interest in sounds did not succumb; that interest was elaborated on the basis of another erotogenic zone, which metonymically colonized the domain of music. The new erotogenic zone thereby records a prohibition of jouissance. This relation between castration and metonymization of the erotogenic zones accounts for what has been identified empirically in the observation that an obsessional patient or a tic sufferer has symptomatic *behaviors*, that he is thus turned toward the outside. But the expression of discharge through motion is obscure and that of alloplastic activity confused, since it distinguishes poorly between exteriority and objectality as long as they are not related to the decisive split accomplished by metonymy, which at bottom dissociates the source and the object of the instinct, the material, and the content of the symptom. The style of hysteria is intent upon identifying the one with the other through the appeal to the movements capable of solidifying metaphors.

For on the subject of metaphors, the obsessional patient and the tic sufferer must also be heard from. They are not unfamiliar with the use of metaphors, but they produce them within the field opened up by the metonymy of the erotogenic zones instead of avoiding it by a plasticity of meaning that fixates it by freezing it.

"Felix had tried to obtain admission to a concert that was sold out; he was standing with many other people in the entrance to the concert hall, when in the crush a man broke a pane of glass and a policeman had to be summoned. At that moment, the tic appeared. Analysis revealed that this particular situation represented a repetition of the eavesdropping scene in early childhood which was closely bound up with the origin of the tic. He identified himself with the man who broke the window, for like him, he too . . . had wanted to force admission *to a 'concert,'* i.e., the sexual intercourse between parents. The policeman stood for the father detecting him in this attempt."[37]

37. "A Contribution to the Psychogenesis of Tics," p. 124; emphasis added.

The metaphoric term here is not crystallized in a movement put on display; it brings into play the harmonics of the musical space opened up by the metonymy of anality. To take up Freud's terminology, which is less paradoxical now, let us say that the affect remains in the psychical domain. In the tic, inasmuch as it represents a step toward the formation of an obsessional symptom, a disjunction is produced between the metaphoric operation and the activity of the erotogenic zone. When Felix seeks to "disrupt the concert," it is no longer in the place of metaphor that his body intervenes. His body remains involved the jouissance in two ways: as a source, in this instance anal, of the drive, and also as a metonymic link that brings about the passage from the noise of flatulence to the musical sounds of the rhythms produced by the body as Landauer described them, to the musical measure that orchestra conductors are able to lead and maintain. A small part of Felix's body perpetuates his desire to participate actively in his father's breathing during intercourse, but the multiplicity of the sequences in which this body part figures indicates that his erotogenic zones have changed status: they can enter into sequences that disperse them. Felix wanted to know why music in the theater had a muffled sound: Was it because the orchestra was in a pit below the stage? He went so far as to criticize a young composer who, in Felix's view, made excessive use of wind instruments. And again, in his admiration for conductors, who are simultaneously capable of directing and of turning the pages of the score so rapidly that the pages make ripping noises, he imagined himself capable of hearing the page noises from his seat.

Might we not say that the function of diversified metonymic relay of the anal erotogenic zone is opposed to the centripetal direction of the metaphors that in hysteria aim to make the oral erotogenic zone into a fantastic space where erotic experiences converge? Participating in the sounds of parental intercourse, Dora comes to terms with this by a disorder of the vocal cords that figures the impossibility of an act of cunnilingus. The entire erotic charge of these later events will, through metaphors, operate a return to *that zone that thereby enters into systems of equivalences rather than of dispersion.* Felix's vocal cords have a different fate: as the operation on his foreskin achieved an imaginary castration, his identification with his father through singing turned out to be prohibited. But his love of sounds was not so dependent upon a particular place in the body that that identification should succumb and be fixated there: instrumental music takes up the theme forbidden to the voice. This abstraction of the erotogenic zone also makes it possible for what is at stake in singing to be taken up by other zones: Felix is fascinated by the conductor's baton that directs the musicians' hands.

The semantic and syntactic organization of the symptom thus allows us to take another look at Abraham's formula: the tic is not, properly speaking, a conversive symptom at the sadistic-anal stage; it is sadistic-anal through one of its aspects, and on that basis it symbolizes the erotogenic zones by a metonymic game, the metaphor intervening not "besides" but on that condition. The tic is hysterical on a different basis, which does not specifically involve the dominant anality: the movement of the tic represents the broaching of a metaphorization confused with movements of the neck and shoulders. Metonymic anality develops the heterosexual identification with the father; the tic crystallizes a bisexual hesitation, which makes rudimentary use of the resources of the Darstellung. *The tic is not conversive where it is sadistic-anal, but it combines the two modes of symptom formation.*

It is indeed on the basis of the articulation of language "on" the erotogenic zones that we can grasp the status of movements in hysteria and in obsessional neurosis respectively. A symptom is a certain style, in the sense in which Roman Jakobson wrote that, in realist literature, metonymy dominates, whereas metaphor reigns in symbolism.[38] But in the field of neuroses, the opposition of these terms encounters the question of the status of the erotogenic zones involved in castration; there are metaphors and metaphors. The resources of metaphor are exploited in hysteria toward the ends of a plastic activity that serves the passion for presence. Metonymy, in the sense of the referential displacements that language translates secondarily, is exercised in this framework; and another metonymy makes it possible, finally, to suspend the excess of reality of what metaphors realize.

In obsessional neurosis, metaphor operates in the metonymic dispersion of the erotogenic zones, through which is resolved the prohibition of jouissance laid upon them. Here in the symbolic, metonymy seizes the instinctual space that the hysterical metaphor attempts to carry to an absolute power.

38. "Two Aspects of Language and Two Types of Aphasic Disturbances," in *Selected Writings*, vol. 2, *Word and Language* (The Hague: Mouton, 1971), pp. 255–56.

Conclusion

Jouissance and Knowledge

Our intention in this study has been to break down or "reduce" the energetistic metaphors Freud uses to designate the erotogenic body. These metaphors actually keep us from conceptualizing the specificity of that body. Hysterical conversion allows the erotogenic body to be discovered, but not to be conceptualized, since the notion of conversion announces a mystery and remains dependent upon the prepsychoanalytic opposition between the psychical and the somatic. Breaking down the metaphor of innervation implied limiting oneself to the erotogenic body, trying to describe it for itself, and doing so by way of a topology rather than an energetics.

Hysterical symptoms then offered the opportunity to pursue the reduction further, to extend it to the language of discharge. Freud himself acknowledged that the word "discharge" should be translated by a term indicating an action whose aim is to procure pleasure; a renewed reflection on the act and the shaping that the so-called conversion symptoms represent then allowed for a juxtaposition with painting, and more precisely with the correlation between motion and vision that underlies painting as well, albeit differently.

At the end of this itinerary, however, there is a remainder. To tell the truth, we still read, in the energetistic language with which Freud describes pleasure, something other than a misunderstanding of the order of the body involved, something other than an analogy with Helmholtz's language of physics. Far from being merely an inadequate formulation, the Freudian vocabulary of pleasure as sensation of discharge and its persistent reference to motion make possible a discourse on jouissance, insofar as jouissance juxtaposes and exceeds all that a subject can symbolize of it.

This other reading does not cancel out the previously accomplished reduction. But it no longer considers energetistic language as an epistemologically inadequate formulation, since it is transposed to a field other than the one in which it has a function of rigorous knowledge. Perhaps a metaphor is needed to express the excess, at least within a metapsychological framework. We no longer presuppose that Freud believes in the positivist status of what he is proposing when he uses energetistic terms; in fact, the language of energetics allows him to approach not only another field, that of the erotogenic body, but an extreme experience of which conversion hysteria provides him with an example, doubtless a privileged one. An extreme experience in that it defies description, for it excludes language. As Lacan put it, no one can say *"je jouis"* ("I am having orgasmic pleasure"). The Freudian energetics constitutes an attempt to sustain coherent discourse about an experience that in itself exceeds discourse.

The most remarkable exercise in the conceptualization of jouissance is undoubtedly Freud's "Project for a Scientific Psychology." This text was written in July 1895, in the heady excitement of an encounter with Fliess, for the first two chapters were begun in pencil on the train that took Freud from Berlin to Vienna. During that period Freud's erotic life was divided between such colloquies, which led him to write, and his sexual relations with his wife, which he had probably not yet given up.[1]

In the "Project," the term motion comes into play in two ways. In the first place, it characterizes a moment of the general functioning of the psychical apparatus: in this functioning, the structure of the neuronic system serves to retain, in addition to the neurons, quantities $(Q\acute{\eta})$, whose function it is to discharge. Discharge is always viewed, in the last analysis, as motor discharge, even when it involves not perceptible bodily movements but rather representations. Throughout his work, Freud continues to view thought itself as an energetistic process, operating at a weak level: the system (ω),

---

1. It was also in July of that year that he analyzed his own dream of giving an injection to Irma; he met Fliess in September. Anna was born in December 1895. In his correspondence with Fliess he mentions that "sexual excitement, too, is no longer of use for someone like me" (October 31, 1897, in *The Complete Letters of Sigmund Freud to Wilhelm Fliess, 1887–1904*, trans. and ed. Jeffrey Moussaieff Masson [Cambridge, Mass.: Belknap Press, 1985], p. 276).

which gives indications of qualities in the psychical apparatus, provided the ego is sufficiently cathected, and which is sensitive only to the periodicity of neuronic movements—not to quantities—is nonetheless the theater of motor discharges. In the system that controls the conscious state, "the discharge will, like all others, go in the direction of motility" (*SE* 1:311). Freud follows up on this decisive text in "Formulations on the Two Principles of Mental Functioning" (1911) and in his 1925 essay "On Negation," where he analyzes intellectual activities in terms of primary processes. For Freud the term primary process designates jouissance, that is, the excessive and immediate discharge of the apparatus of which sexual pleasure consists and which always threatens to overwhelm the regulations, mediations, and detours of the secondary processes. To treat thought and sexual satisfaction in the same terms, except for a difference in energy level, to declare, as he does in 1925, that judging is motor palpation, or else to say that there is discharge in all representative activites—whether they are hallucinatory or subtly mediatized in thoughts apparently unrelated to sexual satisfaction—to do this is to make all thought dependent on jouissance. Eliminating jouissance is another way of satisfying it when judgment "has no practical purpose" (*SE* 1:332), gives up sexual discharge, and seeks a state of "identity" with perception (p. 330). Lacan pursues Freud's thought in this direction when he says: "In other words, for the moment I am not fucking, I am talking to you. Well! I can have *exactly the same* satisfaction as if I were fucking."[2]

But in the second place, we note that on two occasions in the "Project" Freud sets up a relation of disjunction between the order of movement and the order of representation. In the first instance, he is describing the function of the conscious state (ω). Let us take another look at the preceding text. "The discharge will, like all others, go in the direction of motility; and here it is to be noticed that *with the transformation into motion* everything in the nature of quality, every peculiarity of period, is lost" (*SE* 1:311–12).

Motion, or rather movement, here no longer designates every thought inasmuch as thought remains dependent upon jouissance, but rather designates jouissance inasmuch as jouissance excludes the specialized functioning of thought in the contribution of indexes of reality. In the Lacanian formula according to which no one can say

2. *FFC*, pp. 165–66; emphasis added.

"*je jouis,*" we might see a commentary on this passage of the "Project," except that Lacan chooses not to take into account the relation of jouissance to movement, as extinction of thought (in ω).

For Freud, only the consideration of movement makes it possible to describe that reciprocal exclusion of jouissance and discourse—precisely the discourse about jouissance that the subject who is experiencing jouissance cannot engage in. Lacan for his part refers that suspension of thought back to feminine jouissance. Might women experience jouissance without being able to say anything about it?[3] The "Project" did not settle for that expedient. Another passage of Freud's text confirms this: reflecting on the hallucinatory residues in thought, Freud defines the "motor images" in the element of representation as a sequel to the experience of satisfaction that for its part implied movement. Motor images are the trace, in representation, of the jouissance that exceeded it. "The information of the reflex discharge comes about because every movement, through its subsidiary results, becomes the occasion for fresh sensory excitations (from the skin and muscles) which give rise to a *motor* [kinaesthetic] *image* in (ψ)" (*SE* 1:318).

Freud adds, however, that *this representative residue of the experience of satisfaction always risks being transformed once again into jouissance properly speaking, that is, into movement.* "The perception may correspond to an object-nucleus + a motor image. While one is perceiving the perception, one copies the movement itself—that is, one innervates so strongly the motor image of one's own which is aroused towards coinciding [with the perception], *that the movement is carried out*" (p. 333; emphasis added).

Jouissance, then, is described not exclusively in the representative element, but as an exclusive—and consequently violent—relay of representation by way of movement. And the motor image accomplishes the diversion, or rather—for hysteria is nothing else—the conversion into real innervation. Innervation, or the order of movement, is plugged into the Real, in the Lacanian sense. This is important, for, in the same passage of the "Project" we find the crucial statement on objects: "What we call *things* are residues which evade being judged" (p. 334). Does the idea that objects refer to the real of desire mean the same thing for Freud and for Lacan? In what sense does the object or "thing" evade judgment?

3. *Le séminaire*, book 20, *Encore* (Paris: Seuil, 1970), p. 68.

In Freud the ambiguity of the notions of discharge and motor image returns in the ambiguity of the verb used here, "evade." Lacan defines the object *a* in the order of representation, of Vorstellung; it is the residue that eludes symbolization, that escapes assimilation to a specular structure. Freud adds that the moment of the object or thing, as remainder, exceeds any Vorstellung, even a Vorstellung conceived as resistant to specularity. The motor order designates the Darstellung or realization in the presence of jouissance.

Freud's insistence on motion, far from importing an inadequate physicalist vocabulary into the field of the unconscious, far from constituting a psychophysiology of pleasure, characterizes precisely the reciprocal exclusion of language and jouissance. Lacan retained Freud's energetistic language in general, the language that can in fact be transposed into the terms of a language-producing apparatus, of a circulation of signifiers eluded by things that continue to be representative. The excess jouissance consists in is not, by that token, conceived merely unilaterally. The Real is thought only in the register of the hallucinatory, whereas for the author of the "Project" it is also movement, inasmuch as it implies a momentary extinction of discourse and a presentification of the impossible, which Freud identified clinically as hysterical conversion, through a diversion into bodily innervation. In a decisive moment, jouissance is no longer representation, not even real representation: it is movement.

The very ambiguity of Freud's text, in which the term discharge sometimes designates a thought process and sometimes means the extinction of the process in which jouissance consists, merits further attention, because it allows us to differentiate several modalities in the relation between jouissance and language. Does not the misunderstanding that the relation between the sexes consists of arise from the fact that the reciprocal exclusion of knowledge and jouissance has a different aspect for the man and for the woman? No one can say "*je jouis*," to be sure. But if we sum up the relation between expression and jouissance that way, we are neglecting a difference, a disagreement. For that little sentence summarizes and confuses two distinct positions.

The hysteric Darstellung has various aspects. It is always a matter of rendering jouissance present in its excess. The Freudian idea of pleasure as sensation of motor discharge thus does not merely signify that Freud, obsessional as he is, assimilates pleasure to death, presumably because he shrinks from the gentleness of the first initiator in sexuality;[4] his energetistic language also makes it possible to describe relations of exclusion between sexual jouissance and discourse, relations that are experienced by women and men in violence, not only in gentleness. The excess of the hysteric's demand stems from this disjunction, of which the general formula is given by the extinction of thought transformed into movement. To require that discourse be momentarily arrested because thought is failing to cope and because thought alone serves as representative of what discourse keeps at bay—that is, for woman, a banal position. It exists in other forms. Earlier[5] we referred to hysterical theatricalization in the realm of discursive practices: the conversion of the conceptual into something on display owing to a pirouette of language that suddenly subjectivizes the rigor of a development. But by way of these examples, it still seems as though, in the Darstellung of jouissance, hysterics are struggling directly with the symbolic. In other words, we may wonder what type of man makes a woman hysterical.

In what precedes we have discerned a double aspect of the symptom, which is expressed through the conjunction of the rejection of the other sex, as evidenced in the slap Dora gives Herr K., and the actualization of an impossible jouissance by conversion. To understand hysteria amounts to grasping the stakes of that violence. Post-Freudian psychoanalytic theory has given it a name, "penis envy," describing the effect produced on males, male theoreticians, by this aspect of feminine desire. The theory of penis envy constitutes a sort of immediate reaction on the man's part to what is presented in women's dreams as the fear or desire that the man should lose his penis. Sarah Kofman shows that, in Freud, the theory of penis envy functions to protect men who, subjected to the violence of feminine desire, construct an interpretation that turns it to their advantage.[6] But this deconstruction leaves unanswered the question of knowing what constitutes the violence of feminine desire.

The interpretation we have offered of that violence refers to an

4. Cf. Monique Schneider, *Freud et le plaisir* (Paris: Denoël, 1980).
5. See above, p. 166.
6. Sarah Kofman, *The Enigma of Woman*, trans. Catherine Porter (Ithaca: Cornell University Press, 1985).

inability to symbolize an overly threatening lack of jouissance. But in focusing exclusive attention on Oedipal history read in a normative fashion, are we not offering a completely prefabricated version of castration? To symbolize a loss: that is the objective. The superego connotation of such a definition also marked our schema for reading Dora's case. If we proceed too quickly to relate the violence of hysterical desire to what might resolve it, we cannot produce an adequate description of the irreducible misunderstanding that is always present in the relation between the sexes. Invoking the Other and the symbolic makes it possible to avoid stating what is produced in the encounter with another. We had stopped there: the Lacanian interpretation of Dora's case does not escape, either, from a reassuring reconstruction, a new version of the thesis of penis envy. In the seminar known as "L'envers de la psychanalyse,"[7] Lacan interprets Dora's second dream by equating the dead father with the symbolic father. Dora's accession to knowledge about sex presupposes the presence of the father's death as signifying element. The violence of the death wish is thereby dedramatized but at the same time set aside. Its elimination allows the subject to be plugged directly into the symbolic and allows Lacan *to avoid saying what constitutes the other's defiance, which is what its encounter consists of.* Where Freud expressed his terror of feminine desire through the theory of penis envy, Lacan reassures himself by making the hysteric someone who rejects jouissance in the name of knowledge about jouissance, and whose wish for her father's death is only the imaginary representation of her belonging to the symbolic.

What do these women's dreams signify when the death of a man is involved? Let us reread Dora's story in the light of Lou Andreas-Salomé's: the importance, for both women, of acceding to knowledge about jouissance, when certain men awaken the excess of their desire, is the connecting link. We are familiar with the valiantly unifying language that was for Lou Andreas-Salomé a crucial aspect of her relation to the men who mattered to her. Freud often indicated to her that, while he admired her capacity for synthesis and her metaphysical optimism, he could not share them;[8] and that very admiration helped him keep at a safe distance a mode of thought

7. Unpublished seminar, February 18, 1970.
8. Cf. *Sigmund Freud and Lou Andreas-Salomé: Letters*, ed. Ernst Pfeiffer, trans. William and Elaine Robson-Scott (New York: Harcourt Brace Jovanovich, 1972), pp. 60–61, 67, 171.

that he also found seductive. Curiously, to that distance and that rejection, Lou responded with gratitude, as if Freud's fear of being "taken in" by her discourse allowed her to remain undisturbed by the excess of her own desire. On the contrary, the men who were fascinated by Lou, and whom she loved, exacerbated her discourse on the union of body and mind as if, without consciously deciding to do so, she offered that discourse as a spectacle to certain men who desired to hear it, but in such a way that the spectacle became a struggle in which death or insanity constituted the stakes for each of the protagonists, and more radically perhaps for the men she encountered than for herself.

Lou Andreas-Salomé's metaphysics on the union of body and mind stems from the hysterical Darstellung. It is sometimes presented as an autonomous theoretical discourse, but its author knew that, even so, these formulations were conceivable only in terms of reflection on "What arises from the fact that the woman is not the one who killed the father."[9] Language and knowledge for a woman do not have simply the function of killing the thing, or of distancing from the thing, since the man who separates from the mother awakens a desire for knowledge *and* a sexual desire. To name this desire, to approach it, does not mean having to give it up, but means having to await its actualization. And if it is conceivable that a desire for the father should take over from an archaic desire for the mother, is this not in accord with that register where neither language nor knowledge suffices to proscribe? In Lacanian terms we shall say that, for a woman, the symbolic itself may have the function of object *a*, cause of desire. This paradox—that the residue that eludes the symbolic should be the symbolic itself—doubtless has a status analogous to the paradoxes Kant formulated with regard to aesthetic judgment: finality without end, universality without concept. In the face of the heterogeneity of one field or process with respect to another, the categories forged for this latter—the theoretical critique of pure reason or masculine sexuality—betray their limits.

Lou Andreas-Salomé began her writing career by drafting sermons for pastor Gillot, who initiated her into the things of the spirit. Heinz-Frederick Peters, her biographer, explains that that

9. Title of a 1928 article translated by I. Hildenbrand in Lou Andreas-Salomé, *L'amour du narcissisme* (Paris: Gallimard, 1980).

exercise came to an end the day when, instead of preparing a commentary on the Bible, "She wrote a powerful sermon on the well-known words from Goethe's *Faust*: "Name is sound and fury."[10] For the men who fascinated her, Lou always had the same language; she recognized herself in the Nietzschean principle[11] according to which every philosophy has to be analyzed as a confession, every construction that presents itself as conceptual. She addressed to Rilke the well-known pronouncement that precisely pinpointed the misunderstanding in which their encounter was rooted, and that destroyed it: "If I was yours for many years, it is because you were for me the first reality in which body and man were indiscernible, an undeniable fact of life itself."[12]

With regard to Andreas, her husband, by whom she was subjugated in a way that always remained unclear to her, she said, she also wrote: "It seemed to me that this could explain in large measure what was special about Andreas and what was essential in him: *the 'mental' and the 'physical' were absolutely inseparable*" (*Ma vie*, p. 200).

And in each case, Lou adds that a man appears *real* to her when he arouses in her a statement of that sort. "Even though the idea might not be for him directly readable at the level of the body, it was undeniably anchored there; this was confirmed not by a long series of deductions, but by its character of *incomprehensible existence* and of spontaneity."[13]

Lou is reflecting here on what makes *for her* the incomprehensible existence of her husband; and about Rilke she wrote the following lines, in which the reciprocity *seems* to be more secure: "I could have told you word for word what you told me in confessing your love: *You alone are real*" (*Ma vie*, p. 140). Lou quotes Rilke and borrows a sentence from him to describe the Real of their love. But that sentence is not univocal.

When a man lives by producing works in close proximity to the

10. Heinz-Frederick Peters, *My Sister, My Spouse: A Biography of Lou Andreas-Salomé* (New York: Norton, 1962), p. 54.

11. Lou Andreas-Salomé, *Frédéric Nietzsche* (1932), reprint (Paris: Gordon and Breach, 1970). Cf. Nietzsche's letter-preface: "Your idea of reducing philosophical systems to the personal acts of their authors is truly the idea of a 'soul-sister'" (pp. 3, 6).

12. Lou Andreas-Salomé, *Ma vie* (Paris: Presses Universitaires de France, 1978), p. 140.

13. *Ma vie*, p. 140; emphasis added.

point of fragility of the symbolic—whether he is an artist, a linguist, a writer, a theoretician, or a philosopher—he arouses, in a woman he addresses, statements of the sort Lou addressed to the men who mattered to her: that there is no difference in the other between body and mind, or that he knows perfectly well, for his part, that beneath all conceptual thought a subject desires. Curiously, Lou makes statements of this sort to others and about others, yet she has little to say about herself. We may imagine she may have told Nietzsche, Rilke, Freud, and even Andreas that with them, exceptionally, she felt she was recognized both in her sexual identity and in her intelligence, with no distinction between the two. Or rather, Lou may have refrained from having to say that (and sexually she held herself back, except with Rilke), for such a confession signifies that a woman, through a certain masculine desire, is placed outside herself, owing to what is at stake: that eccentric and constitutive point where language has no prohibitory function and does not serve to kill the thing.

These statements or words *cannot be heard* by the man who elicits them from a woman; he cannot allow himself to recognize himself in them without running the risk of impotence—that was doubtless Andreas's case[14]—or death, in Rilke's. For this form of encounter short-circuits the phallic function in a violent way on all sides: the man is confronted directly with what prohibitory language and the phallic function have as their goal to fail to recognize. With such a woman, he cannot occupy the place of a man, since she confronts him with his own femininity and also with other men; in fact, a woman such as Dora or Lou plays at being a man, but always in the hope of making a man abandon his homosexuality and being able to abandon this role by pronouncing these words that confirm the misunderstanding: with you I need not to play at being a man in order to be recognized in my intelligence.

The woman too is placed in a situation of violence: she can experience the proximity of jouissance and knowledge, sexually and intellectually, and that makes her inventive even as it places her in a situation of erotic dependence that is difficult to accept, since what makes her enjoy [*jouir*] makes her, at the same time, intelligent; that is to say, she no longer has the means of knowing that her intelligence is her own, independent of the one through whom

14. Cf. the final chapter of *Ma vie*, "Ce qui manque à l'esquisse . . ."

she experiences jouissance or the one of whom she demands jouissance and who returns her to her insanity. This is what has been called possession, and it would be useful to reconsider the question of erotomania in this light.

On the verge of being caught up in it, Lou Andreas-Salomé holds herself back, at the price of not comprehending the violence she uses against men. In her memoirs she describes her consternation in the face of Rilke's anxieties, which resurfaced, multiplied, during their sexual adventure: "I do not wish to embellish anything. Holding my head in my hands, I struggled to understand what was happening. And I was deeply astonished the day when, in a torn old diary that related only a few experiences, I read this sentence, so baldly sincere: '*I am eternally faithful to memories; I will never be faithful to men.*'"[15]

Lou, who approached men by telling them that body and mind were not separate and that they knew it, never stopped confronting—though she never analyzed the process—the fact that, for the men she met, life and work were in disjunction. She could not accept the idea that death had a different function for them than for her—that they needed to play with death, alone with words, so as to postpone their encounter with the abyss, as Rilke said (*Ma vie*, p. 282, n. 132), or insanity. But she knew—very early in Nietzsche's case and later in Rilke's—their secret: work at the expense of life. Of this operation of the death instinct, she who spoke in the name of life was the fascinated and helpless companion.

In *Encore* Jacques Lacan deals with female jouissance, which he defines as not-everything in the phallic function. Such a proposition comes from a man who is attempting to elucidate the unknown represented by woman's need and woman's jouissance, on the basis of principles elaborated in the description of masculine sexuality. It is the sexual nonrelation seen by a man, who presumes that "the signifier is what brings jouissance to a halt."[16] Since for Lacan it goes without saying that the word is death to the thing, woman's jouissance appears to be beyond discourse: there is always something that escapes discourse in her. Lacan says, too: "There is no woman not excluded by the nature of things that is the nature of

15. *Ma vie*, p. 149; emphasis added.
16. *Le séminaire*, book 20, *Encore*, p. 27.

words, and it must be said that if there is something that they themselves are complaining about plenty at the moment, it is precisely that—simply, they don't know what they are saying, that's the whole difference between them and me" (p. 34).

Lacan's prudence in not spelling out this "something more" (p. 69) is explained by the point he seeks to reach: this "more" can only be an experience of nothingness, that is, a mystical jouissance, an asceticism of the body in the name of a signifier of which women would be the theater.[17] But there is a mirror effect here: the necessary passage of men through the symbolization of death that makes phallic jouissance possible is attributed to women as well. We do not escape here from the narcissism of love. And the logic of this construction rests on the principle according to which language is the death of things.

Now if it is true that women are somewhat out of phase with respect to the phallic function, it is precisely because what causes their desire is that language does not simply bring jouissance to a halt. To describe the excess, one may hesitate at first between two formulations. Is woman situated at the point where sexual jouissance silences the woman herself as well as the man who awakens her desire, or does she enjoy language at the mythical and constitutive point where it would not have the value of a prohibition? It is in fact important to reject this alternative; the point to be described is the equivalence of these two apparently exclusive aspects. For women experience jouissance at the moment when language falls away from its signifying function. Lacan states quite properly that "a subject, as such, does not have very much to do with jouissance."[18] Not very much; all the same, that leaves something. It so happens that women call upon certain men at the point where a subject, as such, has something to do after all with jouissance.

It cannot be said that we are dealing here with a "beyond" of the phallic function, or that a woman is not-everything in the phallic function. For on the man's side this excess necessarily attacks the phallic function, which is at one with language as the distancing of the Thing. The violence of women's desire stems from the effects

17. "There is a jouissance that belongs to *her*, to that *her* that does not exist and signifies nothing" (ibid., p. 169).
18. Ibid., p. 36.

that that desire necessarily exercises on man. Even though woman does not seek to castrate the man she desires, we can understand that man may feel that a given woman wants to take a knife to him, and that she causes him to lose his masculinity, whereas that is not exactly what is going on. What constitutes, for a woman, a formidable appeal to jouissance is to encounter a certain compliance in a man—but precisely not a somatic compliance!—leading him to occupy that mythical and constitutive place where signification loses its right to distance the Thing. No doubt men can confront this point, alone with words, but not in the sexual relation, whereas women can demand of man's body and his genitals a sexual jouissance that presentifies the very excess of their desire with respect to the forbidden.

This can be expressed in still another way. Lacan gives a fairly good description of the masculine position when he says: "Nothing forces anyone to enjoy, except the superego. The superego is the imperative of jouissance—'Enjoy'" (p. 10).

Now for a woman there is no injunction to enjoy but a demand for unlimited jouissance, that is, for a jouissance that signification does not bring to a halt, a jouissance that is instead restimulated by signification. It is a matter of enjoying a man's intelligence as if it were a part of his body, without precluding the enjoyment of his body. But this occurs only with men engaged in sublimatory activities, men who are sensitive to the point of fragility of any symbolic order. Women, through their desire, do not challenge them, contrary to what these men necessarily think; women are fascinated by the cathexis of the symbolic inasmuch as its reference points are not assured once and for all and inasmuch as such men excel in transforming this risk into a work. Women are fascinated, provided these men address them, for they are confronted because of their desire, at that point where sexual jouissance and sublimation need not be distinguished. On this slope the men cannot follow them, but there are several ways of manifesting this.

Failing to grasp the modalities of this excess, Lacan borders the phallic function with a mystical "not-everything." Feminine jouissance exists only when it still responds to the desire of a man for whom language and distancing of jouissance are the same thing. Jouissance then has as its condition that women's bodies become

189

waste products in the name of the signifier. And to be sure, some women—mystics, for example—may fulfill this description.[19] This eliminates the need for men to confront sexually the fragility of the symbolic that they evoke through discourse. The game feeds mysticism, that is, the regime of jouissance in which men approach the excess of feminine desire even as they refuse to allow women to experience jouissance *through them*. As evidence, we may take Lacan's fascination with Bernini's statue—the ecstasy of Saint Theresa—which he reproduces on the cover of his book. Men are quite willing for women to be not-everything in the phallic function, for then angels, signifiers, would bring them to jouissance, but not they themselves, not men; and they give themselves the spectacle of that jouissance.

To describe this feminine position does not make it valid. To propose the excess that inhabits women's desire as more true or as bearer of more value than masculine desire is in no way helpful for describing the sexual relation and nonrelation.

We can only say that men and women approach jouissance in two ways, which tend to be unable to meet in their difference, each position rendering the other unrepresentable. This does not make pleasure or sexual relations impossible, but it does explain why these can be produced only naively, that is, when the circumstances of an encounter lighten the impact of that point of discord or of disembodiment [*dis-corps*], which is a point of truth. What supplements the absence of sexual relation is a game of truth with itself in which lovers are the actors.

This counterpoint between two aspects of jouissance, mystical and hysterical, finally provides an occasion for spelling out one of the stakes of our investigation: clinical and epistemological questions are not truly independent of each other in the psychoanalytic field. A choice of neurosis and a choice of epistemology go hand in hand.

Lacan privileges mystical jouissance, and he raises the question of the status of the body by a reduction of the Freudian energetics to a region of the imaginary, or to a topology. Every symptom that

19. Even then, it is not certain that this eroticization of the body on the basis of the void and of the death of the senses is the exact reflection of the symbolization of death as condition of phallic jouissance for men. There is trickery in the game mystical women play. Hysterics are more naive.

gives positive reality to the body is conceived, on the basis of the fetishism set up as a model, as a veil for a lack, a veiled phallus. The body counts as "minus one"; any appearance of positivity disguises the fact that the body is first and foremost emptiness or gap. That justifies the criticism of the Freudian energetics and puts the various symptoms on the same level: hysterical conversion is read on the basis of symptoms for which the affect remains in the psychical domain, as Freud declared. Along these lines, Octave Mannoni sometimes settles for putting dream-as-rebus and conversion on the same plane.[20] Lacan interprets Dora's rejection of Herr K.'s advances as phallic, when he says that she does not want Herr K.'s gifts, his jewels, since she herself is the jewel.[21] Conversion is interpreted as an erection that is unaware of itself; the attention-getting aspect of motor symptoms is the equivalent of the imaginary experience of the negativity of the phallus. The body as ultimate signified is the cadaver or stone phallus;[22] meaning and metaphor are woven of non-sense and no-sense. This is how Roland Chemama interprets the feelings of paralysis experienced in dreams, which, as we have seen, represent the same thing as hysterical conversion: "If the entire body in these dreams can have the value of the phallic signifier, we understand what Freud emphasizes right away: in his dream, he has the feeling of being paralyzed, let us say medusized."[23] Does every paralysis refer to the horror experienced before Medusa's head? This view can be maintained only if we see the correlation between the perverse instinct and mystical jouissance as the model of every psychical structuration.

Now the most general formulation of this privilege accorded to the head-to-head confrontation between perversion and mysticism is expressed in epistemological terms. Body and language are articulated in the unconscious only as the covering over of two lacks: the incompleteness of every living being owing to the fact of sexualized biological reproduction, and the division of every speaking being

20. Octave Mannoni, "L'ellipse et la barre," in *Clefs pour l'imaginaire, ou L'autre scène* (Paris: Seuil, 1969).

21. Jacques Lacan, unpublished seminar, "L'envers de la psychanalyse," February 10, 1970.

22. Jacques Lacan, unpublished seminar, "La relation d'objet," December 5, 1956.

23. R. Chemama, "Ce que produit le discours de l'analyste," *Lettres de l'Ecole Freudienne de Paris*, no. 25, vol. 1, p. 241.

who is constituted in the place of the Other. An appeal to "the topological unity of the gaps in play" (*FFC*, p. 181) does not resolve the heterogeneity of the two series, each of which includes a point of cancellation; such an appeal rather dazzles with a reflection that is not conceptually effective. In fact, in negativizing biological sexuality and language, that perspective does not escape from the body/mind dualism, whereas Freud's contribution, at its best, consisted in being able to do without that dualism, taking into consideration the erotogenic body, conceived then in such a way that the opposition of the psychical and the physiological was no longer operative.

To tell the truth, Lacan's position is more complex; he knows perfectly well that he cannot confine himself to combining language and biology. To say that *the drive assumes its role* (p. 181) in the functioning of the unconscious by virtue of the topological unity of the gaps involved is to make the drive—a seemingly positive term—the result of the operation that links the two preceding gaps. This result is assimilated to another gap, to a nothing disguised arbitrarily as an object, like the fetish.

"That is what Freud tells us. Let us look at what he says. *As far as the object in the drive is concerned, let it be clear that it is, strictly speaking, of no importance. It is a matter of total indifference.* One must never read Freud without one's ears cocked. When one reads such things, one really ought to prick up one's ears."[24]

Let us look at Freud's text, as Lacan invites us to do. We stumble upon a misreading by Lacan, who was fascinated by the nothing.

> The object [*Objekt*] of an instinct is the thing in regard to which or through which the instinct is able to achieve its aim. It is *what is most variable* about an instinct and is not originally connected with it, but becomes assigned to it only in consequence of being peculiarly fitted to make satisfaction possible. The object is not necessarily something extraneous [*Gegenstand*]: it may equally well be a part of the subject's own body. *It may be changed any number of times in the course of the vicissitudes which the instinct undergoes during its existence [Es kann im Laufe der Lebensschicksale des Triebes beliebig oft gewechselt werden]*; and

24. Ibid., p. 168. On the object as holding the place of the void, see also p. 180: "This object, which is in fact simply the presence of a hollow, a void, which can be occupied, Freud tells us, by any object."

highly important parts are played by this displacement of instinct. It may happen that the same object serves for the satisfaction of several instincts simultaneously, a phenomenon which Adler [1908] has called a "confluence" of instincts [*Triebverschränkung*]. A particularly close attachment of the instinct to its object is distinguished by the term "fixation." This frequently occurs at very early periods of the development of an instinct and puts an end to its mobility through its intense opposition to detachment. (*SE* 14:122–23; emphasis added)

Freud did not state that the object has, strictly speaking, no importance, or that it is a matter of total indifference. Quite the contrary, it acquires its importance from the fact that it makes satisfaction possible, and this to the extent that a subject can accept its variable nature. Lacan's misreading has to do with the little word *beliebig* ("any number of times," "as much as one wishes"), which he replaces by "arbitrary," "indifferent," swallowing up the whole fetishist problematic and the adoration of the no-thing in this false step. In Freud's text, *beliebig* is an adverb that modifies another adverb (*oft*): the object changes any number of times, *as often as one likes.* The nuance of arbitrariness leads not to indifference regarding the object, but to the need to change objects, in order for sexual satisfaction to be possible. The variability of the object of the instinct or drive binds together mourning and sexual satisfaction in the same problematic. In this view, fetishism falls on the side of an impossible mourning and consequently on the side of refusal of satisfaction.

From this confrontation, a decisive one in many respects, we shall retain for the time being the observation that the status of the body for Lacan is determined by the *supposed* covering over of three gaps, the third resulting from the first two, in the conceptual order, in the sense in which desire is said to result from subtracting need from demand.[25] These three gaps are:

—the incompleteness of every living being, owing to the fact of sexualized biological reproduction;

—the division of every subject, each one being constituted by the

25. Jacques Lacan, "The Signification of the Phallus," in *Ecrits: A Selection*, trans. Alan Sheridan (New York: W. W. Norton, 1977), p. 286. The third term, desire and object of the drive, is presented sometimes as the result of a subtraction, sometimes as the product of a disguising (of the gaps).

193

gaps that the distribution of signifying cathexes installs in him or her;

—the lack that is at stake in the variability of the object of a drive, a variability that Lacan transforms into complete indifference regarding the object, taking the place of the void.

Does the unconscious necessity of establishing the rights of the third of these lacks govern the conceptual combination of the two others? For the time being it is difficult to tell where the investigation of that question may lead; the fact remains that here we are encountering the interest, but also the specific difficulty, of what is called psychoanalytic theory in its relation to interpretation: the principles of analysis of the object, the unconscious, are the universalization of certain factors identified in the interpretation of a group of particular fantasies. Is the passage from a fantasy heard in analysis to the concept never assured except at the price of a pirouette? Lacan performs one when he invokes the gaps whose mutual covering over he asserts without conceiving their unity. Added to this is the fact that he neglects to conceptualize the heterogeneity of symptom formation in hysteria, since his whole construction is made to conceptualize something else. That the hysteric challenges language through movement can receive no status other than that of a falling away of signification in the register of the sign.[26] Thus the difference between two modes of annulment of meaning remains unthought: the no-sense constituted by the phallus and the wordplay realized and contested by the hysteric Darstellung. Another sign of this lack of rigor that consists in not saying what one is leaving aside thus marks the passage from listening to a fantasy to a concept that is supposed to define the unconscious in general.

Naturally we do not escape that aporia in our turn. Does conceptualizing the erotogenic body for itself amount to listening to hysteria or to giving a new definition of the unconscious that takes as its principle the "resistance" of jouissance to the symbolic constitution of the subject who nevertheless programs the jouissance that exceeds it? Would it follow that there is no difference in the analytic

26. *FFC*, p. 157: "What did she show by this? One may speculate, but one must refrain from resorting too precipitously to the language of the body. Let us say simply that the domain of sexuality shows a natural functioning of signs. At this level, they are not signifiers, for the nervous pregnancy is a symptom, and, according to the definition of the sign, something intended for someone. The signifier, being something quite different, represents a subject for another signifier."

realm between hearing a fantasy and conceptual thought? Not necessarily: it is important, rather, to note what one is leaving aside in passing on to the concept, that is, to say at what price the universalism of the concept wins out over the hearing of a fantasy. But the one who undertakes that task is doubtless unable to say it, at least not while doing it. Freudian thought ruins every philosophical or scientific idea of truth, not by dissolving the difference between interpretation and theory, but by making it possible to say at what price the universal is constructed—by making interpretation the aftermath of constructions of concepts that pretend to put an end to interpretation.

Bibliography

Philosophy, Epistemology, and Linguistics

Bachelard, Gaston. *La formation de l'esprit scientifique.* 5th ed. Paris: Vrin, 1967.

———. *Le nouvel esprit scientifique.* 8th ed. Paris: Presses Universitaires de France, 1963.

———. *The Philosophy of No: A Philosophy of the New Scientific Mind.* Trans. G. C. Waterston. New York: Orion Press, 1968.

Canguilhem, Georges. "Qu'est-ce que la psychologie?" In *Etudes d'histoire et de philosophie des sciences.* Paris: Vrin, 1968.

Derrida, Jacques. *Edmund Husserl's "Origin of Geometry": An Introduction,* trans. John P. Leavey, Jr., ed. David B. Allison, pp. 155–80. Stony Brook, N.Y.: Nicolas Hays, 1978.

Descartes, René. "The Passions of the Soul." In *The Philosophical Works of Descartes,* trans. Elizabeth S. Haldane and G. R. T. Ross, 1:329–427. Cambridge: Cambridge University Press, 1931.

———. "Rules for the Direction of the Mind." In *The Philosophical Works of Descartes,* 1:1–77.

Didi-Hubermann, Georges. *L'invention de l'hystérie.* Paris: Macula, 1982.

Husserl, Edmund, in Jacques Derrida, *Edmund Husserl's Origin of Geometry,* trans. John P. Leavey, Jr., ed. David B. Allison, pp. 155–80. Boulder, Colo.: distr. Great Eastern Book Co., 1978.

Jakobson, Roman. "Two Aspects of Language and Two Types of Aphasic Disturbances." In *Selected Writings,* vol. 2: *Word and Language,* pp. 239–59. The Hague: Mouton, 1971.

Le Guern, Maurice. *Sémantique de la métaphore et de la métonymie.* Paris: Larousse Université, 1973.

Merleau-Ponty, Maurice. *Phenomenology of Perception.* Trans. Colin Smith. New York: Humanities Press, 1962.

——. *The Visible and the Invisible.* Ed. Claude Lefort, trans. Alfonso Lingis. Evanston, Ill.: Northwestern University Press, 1968.

Normand, I. *Métaphore et concept.* Paris: Complexe; distr. Presses Universitaires de France, 1976.

Serres, Michel. "Le point de vue de la bio-physique." In *Critique* 346 (La psychanalyse vue du dehors, 2), March 1976.

Veight, I. *Histoire de l'hystérie.* Paris: Seghers, 1973.

Psychosomatics and Conversion Hysteria

Alexander, Franz. *La médecine psychosomatique.* Paris: Payot, 1962.

——. *Principes de psychanalyse.* Trans. E. Stern and D. Anzieu. Paris: Payot, 1952.

Babinski, Josef, and Jules Froment. *Hysteria of Pithiatism, and Reflex Nervous Disorders in the Neurology of War.* Trans. E. F. Buzzard. London: University of London Press, 1918.

Boegner-Plichet, M. "Symptômes hystériques et symptômes psychosomatiques." *Entretiens Psychiatriques,* 1963.

Delay, Jean. *Introduction à la médecine psychosomatique.* Paris: Masson, 1961.

——. *Perspectives psychomatiques.* Paris: Masson, 1961.

Deutsch, Felix. "Der gesunde und der kranke Körper in psychoanalytischer Betrachtung." *Internationale Zeitschrift für Psychoanalyse,* 1926, no. 3, pp. 493–503.

——. "Psychoanalyse und Organkrankheiten." *Internationale Zeitschrift für Psychoanalyse,* 1922, no. 3, pp. 290–306.

——. "Zur Bildung des Konversionssymptoms." *Internationale Zeitschrift für Psychoanalyse,* 1924, no. 3, pp. 380–92.

Dongier, Maurice. *Névrose et troubles psychosomatiques.* Brussels: Dessart, 1966.

Hesnard, A., and R. Laforgue. *Les processus d'autopunition.* Paris: Denoël et Steel, 1931.

Hollós, S. "Von den 'pathoneurosen' zur Pathologie der Neurosen." *Internationale Zeitschrift für Psychoanalyse,* 1923, no. 3, pp. 311–22.

Hollós, S., and Sandor Ferenczi. "Zur Psychoanalyse der paralytischen Geistesstörungen." *Internationale Zeitschrift für Psychoanalyse,* 1922, pp. 354–58.

Marty, Pierre, M. de M'Uzan, and C. David. *L'investigation psychosomatique.* Paris: Presses Universitaires de France, 1963.

Parcheminey, G. "Critique de la notion d'hystérie de conversion." *L'Evolution Psychiatrique,* 1949, p. 45.

——. "La problématique du psychosomatique." *Revue Française de Psychanalyse* (1948).

Sperling, Melissa. "Conversion Hysteria and Conversion Symptoms: A Revision of Classification and Concepts." In Index Medicus, *American Journal of Psychoanalysis*, pp. 745–70.

Valabrega, Jean-Paul. "Entretien avec J.-P. Valabrega: Les conceptions actuelles en médecine psychosomatique." *Revue de Médecine Psychosomatique et de Psychologie Médicale* 8, no. 1, January–March 1966.

——. *Les théories psychosomatiques.* Toulouse: Privat, 1954.

Van Bogaert, L. "L'hystérie et les fonctions diencéphaliques." In *Congrès des médecins aliénistes et neurologistes de langue française.* Paris: Masson, 1935.

Psychoanalysis

Abraham, Karl. "Erörterung über den Tic." *Internationale Zeitschrift für Psychoanalyse*, 1921. Translated in *Oeuvres complètes*, vol. 2. Paris: Payot, 1966.

Abraham, Nicolas. "L'écorce et le noyau." *Critique* 249, February 1968, pp. 162 ff.

Andreas-Salomé, Lou. "Ce qui découle du fait que ce n'est pas la femme qui a tué la père." Trans. I. Hildenbrand. In Lou Andreas-Salomé, *L'amour du narcissisme.* Paris: Gallimard, 1980.

——. *Frédéric Nietzsche.* Paris: Grasset, 1932. Reprinted Paris: Gordon and Breach, 1979.

——. *Ma vie.* Paris: Presses Universitaires de France, 1978.

Chemama, R. "Ce que produit le discours de l'analyste." *Lettres de l'Ecole Freudienne de Paris*, no. 25, vol. 1.

Eisler, M. Josef. "Über hysterische Erscheinungen am Uterus." *Internationale Zeitschrift für Psychoanalyse*, 1923, no. 3, pp. 266–77.

Fédida, Pierre. "L'anatomie dans la psychanalyse." *Nouvelle Revue de Psychanalyse* 3 (1971): 109 ff.

——. "Le conte et la zone d'endormissement." *Psychanalyse à l'Université* 1 (1975): 111 ff.

——. "L'hypocondrie du rêve." *Nouvelle Revue de Psychanalyse* 5 (1972): 225 ff.

Feldmann, S. "Über das Erröten." *Internationale Zeitschrift für Psychoanalyse*, 1922, no. 1, pp. 14–34.

Ferenczi, Sandor. "Psychoanalytische Betrachtungen über den Tic." *Internationale Zeitschrift für Psychoanalyse*, 1921, pp. 33–63. Reprinted in *Oeuvres complètes* 3:85 ff. Paris: Payot, 1974.

Freud, Sigmund. *The Complete Letters of Sigmund Freud to Wilhelm Fliess, 1887–1904.* Trans. Jeffrey Moussaieff Masson. Cambridge, Mass.: Belknap Press, 1985.

——. *Gesammelte Werke.* 18 vols. Frankfurt and London: Fischer, 1952–68.

——. *Sigmund Freud and Lou Andreas-Salomé: Letters.* Ed. Ernst Pfeiffer, trans. William and Elaine Robson-Scott. New York: Harcourt Brace Jovanovich, 1972.

——. *The Standard Edition of the Complete Psychological Works of Sigmund Freud*, ed. James Strachey. 24 vols. London: Hogarth Press, 1953–74.

Groddeck, Georg. "Traumarbeit und Arbeit des organischen Symptoms." *Internationale Zeitschrift für Psychoanalyse*, 1926, pp. 504–12. Translated as "Travail du rêve et travail du symptôme organique." In *La maladie, l'art et le symbole*, trans. R. Lewinter, pp. 14 ff. Paris: Gallimard, 1969.

Hermann, Imre. "Organlibido und Begabung." *Internationale Zeitschrift für Psychoanalyse*, 1923, no. 2, pp. 297–310.

L'hystérie. Special issue of *Confrontations psychiatriques* 1 (1968).

Israël, Luce. *L'hystérique, le sexe et la médecin.* Paris: Masson, 1976.

——. "Le victime de l'hystérique." *L'Evolution Psychiatrique*, 1967.

Klein, Melanie. "Zur Genese des Tics." *Internationale Zeitschrift für Psychoanalyse*, 1925, pp. 332–49. Translated as "A Contribution to the Psychogenesis of Tics." In *Contributions to Psycho-Analysis, 1921–1945*, pp. 117–39. London: Hogarth Press, 1948.

Kofman, Sarah. *The Enigma of Woman*, trans. Catherine Porter. Ithaca: Cornell University Press, 1985.

Lacan, Jacques. *Ecrits.* Paris: Seuil, 1966.

——. *Ecrits: A Selection.* Trans. Alan Sheridan. New York: W. W. Norton, 1977.

——. *The Four Fundamental Concepts of Psychoanalysis.* Ed. Jacques-Alain Miller, trans. Alan Sheridan. New York: W. W. Norton, 1978.

——. *The Seminar of Jacques Lacan.* Book 1. *Freud's Papers on Technique, 1953–54.* Ed. Jacques-Alain Miller, trans. John Forrester. New York: W. W. Norton, 1988.

——. *The Seminar of Jacques Lacan.* Book 2. *The Ego in Freud's Theory and in the Technique of Psychoanalysis, 1954–55.* Ed. Jacques-Alain Miller, trans. Sylvana Tomaselli. New York: W. W. Norton, 1988.

——. *Le séminaire.* Book 20. *Encore.* Paris: Seuil, 1970.

Landauer, Karl. "Die kindliche Bewegungsunruhe." *Internationale Zeitschrift für Psychoanalyse*, 1926, pp. 379–90.

Laplanche, Jean. *Life and Death in Psychoanalysis.* Trans. Jeffrey Mehlman. Baltimore: Johns Hopkins University Press, 1976.

Leclaire, Serge. *Psychanalyser.* Paris: Seuil, 1968.

McDougall, Joyce. "L'idéal hermaphrodite et ses avatars." *Nouvelle Revue de Psychanalyse* 7 (1983).

Mannoni, Octave. *Clefs pour l'imaginaire, ou L'autre scène.* Paris: Seuil, 1969.

Montrelay, Michèle. *L'ombre et le nom.* Paris: Editions de Minuit, 1977.

Die Onanie: Vierzehn Beiträge zu einer Diskussion der Wiener psychoanalytischen Vereinigung. Wiesbaden: J. F. Bergmann, 1913. (Contributors include Hitschmann, Sadger, Stekel, Ferenczi, Tausk, and Freud.)

Perrier, François. "Psychanalyse de l'hypocondriaque." *L'Evolution Psychiatrique,* 1959, fasc. 3, pp. 413 ff.

Peters, Heinz-Frederick. *My Sister, My Spouse: A Biography of Lou Andreas-Salomé.* New York: W. W. Norton, 1962.

Racamier, P. "Hystérie et théâtre." *L'Evolution Psychiatrique,* 1952.

Reich, Wilhelm. "Über die Quellen der neurotischen Angst." *Internationale Zeitschrift für Psychoanalyse,* 1926, pp. 422–31.

———. "Über Spezifität der Onanieformen." *Internationale Zeitschrift für Psychoanalyse,* 1922, pp. 333–37.

Ribot, T. *Problèmes de psychologie affective.* Paris: Alcan, 1910.

Roudinesco, Elisabeth. *Histoire de la psychanalyse en France.* Vol. 1. *La bataille de cent ans.* Paris: Ramsay, 1982.

Sadger, J. "Ein Beitrag zum Verständnis des Tic." *Internationale Zeitschrift für Psychoanalyse,* 1914, pp. 354–66.

———. *Über Nachtwandeln und Mondsucht: Eine medizinische und litterarische Studie.* Leipzig: Franz Dentike, 1913–14.

Schilder, Paul. *L'image du corps.* Trans. F. Gantheret and P. Truffert. Paris: Gallimard, 1968.

Schneider, Monique. *Freud et le plaisir.* Paris: Denoël, 1980.

Sharpe, E. "Mécanismes du rêve et procédés poétiques." *Nouvelle Revue de Psychanalyse* 5 (1972): 101 ff.

"Sur l'hystérie." Special issue of *Revue Française de Psychanalyse* 37 (May 1973).

Index

Freud's name is not listed below, as references are too numerous; "hysteria" is omitted for the same reason. The concepts listed include only those developed in some detail in the text.

Index

Library of Congress Cataloging-in-Publication Data

David-Ménard, Monique.
  [Hystérique entre Freud et Lacan. English]
  Hysteria from Freud to Lacan : body and language in psychoanalysis /
Monique David-Ménard : translated by Catherine Porter : foreword by Ned
Lukacher.
      p.   cm.
  Translation of: L'hystérique entre Freud et Lacan.
  Bibliography: p.
  Includes index.
  ISBN 0–8014–2100–4.—ISBN 0–8014–9617–9 (pbk.)
  1. Hysteria.   2. Conversion (Psychology)   3. Sex (Psychology)
4. Freud, Sigmund, 1856–1939.   5. Lacan, Jacques, 1901–   . I. Title.
RC532.D3813   1989   616.85′24—dc20   89–42870